Mastering Real Wellness

Mastering Real Wellness

A self-mastery framework to create holistic health and optimal living

DR SUSANNAH WARD

Specialist Rehabilitation Medicine
BMedSci (Hons) MBBS (Hons) FAFRM RYT® 200

The information provided within this book is conceptual, general, and educational and does not purport to offer medical advice, nor should it be taken as a substitute for such. The content is not a substitute for professional healthcare. Always engage with a qualified healthcare professional to receive personalised advice and treatment. The contents of this book may not resonate or be applicable to every reader's personal circumstance or beliefs. The author disclaims any responsibility or liability for any direct, indirect, incidental, consequential, or any other forms of damages arising from the use or interpretation of the information contained in this book. This includes, but is not limited to, health-related issues. The information in this book reflects knowledge available at the time of publication and the correctness of information should be considered. Case studies are examples for illustrative purposes. The reader should not construe any example as reflecting any real individual, living, or deceased, or actual events.

Mastering Real Wellness
First published in 2024 by Dr Susannah Ward

Text copyright © Dr Susannah Ward, 2024
Design and typography copyright © Dr Susannah Ward, 2024

Dr Susannah Ward has asserted her moral rights to be identified as the author of this work.

This work is copyright. All rights reserved. No part of this publication may be reproduced, distributed, or transmitted in any form or by any means, including photocopying, recording, or other electronic or mechanical methods, without the prior written permission of the publisher, except in cases permitted under copyright law.

Please send all permission enquires to hello@ataraxaicollective.com.au

A Cataloguing-in-Publication entry for this work is available from the National Library of Australia.

ISBN 978-1-7636349-1-6 (Paperback)
ISBN 978-1-7636349-0-9 (eBook)

Cover design: Christa Moffitt
Cover images: Christa Moffitt
Editor: Anne Reilly
Typesetting: Kirby Jones
Author photo: April Wertz Photography
Printed and bound in China by Book Printing China

Contents

Introduction   1

Part 1: Real Wellness   11
1 Real Wellness Is Not …   13
2 Real Wellness Is Living with Self-Mastery   21
3 How to Create a Life with Real Wellness   29

Part 2: Pillar 1 – Self-awareness   43
4 Mindfulness   45
5 Our Two Worlds   57
6 Values   75
7 Priorities   85
8 Intentions   94
9 Beliefs   107

Part 3: Pillar 2 – Self-acceptance   121
10 Acceptance   123
11 Self-compassion   136
12 Self-honesty   149

Part 4: Pillar 3 – Self-management   155
13 Ideal You   157
14 Goals   164
15 Attention Regulation   176

16 Internal-world Regulation	188
17 External-world Regulation	216
18 Compassionate Self-discipline	229
19 Self-care	240
20 Self-soothing	253
21 Habit Autonomy	262
22 Holistic Skills for Self-mastery	280
Final Words	289
Acknowledgements	295

Introduction

Hi, nice to meet you, and thank you for taking the time to read *Mastering Wellness*, which is my first published self-help book. I am a Specialist Physician of Rehabilitation Medicine based in Newcastle, New South Wales, Australia. I have a special interest in holistic health, wellness, and human-mastery. I have trained in medicine and medical science with honours at Sydney University. I am a yoga and mindfulness teacher and the founder of Ataraxia Collective (www.ataraxiacollective.com.au – please join the group; you can also follow me on Instagram @axcollective).

In my daily professional and personal life, I use a set of skills and concepts that I call **real wellness**, which I share with you in this book. I developed and refined them over years of self-study, research and professional support. These are tools I use to cope with and make the most of every day. All my life I have been anxious: I have a highly sensitive disposition – I am prone to intense thinking and feeling.

But I am proud to say that since consistently applying the strategies outlined in this book, I feel well, show up most days as the best version of myself, and I can honestly say I live my best life. I truly feel I have mastered the art of **real wellness**.

Crucial to my **real wellness** is that I intimately understand and accept my humanness, and the inevitable role the past and my conditioning intricately play in my reality, health and lived human experience today. Having developed a strong sense of self-agency and self-mastery, I live with the loving intention of making the most of whatever I'm working with when I wake up each day, while accepting and holding huge gratitude for what I am and have in my life.

In turn, these insights have informed my work, and I have learnt to help my patients achieve the same clarity. Nowadays, my passion is helping people everywhere to understand, embrace and optimally manage their humanness to live this brilliant life fully and freely to the best of their abilities, which is my motivation for writing this book. I hope to reassure others that it is perfectly normal and valid to live as a flawed and imperfect human with struggles, and this does not mean you can't live well and enjoy a life of rich meaning and value. We all absolutely can.

*

During my years at university, I learnt in detail about the body, its systems, how it is affected by disease, and how to treat illness. But despite this privileged education, something felt lacking. There seemed a dearth of information on the mind–body–world connection and how it all comes together to cultivate our lived human experience and health outcomes. There was clearly more to health and wellness than simply having good heart health. Where was the chapter in Harrison's and my other medical textbooks on the intangible inner human world and how it contributes to our choices, actions and inner peace? I wanted to learn about the role our sensations, thoughts, emotions, and urges play in driving our behaviour and mood. I wanted to learn about the whole human self, our holistic health, and how our environment also impacts

INTRODUCTION

our function and health outcomes. I wanted to understand my humanness and develop self-agency, and then to work out how to support others to do the same and make healthier choices for healthier lives.

As human beings we all have a complex and often chaotic inner world to manage, along with a vulnerable physical form to care for, and a social context and environment to consider. My hunger was to understand this dynamic interplay and how it influences health and wellbeing. In tandem with my formal medical studies, I began my self-study on being human, the lived human experience, and how to optimally manage this complex state of affairs. From this personal pursuit emerged my knowledge about unlocking and mastering **real wellness**.

Many non-communicable illnesses can be prevented, and all illness and disability is impacted by lifestyle and health behaviours. During my training, it quickly became obvious to me that it didn't work to tell a patient they were at risk of illness and needed to make a certain change. People need more guidance than that. The approach I came up with is to start with a deeper look at the 'why': people need to understand why they make choices, how those choices affect their health and why different choices are worth the effort for them. Then comes the how: specifically, how to change unhealthy behaviours. From what I could see, most patients lacked the self-mastery for this, yet I discovered that these skills can be learnt, and I show you how on these pages.

Self-mastery is relevant to all people keen to live their best life and find inner peace. Our own behaviour immensely impacts our precious and fleeting lives, and that includes our health and wellbeing.

Many of us quietly struggle with autonomy over our choices and behaviour, which can erode our self-worth and self-esteem. But it needn't be this way. Having autonomy over your choices breeds inner contentment and peace, and this skill can be acquired.

The opposite – a lack of life meaning, purpose and mastery – unless attended to, can lead to discontent and even depression and mental illness. At worst, some people develop addictions and lose all control over their lives. We can give up on ourselves and our lives – hopefully long enough to glimpse the abyss then decide to learn to live with and manage ourselves better. Whether that is your story or if, like me, you have a passion and commitment to making the most of who you are and this incredible life – old or young, sick or disease-free, disabled or fully abled – you will be looking for ways to live optimally and feel well.

Wouldn't it be ideal to grow up with these skills and insights? If we learnt this in childhood, a lot of people's suffering might be avoided. Self-mastery is particularly relevant to teens and young adults. Young people need to understand themselves, their worlds and how to manage it all so they can have the best chance of living well and avoid adopting coping mechanisms that contribute to illness, such as smoking and binge-drinking. For many, this is the age of experimentation – a time of increasing adult freedom with fewer boundaries – but it coincides with having to learn to cope with stress. Destructive health behaviours may form when life starts to become complicated and increased stressors are paired with maladaptive coping tools.

By the time people are in their 30s, coping behaviours are typically deeply ingrained and may feel impossible to outgrow. By the time people are in their 40s, the previously hidden, yet compounding, health consequences of harmful behaviours start to become visible and tangible. These may be rising blood pressure and weight. By our 50s and 60s (or earlier), we may live with diagnosed illnesses caused by harmful habits, such as emphysema from a lifetime of smoking. These cascading effects may be preventable if we learn the art of adaptive self-mastery from youth.

For all of these reasons – and so many others – I have written this how-to of human-mastery, which is the essence of **real**

INTRODUCTION

wellness. In my opinion, if you are a human being, then this book is relevant to you. So, if you aren't a robot or God, then I urge you to keep reading. If you feel unwell or stuck in some way, then definitely keep reading! Even if the messages of this book do not resonate with you personally, they may help you understand other individuals who feel unwell or stuck and perhaps enable you to care for them.

In this book, I debunk some myths around 'wellness', introduce alternative views, and empower you to claim your own unique journey of **real wellness** regardless of your circumstances. Let's get realistic, brutally honest, inspired and empowered. I hope to convince any reader who may feel stuck, lost, ashamed of their humanness, and lacking in wellness – for example, due to chronic health issues – that you too are capable and worthy of **real wellness**. Living, feeling and being well is a birthright accessible to all, regardless of circumstance.

*

I wrote this book a little disheartened with the wellness industry, with its endless parade of fads and its hype. While there are certainly exceptions, one could argue that the wellness industry is generally made up of businesses that profit off our vulnerabilities and ignorance. Personally, I often have reservations about what is promised – especially when it's some wonderful state of being that seems attainable only by spending money and, even more so, when it's to achieve a particular aesthetic. Too frequently, the subtext is that we can be 'perfect': healed, immune to health challenges, feeling bliss all the time, or that we can defy the ageing process to live longer and retain the hallmarks of youthful health, free of symptoms and physical issues. But not unless we look a certain way, purchase certain products or programs, and invest in glorified self-care routines. Not only does the wellness industry contribute to consumers' false expectations of their health and the realities of being a vulnerable human, but it also takes people's money for products that may not be helpful to their **real wellness**. By and large, the focus is on tangible goods and activities because these can be sold. But what about self-mastery and the relationship you hold with yourself? Can you buy this?

Whether an act of self-care meets a need is determined by the intention you hold behind your choices, how informed you are, and what is motivating you. In the final analysis, your journey to **real wellness** is yours alone to experiment with and conduct. I hope this book helps keep you in the driver's seat as you navigate your way.

Engaging with and enjoying the fruits of the wellness industry can be to your benefit, if you are informed about your choices and clear on your motivations. If whatever you are buying – and buying into – is working for you, then great! However, many people fall for the hoopla and then live in a delusional pursuit of 'wellness' at the expense of making the most of what they have got and enjoying the here and now. The brutal truth is that no supplement – or other wellness offering – can make us live forever, avoid health challenges, make everyone admire us, and prevent pain and suffering. What we can expect as humans is a life of **real wellness**, which I define in the coming pages of this book along with providing practical concepts and skills to cultivate this destiny.

There is plenty of great news: to achieve **real wellness**, we don't need to invest in gadgets, clothes, vitamins, gimmicky superfoods, particular practices or whatever you are led to believe you need to buy in order to thrive and feel good enough. Rather, we need to show up for ourselves, learn a little about our inner world and develop some mastery over our thoughts, emotions, impulses, and behaviour. Forget overpriced lycra pants: the most natural way to feel well is through self-mastery.

INTRODUCTION

My hope is that the words in this book give you permission and encouragement to be you: to be a vulnerable and imperfect human being who has both good days and tough times, who will age (hopefully), and face life's pain with courage and care. There's no need to be anyone else. There's no need to appease anyone else.

When you self-appraise your wellness, what is paramount is the relationship you foster with yourself. If you feel proud, safe and 'good' enough, you will feel well. This, my friend, comes as a result of living with adaptive self-management skills, insight into yourself and your ways of being, but also self-compassion and the ability to accept yourself as you are today, which is good enough.

Let's celebrate our messy selves – works in progress for ever. Let's connect and share our truth, which is that we all struggle to feel well at times, and that we want to be loved and feel good enough. Let's revel in the fact that these realities and urges are common to all and that the comforts we yearn for stem from ourselves, and not by taking a supplement.

I hope this book validates for you that, even if you have chronic disease and health issues, even if you're not the perfect picture of mainstream wellness depicted in marketing, even if you don't like herbs or can't afford them, and even if you don't do any of the things commonly advocated by the wellness industry, *you can still be well* and that this power lies within you.

You are allowed to be human: you don't need healing or to be made perfect. You need understanding, acceptance and skilful self-management. Empower yourself with knowledge, skills, tools and practices that build these things.

*

Living a life of **real wellness** isn't rocket science, but neither is it necessarily easy! It should not be assumed to be inherent to us in the way that something like breathing is, nor should it be expected that the required knowledge and skills are passed on by parents and teachers. That said, self-mastery is a skill that can be taught, learnt and practised at any age by anyone who is motivated.

Numerous internal and external barriers can get in the way of your self-care. I try to highlight potential obstacles that may hold you back from living *your* life really well, so you can learn to overcome them, or at least understand and accept them to reduce any self-judgement and shame around your humanness.

The aim of this book is to conceptualise what it is to be human, what it is we must manage on a day-to-day basis, and how to best do this in a way that works and means we live optimally.

Life is amazing, wonderful and beautiful, but being human can be messy, ugly, and downright hard at times. Being human means living with a monkey mind – a term that describes how our thoughts ping around constantly as our brains ceaselessly process information, memories and future possibilities – inhabiting a sensate and vulnerable body that can fail our ego and test our tolerance; knowing that we make mistakes and can be unlucky and get into accidents, and surviving inevitable grief, pain and loss.

Despite this shared fate, each of us is capable of leading a life of **real wellness** via understanding our humanness, accepting it and being able to optimally manage it regardless of our circumstances. It means making the most of what you've got to work with today. It means fostering a healthy and reliable relationship with yourself through a lifelong commitment to self-care. With this realistic self-awareness and a healthy sense of self, you will feel well.

This book is all about embracing our humanness and learning how to make the most of it. It explains how to cultivate **real wellness** using concepts and skills. *Mastering Wellness* provides insights into some of the self-mastery required for **real wellness** that is available to all people, at any stage of life, no matter what challenges and adversity they may be dealing with.

INTRODUCTION

The first part of the book debunks the marketing myths around wellness and offers a more authentic definition of **real wellness**. It then explains the pathway for cultivating a life of **real wellness**, which is a life of self-mastery and requires three key skills:

1. self-awareness
2. self-acceptance
3. self-management

These three self-mastery skills – which I talk about in Parts 2, 3, and 4 respectively – can be developed and practised over a lifetime. It's a commitment to living a life of self-mastery that paves the way to **real wellness**, where your relationship with yourself is one of self-compassionate discipline and care. You cultivate the ability to meet your holistic health needs in unique and authentic ways that suit you and only you. This quest fosters a deep and meaningful relationship with self where you feel proud, safe and trusting living as you.

I hope *Mastering Wellness* motivates you to be kind, accepting and gentle with yourself and your reality as you work with all you are capable of, knowing you are perfectly imperfect as you are today. Remember, you are not alone in your human journey.

Enjoy!
Susannah

PART 1

Real Wellness

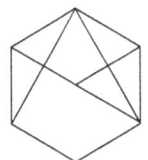

1
Real Wellness Is Not ...

It may feel upside down to you to start this book by going through what wellness is not. But it feels right to me to firstly clear that up. There's a lot of mis-messaging coming at us, mostly thanks to the marketing activities of the lucrative wellness industry. It concerns me when I see people taking up ideas that may be unhelpful and even harmful.

Real wellness is not necessarily living free from disease and challenges, and your capacity to be **really well** is not dictated by your age, physical or mental capability, or body shape. Looking a certain way, owning certain things – like an organic yoga mat or gadget to change the pH of your water – or participating in specific activities – colonic irrigation or whatever the latest wellness fad may be – is not necessarily your path to **real wellness**. Achieving **real wellness** is not a 'one size fits all' process, and what you see in marketing may not suit you.

There is no quick fix for attaining **real wellness**, nor is it something we gain and then it is done. It is not a task on your to-do list that you can achieve in the course of a day or month and then tick off. Lastly, the pursuit of **real wellness** will not be a perfect journey by any means. Don't expect artificially intelligent or divine progression: you are not a robot or God.

*

A culture has arisen of what I call toxic wellness. Do you see wellness advertisements and feel inadequate? Do you follow wellness ambassadors on social media and assume they live a contented life with constant inner peace? Do you compare yourself to these people? The multibillion-dollar wellness industry feeds off our tendency to compare ourselves to others, and the myth that to be well, we need to look a certain way, eat and drink certain things, and do life in a certain way. This is all about creating a need in consumers and then meeting it: the ultimate aim is to sell things to you and take your money. This is not **real wellness**.

The mythmaking is done so skilfully that it's hard *not* to fall for it. Mainstream media understands and exploits our drive for pleasure and inclusion. It takes advantage of our insecurities, our cravings to look better, feel better, and be loved. But, maybe we look fine just as we are, maybe we are loved and need to work on recognising that, and maybe we don't need to feel better all the time? Maybe sitting with challenging sensations, emotions and our humanness is masterful at times and even necessary for wellbeing?

In this culture of toxic wellness, there is an emphasis on fitting in: you do this by making sure you look 'right'. This focus on aesthetics in order to access social safety is not **real wellness**; it can never properly work. It is up to us as individuals to accept ourselves and create a foundation of safety and self-worth through healthy self-mastery.

Can you trust something that is so obviously about chasing profit, that presents as fashion? Have you noticed how quickly wellness trends change? Take goji berries. Up until a couple of years ago, hardly anyone had heard of goji berries. (Meanwhile,

I eat and love goji berries but I also know they are not my holy grail to **real wellness**.) Then, they started being featured in magazines and being included in cereals; health food shops stocked them. Once consumers were educated about their high levels of antioxidants – linked with improving age-related macular degeneration – sales took off and goji berries went mainstream, turning up on supermarket shelves. But now they're so 'last season' and – as I write, but who knows for how much longer – dried Inca berries seem to be the latest antioxidant fad. What will the coming season's hot new product be? Something new from a little-known corner of the globe perhaps? This is not **real wellness**.

Please always be wary of messaging in the media around wellness. Not only could it be irrelevant to your unique wellness needs but, ironically, may serve as a barrier to living well. You may not need to invest in expensive 'superfoods' if you eat a fresh, balanced diet. Just because everyone seems to be doing ice baths right now, it doesn't mean that to be well you need to do this too. If you're a cold frog like me – I have Raynaud syndrome – then you may prefer to give it a miss.

*

Take a moment to tune in to a common wellness stereotype. Can you see in your mind's eye a youthful, slim, white person meditating in some bendy yoga position appearing totally Zen and at ease? It would be surprising if you can't: those images are everywhere. Next, try to picture a relaxed and healthy version of *you* feeling well. For me, what comes up is a vision of myself sitting outside, feeling the warmth of the sun, smelling the fresh air, enjoying the breeze, hearing the birds, and feeling comforted by nature.

This second image, the one *you* conjure, is likely to indicate *your* path to **real wellness**. Chances are the two images are quite different. That's because you are not a stereotype. You are uniquely you! You live with your own physical and mental state within your own environment — all the while with *your own* values, priorities, and goals. Your path to **real wellness** is likely not the same as what is socially normalised or pictured in mainstream marketing.

You don't need to be young and shredded, eat ancient grains or do yoga to cultivate **real wellness** and be well in *yourself*. You don't need to own a particular blender, live in a particular postcode, partake of a particular pastime or wear activewear of a particular brand. You don't even need to meditate! Please don't think I'm slamming things like this: in fact, I partake in a lot of them. But that's because I've tried all kinds of activities and practices over the years and have found the ones that keep me well, and I choose them for myself to meet clear self-care needs in an empowering, masterful way. Essentially, this is what this book encourages you to do too.

*

Real wellness is not unrealistic. Perhaps you hold an image of wellness as a past or future version of yourself that you idealise. If so, it's unlikely to be attainable, which is not **real wellness**. **Real wellness** is not you 20 years ago, or you if you changed in some way from the perfectly imperfect version of you as you are right now. It is not some unrealistic fantasy that shames you in comparison. **Real wellness** is not about healing your brokenness, or striving to be better in some way while judging yourself harshly as you are today.

At the start of this chapter, I mentioned the mistaken but commonly held belief that wellness is the state of living disease- and symptom-free. Perfect health is not an attainable existence for most humans. In advanced age, for instance, we all eventually live with disease or disability. While the healthcare industry presents wonderful, sensible science-based options that I wholeheartedly support, a large segment of it cultivates the delusional pursuit of perfect and immortal 'health'. There is money to be made by selling these ideas.

Accepting the inevitability of imperfect physical health and our natural human morbidity is neither appealing nor desirable. But there is plenty you can do to optimise your health, which is what I live and breathe. By looking after yourself optimally and making the most of what you have got – with proper nutrition, rest, nurturing supportive relationships and connections, cultivating a sense of spirituality, self-care, daily exercise, good sleep and other things that make you feel your best – you not only enjoy yourself today but are laying the foundations of a healthier future. Your lifestyle at 40, in part, determines your health and ageing at 60. So, although ageing and disease are inevitable, our behaviours and choices have the power to make things worse or better.

If you've bought into the false goal of attaining 'perfect health', chances are you have a sense of failure. I repeat: for practically all of us, 'perfect health' is an impossibility. But it's not all or nothing. Rather than shaming and blaming yourself for being human with a vulnerable physical and mental form, embrace it, make the most of it, and try not to make it any worse. It is okay to not feel on top of your game all the time, to manage mental illness, be challenged by addictive behaviours. If you live with and must manage chronic illness, it is still possible to care for yourself optimally to feel proud and as well as could be. These human experiences do not exclude us from **real wellness**. Be kind to yourself.

All human beings have physical and mental weakness: this is part of the shared human condition. Our morbidity and mortality are the source of our humility: they keep us humble during our fleeting and impermanent lives. The inevitable physical deterioration faced by humans brings meaning and value to our life while it lasts. The fact that I won't live forever, and my body will become old and frail with time, means I don't take each day for granted. I view my physical self as special and honour its need for special care and attention. With infirmity and weakness come opportunity for personal growth and gratitude for what is. Our human mortality is a matter of fact that requires acceptance if we are to limit suffering.

So, please, no matter your circumstances, don't feel any failure of health if you do manage chronic illness or impairment. Any wellness-related stigma around these shared human challenges is simply ridiculous and unreasonable!

Do you live with a disability? Are you getting older? Are you at a stage in your life where you're noticing physical limitations? You can live with and through such challenges and still be well. While perfect health and living without disease and disability is unrealistic for most of us, what is attainable in life – and for all people – is living with a sense of **real wellness**, which I define in the next chapter. So, let's next learn more about what **real wellness** is.

Case study

Ayaan is intelligent, kind, and simply one of the nicest people I've ever met. Unfortunately, he was born with poor respiratory function: he's always suffered quite serious asthma. Unlike me, he didn't grow out of his childhood chronic obstructive lung disease and must always carry a Ventolin puffer with him.

However, he's never let this hold him back. Ayaan has travelled the world, held many high-profile jobs and is now a wonderful dad of two gorgeous kids (both with great lungs) who are thriving. He's always done everything in his power to live his best life. He's never smoked and is committed to his medical and health care as prescribed. For example, he's always prioritised his vaccinations.

Ayaan lives with a constant slight cough but doesn't focus on it as a flaw or hardship. He has accepted his chronic health condition as a part of his life and works with it.

If you saw Ayaan out and about, you would never mistake him for a wellness model. He is not Anglo-Saxon or fit-looking, nor does he wear the latest activewear. He is not the stereotype of the wellness marketing industry by any means! But to me, Ayaan is a brilliant example of someone who is the picture of **real wellness** as he works towards optimally managing an irreversible and serious health condition in a masterful way, with a compassionate relationship to self.

Take-home messages

- **Real wellness** does not require you to look a certain way or participate in certain activities. Be wary of unhelpful media messaging.
- **Real wellness** is not a 'one size fits all' thing.
- **Real wellness** is not about finding dissatisfaction with your reality.
- **Real wellness** is not reserved for those with perfect health. It is not living free of disease, disability, stress, or symptoms. Those things are an inevitable part of the human experience.
- **Real wellness** is not a perfect journey: expect the very human lows and slips.
- **Real wellness** is not a fixed state: it's constantly changing, flexible, and adaptive. It's a lifelong commitment. It's a lifestyle and you must do the work.

Try this

Spend time identifying and studying some of the wellnessy content you see in the media. Ask yourself if these media images and messages are empowering to you or not. Do the stereotypes make you feel adequate or inadequate? If the latter, do any make you feel ashamed or guilty? Do the ads suggest certain wellness rules to you and, if so, are they helpful?

Get rid of obviously unhelpful influences. A good start is to unfriend and unfollow any social media accounts that don't empower you in a healthy and useful way. Make social media work for you, not unnerve you.

Rewrite the stereotype and embody an image of *yourself* feeling **really well**. What do you look like? What are you wearing? What are you doing? How does your body feel? What emotional state are you in? What is happening in your mind? Where are you? What is happening around you? How are you carrying yourself? How are you interacting and treating others? How are you making others around you feel?

2

Real Wellness Is Living with Self-Mastery

There is no universal definition of 'wellness'. The term is too broad. Plus, it has to do with feeling, which is highly subjective: I can't show you what feeling well means to me, and I can't be totally sure what you mean when you tell me you feel well either. The bottom line is that you define for yourself what wellness means to you.

So far, we've identified that a lot of the wellness that's marketed to us is fantasy. This book is dedicated to wellness that is real – though feel free to switch out the adjective 'real' for whatever language resonates for you: bone fide, authentic, legitimate, the real deal, realistic, attainable, honest, or human, for example. It's *your* subjective experience, so choose the best words for *you*.

*

Real wellness is authentic to you. It is about making choices that work for *you* and leave *you* feeling empowered, vitalised, grounded, and well! It's an entirely unique journey for everyone, requiring different skills and tools depending on your priorities, values, intentions and truth. Because there's no one recipe for **real wellness**, you must work it out for yourself by reflecting and experimenting. Your recipe is unique to *you* and will only be cultivated through experimentation with ideas that resonate with *you*. Forget what others do and cease making comparisons. Instead, tune in to what's happening within you and what you need.

Your wellness journey is about embracing *you*, realising what *you* need and love, and accepting *your* reality – physically, mentally, and environmentally – all while living in tune with *your* values and priorities, and hopefully kicking some life goals. Drop any judgements or standards and focus on yourself, your unique needs and circumstance, and what is workable for you. Your wellness journey is one you take as an individual. It is created by you and for you.

*

Real wellness is realistic and within reach. It is very much about working with yourself as you are in the present moment, and not some fantasy of the past or future. Ensure your version of wellness is realistic, achievable, and sustainable. Work with that. Any unfair expectations you may hold for yourself deep down – and likely all of the comparisons you make – will only stop you from being well and may even cause you suffering. Let go of those.

Real wellness is attainable. It's not you 20 years ago, or you if you changed in some way from the perfectly imperfect version of you as you are right now. This is a key point, and one that it's worth taking the time to understand and accept. Wellness needs to be cultivated by accepting who you are *today*, facing and accommodating any challenges, diseases and/or infirmities you live with *now,* and living in an adaptive way – that you choose for yourself – that works and meets your holistic needs. It fundamentally requires self-acceptance and self-compassion.

Real wellness requires focus on and respect for *your* reality – for what is possible for *you,* and what *you* can do today to care for yourself. The more gracefully you manoeuvre your precious self through the day, the better. If you take this approach, then the relationship you foster with yourself will thrive. Without a mindset of self-care and respect, it may languish and deteriorate.

*

Real wellness is spiritual: it manifests when you connect with others, express yourself fully and intuitively, and allow your whole self to be seen, heard, and loved for the greater good. It takes hard work and gutsiness. It's never achieved by living a life of complacency and, what I call 'Fuck it' moments – those moments where you reach your tipping point and give up on your goals – and it's not about living egotistically for your own gains. Rather, it's about rising to your best capacity and function, to contribute your unique strengths and make the world a better place. When we share our gifts with the world, partake in random acts of kindness, are of service, and advocate for positive change, our soul is nourished and we feel well.

Real wellness is living aligned with your truth and participating fully in your life in ways that work for you. As you now know, it's far more than the sum of the commonly discussed parts – physical health, nutrition, exercise, weight management and so on – but is defined by the relationship you hold with yourself, and includes your values, priorities, intentions, and ability to meet your heartfelt yearnings, all of which are discussed more in coming chapters.

*

Real wellness is an imperfect lifestyle – a life-long commitment to living authentically – and by definition we humans are far from perfect. Part of the goal of **real wellness** is accepting that imperfection, so expect the unexpected, the challenges and all the slips. Seek understanding and forgiveness during times you don't behave ideally. I eat a ton of fresh foods and veggies but at night you'll also find me getting into chocolate, and I love cake! Sometimes I eat too much of a good thing and have remorse when my belly aches or I have a bout of constipation but, hey, I'm human. When I notice I've strayed from my path, I pause, take a moment to redirect myself, then get back to my generally healthy and balanced diet. Know that you will make both mistakes and gains, and your path will be constantly evolving. It is this fluctuating, flexible, and self-attuned lifestyle that will deliver you the benefits of **real wellness**.

Just as your path to **real wellness** is unique to you, the consistent work it requires has to come from you. It's up to you to keep a keen eye on your choices and self-care and put in the effort. Although there is a world of support out there, ultimately, no-one is coming to hands-on help you do the personal work. No-one can do it for you. Important to living with **real wellness** is that you commit to a lifelong lifestyle of self-awareness, self-acceptance and self-mastery, and enjoy your journey as a human doing your best.

*

Real wellness is available to everyone. You can be old or young, any weight, living with illnesses, less fit than you used to be, eat junk food occasionally, and still be well.

You can enjoy **real wellness** despite any health challenges and functional limitations you may face – now or in the future. If you live long enough, you will develop chronic symptoms and health conditions. However, no matter what you experience, it's possible to live and feel well if you manage yourself in ways that makes the most of your situation.

So, what is real wellness?

*

Let's finally turn our attention to what I mean by **real wellness**! 🥁 Simply put, I propose that **real wellness** is defined by living with self-mastery and cultivating a compassionate relationship with yourself.

Self-mastery for **real wellness** is the ability to manage yourself optimally, so you can meet your needs, most of the time. This mastery requires three things: self-awareness, self-acceptance, and self-management, which I refer to as the three pillars of **real wellness**. As you grow in all these areas, you will also develop your capacity for self-compassion and foster a healthy relationship with yourself. All three pillars can be learnt and built on, which is why I wrote this book.

When you live by your personal standards and stay true to what is most valuable and meaningful to you, you will be well. To put it another way, you are on your path to **real wellness** when you get yourself, own your shit and can take care of it.

While I don't want it to sound too simple – because it sure isn't – it is also definitely achievable, provided you commit to it. Essentially, it is everyone's life's work, and I'm offering you the chance to get there quicker and more effectively. It is accessible to all, but you need to do the self-enquiry and the work (behaviour change).

In the following chapters, I provide you with a practical framework to conceptualise your humanness in order to develop your self-awareness and self-acceptance and make it simpler to manage your humanness. I will introduce key skills you can use to achieve **real wellness**. You will find a bunch of concepts and tools to aid your self-efficacy as well as stories that offer inspiration and allow you to learn from others different ways to understand the messages: we all learn differently. With knowledge and actioned strategy, it is possible to live meeting your holistic health needs, regardless of all the shit life may throw you. Being able to live this way is what I call **real wellness**.

Case study

When Janet was growing up, she did not have great role models. Her mum smoked, was emotionally avoidant and ate like a bird. Her dad, on the other hand, loved his food a little too much and was extreme in the amount of TV he watched.

Janet probably had a genetic predisposition to eating disorders and suffered from undiagnosed ADHD. She grew up struggling with boundaries, structure, and routine. She found it difficult to keep focused in class, and completing homework was often a losing battle. She was repeatedly in trouble at school, which only left her feeling more outcast and inadequate. She didn't understand why she was so different and felt a deep sense of shame within. She pacified her inner pain by controlling her food and weight. Watching television was Janet's safe place because it allowed her to block out and avoid the challenges of her young adult life.

But by the time Janet hit her 20s, she yearned for more. She didn't want to live in shame and isolation. She didn't want to end up like her parents. She wanted to feel secure and safe in herself. She confronted her demons and spoke to her GP. He referred her to a psychologist, who taught Janet skills in self-awareness and performed a battery of assessments that indicated she had ADHD. She read widely on the diagnosis and learnt strategies to overcome her challenges. She became less self-critical as she grew to understand and accept more of herself.

When I met Janet, she had been able to develop a healthier relationship with herself and learn self-care. She had embraced her unique brain and temperament and harnessed it into a creative superpower that helped her write several novels, fulfilling a long-held dream. Janet felt well, secure and proud of who she was – struggles and all.

Take-home messages

- **Real wellness** is unique to *you* and needs to be based off *your* reality today.
- **Real wellness** is spiritual and means connecting with others and participating fully in your life.
- Living with **real wellness** requires a lifelong commitment to an imperfect path. Expect long term gains with plenty of mistakes and lessons.
- **Real wellness** is possible for all people, regardless of their circumstance. Anyone can feel well, no matter what their circumstances are.
- **Real wellness** is living with self-mastery, which requires self-awareness, self-acceptance, and self management.
- **Real wellness** is living with a healthy relationship to yourself where you treat yourself with comfort, safety and respect.

Try this

Spend some time considering the health and status of the relationship you hold with yourself. Have you considered how you treat yourself? Would you rate self-care as important to you? Do you show up for yourself when you need it most; for example, getting out of bed and seeing your therapist when you're tempted to lie down all day? When life is stressful, can you do the things you need to do to restore, recover and cope in healthy ways? Are you able to parent yourself?

If the answer to any of these questions is no, ask yourself why not. Why don't you care for yourself the way a healthy parent would look after their child? Try to simply notice without judgement how you respond to these questions. Noticing is the first step toward any required change.

3

How to Create a Life with Real Wellness

You now know the exciting and empowering fact that **real wellness** is available to us all – no matter our circumstances. The power to be well lies within you! Accessing that power requires you to understand and radically accept what you are – a flawed and vulnerable human – and that you're living in a chaotic world, where among the few certainties are constant change and finite control. You use the power to be well when you manage yourself in ways that holistically work for you and meet your needs most of the time, while practising self-compassion when you slip. Granted, this is easier said than done, but the greatest skill of adulthood is making yourself do hard things.

Now that you know what **real wellness** is, and what it is not, let's turn our attention on how to develop this self-mastery.

In my work, I've learnt that humans like having a tried-and-tested blueprint to follow. So, here is a **real wellness** self-mastery blueprint that has helped me be well, and I am confident it will for you too.

There are three key pillars to **real wellness**:

1. self-awareness,
2. self-acceptance, and
3. self-management.

It's my passionate belief that looking into these three pillars of **real wellness** in detail over the coming chapters will serve you well in terms of how you function as a human and relate to yourself, and support you to find some inner contentment and peace of mind living as *you* in this life. The rest of this book is a deep dive into how we may cultivate and evolve these abilities over a lifetime. I introduce some concepts and skills for self-awareness in Part 2, self-acceptance in Part 3, and self-management in Part 4. But first let me describe each pillar in a little more detail.

*

The first pillar of **real wellness** is self-awareness, which requires self-examination. Makes perfect sense, right? If you want to build your self-awareness, then you need to dedicate some time to enquiring within, and maybe you need to learn skills in order to do this. It is cultivated with mindfulness and other self-reflective practices. The desired outcome is building an understanding of what it is to be human as well as your uniqueness and individual values, priorities and needs. It is about discovering more about who you are, why you are as you are, and how to best care for yourself. It is also about sharpening your sense of who and how you wish to be and why you wish to be as you do.

Developing skill in this first pillar of **real wellness** takes identifying your intentions, values and priorities, becoming familiar with your two worlds – your inner world and your outer world – and their intricate relationship, and learning your core beliefs and how they affect your perceptions and filtering of life. I go through this more in Part 2.

*

Self-acceptance, which is the second pillar of self-mastery for **real wellness**, necessarily follows on from the work you do in building self-awareness. That's because in order to accept yourself, you first must understand what it is that you're accepting. Self-awareness also draws on self-compassion, self-honesty, and general acceptance.

You're well on your path to living with **real wellness** when you approach daily life aspiring to experience your full potential while accepting yourself as you are now. It doesn't mean giving yourself a free pass if, for instance, you're doing harmful things to others. The focus of self-acceptance is to be able to meet your gaze in the mirror without looking away. There may be things going on for you or things you discover about yourself that you perceive as less than ideal or don't choose for yourself long-term, and that's perfectly okay! It's essential to honestly accept your reality with compassion. A compassionate view is that you are not inadequate or defective, you are not broken or a lost cause; you are a human who needs kindness and care. With a compassionate and honest self-appraisal, you're in a good position to identify any painful truths that require growth and change and then to figure out how to go about that change, then gently work towards the shifts you choose for yourself.

Why do I keep emphasising compassion? Our brains default to the negative; in other words, our tendency is to beat ourselves up when we look inside. Whereas a mindset of self-acceptance cultivates an internal loving vibe conducive to **real wellness**, self-loathing has the opposite effect. If you approach any change process with negative self-judgement, your whole life will be unpleasant. If you can accept how, who and why you are as you are now, with the goal of optimising yourself, then you will be well as you grow – which you will do for the rest of your life.

Earlier, I mentioned that general acceptance has a role to play in self-acceptance. By general acceptance, I mean important overarching realities also requiring acceptance. Heading the list is that life is not fixed but is forever changing; the world around you is in a constant state of flux; the demands on you are always evolving; and your body, mind and soul are forever changing. To be well, we must accept this changing nature of living. We need to accept love and loss, joy and grief, newness and ageing. We need to be adaptive and flexible and flow with it all as best we can.

Keep the intention top of mind that your pursuit of **real wellness** is simply the commitment to live your best life and be your best version of yourself – accepting that this will fluctuate and change throughout your lifetime – and always accepting yourself as you are today as you work towards making the most of all that comes at you. Anyhoo, there is more on this to come in Part 3.

*

The third pillar to self-mastery and **real wellness** is self-management. Once you understand and have accepted your humanness and your current circumstance in life (Pillars 2 and 3), then the focus becomes optimally managing it all. This is where the 'making the most of it all' comes in.

Part 4 of the book is all about empowerment, inspiration, and skills acquisition to cash in on yourself and enjoy living as you in the most masterful way you can manage. These skills are not inherent and should not be assumed. They are a hidden curriculum of the school of life. Think of the self-management skills in Part 4 as a sort of self-compassionate human manipulation, where you are learning tools to work with your humanness and cultivate an adaptive and thriving relationship with yourself. Acquiring and practising knowledge and tools like these, in my opinion, will equip you with the best chance of making the most of all you are.

Our ability to manage ourselves can be optimised by utilising skills in Ideal Self–management, including goal-setting, habit autonomy, attention regulation, self-care, self-soothing, self-compassionate discipline, internal- and external-world regulation, environmental management and other holistic skills. Part 4 of the book outlines these wellness techniques and tools that you may want to adopt for your self-management toolkit.

The skills and concepts I introduce in Part 4 are for you to play around with – they are simply offerings. There are many, many, many more books on many, many, many more techniques for human-mastery out there, which is exciting and awesome. What I have highlighted has been most effective and efficient for me and many of my patients, and I believe it could also be for you. But do keep up your self-study and open mind. The choice of skills you decide to cultivate is up to you. You are the decider of the things you experiment with, and only you can know whether they resonate and are of use to you. Your evidence base is your lived experience, so experiment with yourself and your life.

Do your best to adopt an attitude of experimentation for personal transformation. The idea is to try, observe what you like and what you don't; be prepared to falter and/or succeed; and to learn from the process.

Learn to embrace, or at least accept, failure as a part of personal development. Flipping your perception of failure is a tried and tested hack for living a limitless life: instead of seeing failure as a bad thing and to be avoided, view it as a precious experience bringing new information. Failure means acquisition of data you would not have otherwise received. So what if you try something, don't like it, and are not much good at it? At least having tried you have learnt something about yourself and can move on to the next adventure life brings.

Be willing to do things you might not be good at, just for the fun of it. Try new stuff and invite experience for growth. If you come across any skills that seem like a good fit, are not harmful, and not unattainable to you, then give them a go! Why not? Be open to change, even if that means facing uncertainty and doubt. Rise to the challenge.

That said, while I am encouraging you to be open and try new things, once again I recommend being wary of cleverly marketed wellness claims. I do get nervous about people trying supplements and other alternative medicines that lack clear guidelines and solid evidence for their use. While I have met patients who seem to get good results with wellness schemes and interventions, in my view, the placebo effect is likely to have a lot to do with this and my preference is to go with peer-reviewed research. Although I want to offer my patients more options and hope, I also don't want to falsely advise and waste their money. Generally, evidence to support the use of holistic strategies is difficult to find: there is a dearth of quality research to guide me as an evidence-based physician – for various reasons that I won't go into right now as it is a huge topic to explain. Long story short, if my patient's experience is that such interventions 'work' without harm – other than to their bank account – and they can afford it, all I can do is point out the facts and leave them to make their own informed investments. But please don't fall into the trap of spending your money on anything that lacks credible evidence – and especially if money is tight for you!

Most of my patients flourish without purchasing their way to health, but by attending instead to their needs. I truly believe that moving your body every day, getting a good night's sleep when you can, cuddling the beings you love and nurturing your connections with community, drinking enough water, cutting out alcohol and cigarettes, and eating fresh healthy foods is the most economical and effective prescription for health. We don't necessarily need the latest costly wellness fad. This path to **real wellness** is not sexy, quick, or easy, but it is true that the best things in life are the things that are sensible, common-sense ... and free.

*

There'll be plenty of times when you find yourself feeling run-down, grumpy, hungry, tired, sick, or in a position you'd rather not be in. Maybe you are newly facing unexplained symptoms or managing chronic health issues that get you down. For some of us, these are the challenges of everyday living. But in these situations, you can still have a profound sense of **real wellness** if you hold a healthy relationship with yourself and are able to adaptively meet your needs.

Please note: the messages and content of this book are not appropriate for or directed to people facing acute illness, addictions, or life-threating, unsafe, and/or violent circumstances. In such potentially tragic situations, people must engage in crisis care and seek urgent professional help to survive. When I speak of **real wellness**, I am speaking to people who feel stuck, trapped, unwell, unsure, in a slump, or frustrated with themselves and suffering, who are otherwise safe, stable, and have the motivation to live differently but need to learn how in a practical way.

For the majority of us, I propose that how well we feel is a matter of self-appraisal. How well you feel is a reflection of the health of the relationship you hold with yourself. The way you view, speak to and treat yourself, how you manage yourself, and the thousands of daily choices you make all contribute to your perception, view and judgement of self, your quality of life, and ultimately your sense of **real wellness**. This is the single most influential relationship you'll ever have. It will heavily determine your life and health outcomes. Do you get that? If you can radically accept yourself and care for yourself in healthy ways most of the time, you'll avoid illness that results from the harmful habits and coping mechanisms that we humans are prone to when living in denial, destruct, and disregard mode.

If you live using the skills of self-mastery – self-awareness, acceptance, and self-compassionate care – you're most likely going to thrive. You will feel safe and trusting of yourself. You will learn you can rely on yourself to be there when needed and meet your needs. Living this way is fulfilling and creates an internal foundation of predictability, reliability, safety, and wellbeing. You will cultivate self-determination and inner peace. Inevitably, your self-worth will build, and because you are caring and relating to yourself in an accepting and loving way, with discipline and boundaries, you will inherently like who you are and enjoy living as you. With self-mastery, you relate to yourself in a healthy, adaptive and functional way. This self-mastery creates your quality of life and determines your wellbeing.

What it looks like is someone who can show up for themself each day, like a caring and reliable parent, and provide themself with a safe and predictable routine (shower, balanced meal, book and bed in the evening, for example). They do this even on the tough days, when they may feel down or overwhelmed. The next morning, they wake refreshed and ready to start a new day.

Now, picture how a human who lacks these self-parenting skills might behave at the end of a challenging day. Maybe they wallow in feelings of self-loathing and disregard their physical needs – skipping the gym and going straight to the couch. Maybe they smash down a tub of ice-cream or work their way through the drinks cabinet or stay up late doom-scrolling. It is not that these behaviours make them a 'bad' person or unethical in some way. But they won't wake refreshed and may probably need a lie-in and kebab for brekky. These coping choices are not conducive to a state of **real wellness** in the long term. But more important to their sense of wellness is their lived experience of not being able to care for themselves in the way they need when they need it most. This behaviour is likely, over time, to leave them feeling unsafe, vulnerable to stress, and unhappy – culminating in a poor self-relationship. At worst, their behaviour reinforces any existing belief of being unworthy, untrustworthy, and unsafe. Living controlled by these beliefs is never going to be conducive to a life of **real wellness**.

Scrupulously nurture the relationship you hold with yourself. To be well, you must learn to consistently show up and care for yourself as a healthy parent would, and be there for yourself in times of need, even when it feels hard, and you may want to 'clock off'.

Absorb the information in Part 4 to invest in this journey. If you feel like you are at the starting line for all this, then I welcome you, as this book is the best place for you to start. Don't be overwhelmed, be excited! Go slowly and lovingly. Just read one page or chapter at a time and come back to anything that resonates with you and re-read as you need. Grab a highlighter and pen and mark the shit out of this book to grab attention and keep a record of parts that work for you. If you are across a lot of this information, then I hope you use the information in this book as a series of prompts to reinforce what you know. Maybe coming at it from a fresh perspective is all about a reset, a chance to wholeheartedly re-dedicate yourself to your wellness.

*

Many patients I see are stuck or unsure of what they need in order to be well. Sometimes the root cause is caring so much about how other people perceive us that we disconnect from ourselves, lose insight into our needs and start to do things like people-please. I'm a big believer in the idea that within us lies considerable wisdom –

that, deep down, we do truly know ourselves and what we need. But tapping into this store of self-knowledge is near impossible when we're distracted, confused, or overwhelmed by the noise and busy-ness of life. Using the skills outlined in this book will help you connect to what matters most to use, and mindfully manifest your dreams.

A good starting point is to take yourself to somewhere quiet, give yourself some relaxing breathing space and spend some time tuning in. Somewhere inside us is a voice of reason, and if we're quiet and focused enough, we can hear its wise message. From it you can learn your values, priorities and intentions, then proactively use them to anchor yourself (this is discussed in Part 2).

One of my favourite sights is the look of relief on the faces of patients when they connect to the wisdom within them and start to find the answers to their wellness questions for themselves.

Reading this book is another effective way to quieten the busy-ness of life, focus on yourself, and enquire within. So, congratulate yourself for picking it up and gifting yourself with this opportunity to connect with your inner wisdom. Keep going!

*

Remember that because we're human, we will inevitably let ourselves down and falter in self-discipline and insight. There's a good chance that, at times, we will resort to vices and coping mechanisms that may not be ideal or in line with a gold-standard picture of wellness. One day you may be living virtuously and another a little sloppy – that is normal and human.

This truth also applies to the wellness stars of Instagram. Naturally, we're unlikely to see off camera any cheat eats, cigarettes, boozy drinks or substances they consume. In the same vein, we need to be acutely aware of the role of artificial intelligence and picture editing when it comes to how influencers depict themselves. A lot of marketing materials and information we click on is not real. So, take what you see and read with a grain of salt and be careful where you find your role models.

Crucially, if you stuff up in any way, don't let that be an excuse to give up on your quest for **real wellness**. Learn to forgive yourself; learn from mistakes. Provided you keep trying to live well with self-care, the improvement in overall picture is so worth the effort. And it's never too late to make a positive difference to your wellness. Never give up on yourself – commit yourself to living your best life, challenges, slips, relapses and all. Remember that **real wellness** is a lifestyle. It's a journey, not the end game. It's about long-term commitment and ongoing effort, responding to stuff-ups by directing yourself back onto your wellness path. It's not something that can be achieved that will then be fixed forever; and there is no such thing as a perfect path.

While **real wellness** is a never-ending journey of building self-mastery, it's also one that may be enjoyed with gratitude. To me, daily cultivating and practising self-mastery isn't a chore but an abiding passion and privilege.

Because we live in an era of constant connectivity and are used to the quick fix, it may be disappointing that you can't nail the blueprint one day and then the job is done. But don't fear: you won't be bored along your journey of **real wellness** as there is more than a lifetime's worth of skills to experiment with and learn for your optimal wellbeing. This book could be never-ending, as I continually discover new skills and techniques that build my capacity for these three pillars of **real wellness**. But think of this book as your starter pack. Once you've absorbed the materials in the chapters ahead, it will remain up to you to continue to try new things and build on the skills, concepts and tools introduced.

*

Much of what occurs in our world is both challenging and beyond our control: we can't stop it from happening or modify it. Where our personal power lies is in our reactions and responses. How we conduct ourselves is in our hands, so let's find ways of responding that work for us. For example, you may not be able to change a health diagnosis, but you can certainly change your attitude towards it and adapt your self-care to accommodate it. Rather than ignoring and denying hard stuff, you can learn about it, accept it and work out how to better care for yourself in light of it. With this kind of self-awareness, self-acceptance and self-management, you can live really well. If you take this approach, you're more likely to at least not make matters worse for yourself; potentially, you might be able to reverse to some extent whatever it is that ails you.

To recap: to live and be well requires you to understand, accept and care for yourself appropriately – that is, in the ways you need – most of the time. In Parts 2 to 4 of this book, I explain how to do that, what self-mastery looks like and entails. But it's up to you to sift through the knowledge, concepts, and skills I set out and see what you can work with. Hopefully, you will acquire greater insight into yourself and the things to try to best manage yourself to live well. At the very least, I hope you will feel liberated from any perceived norm of wellness that isn't tailored to you and empowered to craft your own understanding, accepting and caring relationship with yourself. I hope you feel validated that you are still okay and can be well, even if you live with chronic health issues or feel a bit different in some way from most other people.

Case study

Sandra needed to invest in professional psychotherapy to understand herself. She struggled with speaking up and asserting boundaries. A classic people-pleaser, Sandra found herself in unloving relationships that not only didn't meet her needs but where she would end up 'rescuing' her partners. Her therapist was well versed in chronic post-traumatic stress disorder and was able to explain to Sandra how, as a child, her needs had not been met and those experiences had affected her self-perception and current behaviours.

Once Sandra understood herself, her pattern of behaviour, where it all came from, and why it was present in her life, she was able to forgive herself, accept herself, and develop compassion for her struggles. Instead of viewing her behaviours as evidence of character flaws, she started seeing them as a perfectly understandable and predictable human response to her environment and conditioning.

Following this growth in her self-understanding and self-acceptance, she was then able to focus her attention on adaptively managing it all. Years later, Sandra still notices self-deprecating thoughts and urges to 'save' others, but she uses her skills to let these impulses go and turn her attention to healthier things, like her incredibly gorgeous garden, which grounds her rain, hail or shine.

Take-home messages

- **Real wellness** requires self-awareness, self-acceptance, and self-management.
- **Real wellness** is determined – in part – largely by the relationship you hold with yourself.
- Self-awareness requires an understanding of the worlds you inhabit, a capacity for mindfulness, and identification of your values, priorities, intentions, and core beliefs.
- To be well, you must live in the moment and radically accept yourself.

- Self-acceptance requires skills in self-honesty, self-compassion and acceptance.
- Self-management involves holistic tools such as habit autonomy; goal setting; attention and internal-world regulation, self-soothing, and self-discipline.

Try this

If you aren't yet sure of your unique 'recipe' for wellness, start by reflecting on past experiences of living as you. Have there been times when you've felt more well than usual? Try to recall them in detail and see if you can identify clues to your path towards wellness. When feeling more well, did you have more support from a good GP or a psychologist, or were you engaged in a hobby that promoted wellbeing, like art lessons? Keep going with this investigation: what are your needs and how, in the past, have you met them? For example, being in a choir allows self-expression, community connection, creative release, musical stimulation, and vagal toning (to name a few things). So, if participating in a choir has previously made you feel good, it may be because these benefits are important to you, and it could be worthwhile picking up this activity again. If you can't find the right kind of choir, are there other local groups or creative activities where you could meet some of these needs? Maybe getting out of your comfort zone helps you feel well? Maybe it's being in nature?

If you feel stuck and unsure, consider accessing professional help: you need and deserve it. A clinical psychologist has the skills and qualifications to assist us to understand, accept, and manage our humanness much faster than we can do so on our own. You'd be in great company if you found yourself seeking such professional help, so please drop any stigma around servicing your health in this way.

PART 2

Pillar 1 – Self-awareness

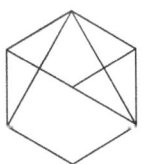

4

Mindfulness

In my opinion, mindfulness – present-moment awareness – is the foundational skill for developing self-awareness, the first pillar of **real wellness**.

A famous definition of mindfulness comes from Dr Jon Kabat-Zinn, the pioneer of Mindfulness-Based Stress Reduction Therapy. He has explained mindfulness as 'paying attention on purpose to the present moment with openness and curiosity'. When we focus our awareness on the present moment, we do so with a sense of acceptance of and non-judgemental attention to all that we notice, like the thoughts and feelings that come up in the process.

Mindfulness is about noticing stuff – both the things we intentionally focus on and the things that come up spontaneously – and we can't be aware of what's going on without noticing! With constant practice, we become more tuned in to the inner workings of our minds – self-aware, in other words.

If being mindful is like shining a light on yourself and the world around you with the aim of seeing what it is you're dealing with at any one moment so you can prepare yourself to deal with it appropriately, living unmindfully is like trying to navigate life in the pitch black of a moonless night. You may get some things right sometimes, but chances are that would be through luck as opposed to measured choice. Even if you're currently happy with winging your way through situations, it is wise to acquire this skill to explore its potential benefits, such as noticing how stress manifests in your body; enhancing your ability to self-inquire; gaining insights and better emotional regulation.

Mindfulness is a practice: something you can build into your self-care routine. It can be practised informally in everyday activities or movement-based pastimes like tai chi. You might prefer meditation, which is a broad term for formal practices designed to cultivate mindfulness. Regardless of the approach you choose, the aim is to find an anchor for your attention and then keep this focus without judgement or getting carried away by distractions. This allows you to improve your concentration and deepen your capacity to notice sensations, emotions and thoughts. Thinking – the incessant mental activity of the monkey mind – is the most common distracter when practising mindfulness. In addition to mental distractions, your focus can be challenged by sensations within you – like the sudden desire to scratch your eye or sensations of pain that seem more intense if, for example, you are being still – and from your environment – like distant traffic noise or the sounds of people moving around. When practising mindfulness, you inevitably lose attention. You can't prevent thoughts and other distractions. Mindfulness is about the intention to avoid losing your attention to judgement or other factors, and practising turning your attention back to presence when it drifts.

Because our thoughts are ongoing, in a mindfulness practice the emphasis is on choosing not to engage in mindless rumination. Rather, you allow rumination to occur but repeatedly re-attend to the present moment non-judgementally. You aren't stopping thoughts – that's an impossibility – just holding your attention elsewhere as best you can. When practising mindfulness, you bring your attention back to your focus – from the distraction of thoughts – over and over and over again until you finish your practice. It can be exhausting and frustrating. The trick is to relax, practise without expectations or striving, and to accept that mindfulness is practised in the face of inevitable distraction. If you're encountering a lot of distractions, you're practising well.

While you are gently looking within – and noticing whatever comes up without following it down a rabbit hole – cultivating a sense of openness and curiosity reduces shame and blame.

I see mindfulness as aiming for a state of pure sensory reception, where you try to perceive data without processing it further. You receive data, but aim to avoid doing anything with the received data – no analysis, no planning, no labelling, no reflection, nothing more than noticing (this is hard for me as I love planning!). It's as if you're taking a break from your thinking self. When you find that you're thinking – which, unavoidably, you will do – gently turn your attention back to a state of pure awareness, a state of simply noticing, experiencing, feeling, and being. Take the example of mindfulness of breath. This is a practice of noticing your breathing without critiquing it, trying to change it, or creating a story around it in your mind. It's focusing your complete attention on feeling the breath as it naturally occurs within you – nothing more, just a simple and easy resting of attention there. When your mind wanders from the breath – as it is bound to do – you simply turn your attention back to it.

When practising mindfulness, the focus of your attention can be whatever you choose. It could be one specific thing, such as paying attention to the flame of a lit candle, or more of an open awareness of multiple experiences and stimuli occurring simultaneously, such as noticing a garden and all that it contains in that moment of awareness. It could be something going on inside you, like your breath, or something in the world around you, like sounds. Different foci require different senses. For instance, while focusing mindfully on a flower, you use your vision to see, touch to feel, and olfaction to smell. You'd probably leave out taste – as most flowers are gross to eat – and hearing – as flowers are generally pretty quiet.

If you try to notice without judgement and, when distracted, pull your attention back to your point of attention, then you're practising mindfulness. If, like all beginners to this skill, you find yourself noticing a lot of judgements and distractions, then you're working really hard and ought to be commended for your efforts!

Practising mindfulness is simple if you follow these three steps:

1. Notice something objectively (without critical appraisal and thinking) and focus on it as best you can, e.g. the sounds going on around you.
2. As soon as you notice you're distracted, gently and without self-judgement turn your attention back to your focus. In this example, it's likely you'll start identifying the origins of the sounds; when that happens just stop, don't judge yourself, and simply turn your attention back to sound.
3. Repeat Steps 1 and 2 over and over and over.

A favourite practice of mine, which I highly recommend, is mindfully drinking a cup of coffee. If you give this a go, try to really notice the smell, taste, touch, and look of your coffee. It's as if time slows down a little and you experience the coffee more fully. I have committed to this as a daily practice, probably because I love coffee and it heightens my enjoyment of drinking it. I do notice judgements and other distractions, but the practice of mindfulness brings a conscious attention to my sensory experience of the coffee.

When you start learning mindfulness, it may require a lot of effort. It's likely that you're beginning to train yourself to exist in a way to which you're altogether unaccustomed; you probably haven't closely examined the world around you in this manner since your early childhood. We're born being present, unrushed, noticing: I see this state of pure mindful presence in my young son, who's forever in the moment and in awe of all he sees. However, sometimes people find reclaiming this skill challenging and draining. All the thinking, planning, judging, problem-solving and ruminating we learn to do as adults makes being present difficult. However, mindfulness is natural to us as humans, and with time it becomes easier. The speed at which you develop this skill depends on your frequency of practice. It's all about the reps!

*

Neuronal plasticity refers to the brain's ability to rewire, sprout, prune, and alter itself, depending on how it is used. The brain and the nervous system are in a constant state of change and development. Hence the term 'plasticity' – the brain and nervous system are malleable and not fixed. They grow in ways based on what you do and how they are used. If you spend a lot of time on a particular activity, like riding a bike, the neural pathways involved strengthen. Eventually, with practice, riding becomes easier and even effortless, thanks to the processes of neuronal plasticity.

Just as capacities you frequently use strengthen and grow, the less you use a capacity, the more the relevant neural pathways get pruned back and weakened. Hence the phrase 'use it or lose it'. As we get older, we need to purposely practise balance and mobility exercises to keep those pathways strong and combat age-related degeneration. More evidence around neuronal plasticity is emerging, which is opening exciting new avenues of scientific enquiry.

On a simple, human behaviour–focused level, if you practise mindfulness regularly – the more the better – the region of the brain used for non-judgemental awareness develops. This means that your practices eventually feel easier and that in your everyday life, even when you're not intentionally engaging in a mindfulness practice, you're more likely to tap into a mindful state. That's right, you read correctly: if you consciously practise mindfulness, you can rewire your brain to be mindful without trying.

After years of practice and mindful yoga, I still notice my monkey mind causing internal stress and I need to consciously choose to switch into mindfulness to relax and reset. However, in general, my mental state is way more effortlessly mindful compared to how it was before I started to develop this skill. I'm more aware of my body and environment and less in my head. In my work as a doctor, I've noticed that I'm more in tune with my inner world and the demands of my environment, and better able to manage how I react to people and situations. This has allowed me to operate with more equanimity: I can mindfully take in all the hassles that come with my job and respond with measured consideration – rather than propagating the stress and pressure I perceive around me.

*

A decade or so ago, few people had heard of mindfulness but today it's a widely taught skill. I've seen it covered in textbooks, at leadership courses, and even on the Australian Institute of Company Directors course. Most high-profile athletes, businesses and organisations promote mindfulness, not only for wellbeing, but to enhance productivity and organisational health. It would be a mistake to dismiss this practice as too 'woo woo' for you.

Once you understand what mindfulness is and its relevance to your self-mastery, you can begin to play around with it in your life, further opening up the path to **real wellness**. In a state of mindfulness, amazing and special things can happen. You notice the nuances of your mind, the patterns of your reactions, and you may even start to see the connection between your internal experiences and your external behaviours. If you have limited awareness, then it's pretty tough to be able to respond appropriately and optimally to the needs of your whole self and environment.

This is something I learnt the hard way because, as a student doctor, I suffered from imposter syndrome. Lots of distracting worries and doubts about my competence used to run through my head. This affected my ability to enjoy my everyday work life and notice the good moments, like shared connections with other people. It also limited my ability to dive into a state of free learning and discovery, as it hindered my ability to focus on tasks, as did the related fear of failure or judgement. So, if a senior asked me to examine a patient's knee as a learning experience, rather than enjoying the privileged opportunity to learn from an experienced and willing teacher, I would be overwhelmed by unpleasant feelings and distracting negative thoughts. Once I learnt mindfulness, I found ways to function better despite this suffering. Gradually, I noticed patterns in my thoughts and found opportunities to choose differently. For example, by focusing on my breath as an anchor to the present moment, I could disregard my monkey mind, with all its catastrophic stories, and redirect my attention to the tasks at hand. I simply noticed all that internal stuff, let it go, and turned my attention back to my work. By letting go of my internal distraction, I was able to notice more of what was going on around me, then I was better equipped to respond to problems as they arose.

When working, I still use mindfulness to let go of distracting and unhelpful internal-world currents in order to devote my attention to the person in front of me. I focus on their needs so I can help them.

A lovely side effect of mindfulness is that you may find it especially relaxing. I started teaching and hosting mindfulness sessions at my hospital when I was a trainee. Although the classes were available to all hospital employees, most of the attendees were administration staff. One day, I asked why so many secretaries came along. The explanation was that their job was very stressful, and the mindfulness helped to relax them. Not only did this underscore the potential of mindfulness to aid relaxation but it taught me that hospital admin staff may well be the most stressed of us all. Ever since then, I've been mindful to be grateful towards the secretaries I interact with in my workplace!

Certainly, the more relaxed you are when practising mindfulness, the easier it will feel and the more likely you will be to continue the habit. Relaxation is probably the best side effect I can think of.

*

The most effective way to start learning mindfulness is with a guide or teacher. This can be face-to-face with a psychologist, via an app, online tutorial, or even a podcast. My favorite mindfulness app is Headspace. I love an English accent and I think the host, one-time Buddhist monk Andy Puddicombe, is quite pleasant to listen to. There are many online resources and books dedicated to mindfulness. I encourage everyone to consider partaking in a Mindfulness Based Stress Reduction course.

Begin your mindfulness journey by first educating yourself a little on what it is, its benefits, how it works, the various techniques and approaches, and all the ways you can practise it. There are many good books that deal with this. As you learn about it, be sure to be practising it as well. It is by doing the skill that you will grow to understand its utility, relevance and what exactly it is. You will never grasp mindfulness without the practice. Just like riding a bike, no matter how much you have intellectualised the process with reading and research, you cannot master it without the practice. You need to do the skill.

If – like me, with my restless body – a seated mindfulness practice is not for you because you struggle to sit still, then don't bother with it. Try something more active, like yoga or mindful walking. Find a resource and version of the practice that works for you and stick with it. Be consistent and give yourself plenty of time – like years of committed practice. Don't expect a quick acquisition of this skill. Do get curious about its effect on you. Set yourself a fun goal of practising daily for a month to see how it changes your lived human experience. Keep a diary or do it with a friend and share your growth over coffee or a walk.

*

In my opinion, a regular mindfulness practice is a requirement for building self-awareness, but it is a tool you can use to develop all three of the pillars of self-mastery for **real wellness**. It is essential to perceive yourself as accurately as you can in order to effectively manage yourself optimally. The more mindful we are of what's going on inside and around us and how this is affecting our physical actions, choices, and life outcomes, the more human-mastery we can achieve.

Over time, mindfulness reveals to us the patterns of our thoughts and actions; it shows us our biases and the underlying beliefs that drive our behaviour, as well as triggers. This is powerful knowledge as it allows us more opportunities to respond to situations with wisdom as opposed to impulsively or reactively. It is like we can insert a stop sign between noticing and action. In that pause, we have the chance to decide to embody our chosen values. With mindfulness, we can work towards breaking unhelpful habits of thinking and develop distance from self-limiting beliefs and flawed perceptions. For example, if negative thoughts and associated unpleasant feelings are deterring you from completing tasks you need to do – thoughts like, 'You'll never get it all done' and associated feelings of doom and gloom – with your newfound mindfulness skill, you'll be able to notice these distractions, let them go, and focus on doing the task.

The light shed by mindfulness allows us to grow. Build this skill and allow it to form the foundation and basis of all the other skills for self-mastery.

In the next chapter, I introduce a simple but powerful concept that will also help you to develop your self-awareness and mastery.

Case study

For years, David regularly practised yoga, and as a part of his yoga studio membership, he also took part in weekly group mindfulness sessions. Although David found it hard to do – at times he would feel restless – unexpectedly, he experienced benefits from the mindfulness practice. During his exams, using mindfulness skills reduced his experience of stress and helped him relax. But it was during his end-of-year training exams that he realised the complete benefits of his regular practice.

His exam was performance-based. He had to cycle through 12 different examination stations, each with a different task to be completed under time pressure. There was no time in between for rest and recovery. As he moved from one station to the next, he used his mindfulness skills to let go of his performance and any worries or thoughts he noticed around whether he might have passed or failed the previous task, and to clear his mind ready for the upcoming one. When he entered the station, he focused his attention on the new task.

Mindfulness had trained David in focused attention, noticing distraction and turning his attention back to the task at hand. In this circumstance, rather than using the skills for self-awareness or relaxation, David was accepting his circumstances and remaining focused on completing the exam to the best of his ability. He topped his class in that exam.

After that experience, David reflected that distractions during exams are much like the distractions he noticed when trying hard or new things, fighting unhelpful urges, and changing his habits. Henceforth, he nurtured the skill and started applying it for self-mastery in all areas of his life. Mindfulness is now a lifelong cherished skill that has helped him not only relax when under stress and to nail exams, but also to optimise his self-management and capacity for **real wellness**.

Take-home messages

- Mindfulness is noticing without thinking about what you're noticing.
- Distractions are inevitable, and turning your attention away from these and back to your focus is part of mindfulness.
- You need to practise being mindful over time in order to develop the skill, but thanks to neuronal plasticity – a fancy term for the brain's capacity to be rewired – mindfulness becomes easier and even starts to happen when you're not expecting it to. So, it's worth the effort!
- Mindfulness reveals your inner world, the patterns of your mind and behaviours, and it sheds light on all the things in your environment that impact your choices.
- Mindfulness is the base skill for self-awareness, the first pillar of self-mastery, but also helps build all other skills for **real wellness**.

Try this

Find a comfy position where you can be both relaxed and alert and you won't be interrupted. Close your eyes, if you feel comfortable doing so, and take some deep, full breaths. Focus your attention wholly and completely on your toes. Notice the sensation of your toes. Allow your mind to rest its attention on the experience of feeling your toes.

You will notice other things going on inside and around you. Let go of these distractions and turn your attention back to your toes. Commit to two minutes of mindfulness of toes. You are not thinking about them, but rather keeping your attention on them. It is a practice of noticing, being distracted, and refocusing on your toes.

5

Our Two Worlds

Before I introduce the **Two Worlds** concept, allow me to explain why I use so many concepts in this book. Concepts are integral to how we function. Humans use concepts to learn, understand, make decisions, and reflect. According to the latest neuroscience, our brains are wired for concepts. Our environment is highly complex, and to manage this, the brain uses concepts to create categories – groups of things based on their function, such as foods that fuel us. Developing categories and concepts allows human beings to make sense of stuff, find meaning and value in stuff, integrate with and function in our world – and survive it all.

As I explained in the introduction, concepts around our humanness seem rarely taught to the masses. This is where the **Two Worlds** concept comes in. It is simple – designed to be easy to use – and its purpose is to increase your clarity about what you must manage and live with day in and day out, the influences affecting your choices, and how to optimise your autonomy over your behaviour and responses, thus fundamentally improving your wellbeing. It certainly has for me. When building self-awareness to cultivate **real wellness**, conceptualising yourself and your lived human experience (your experience of living as you) may be the single most helpful thing you can do (after mindfulness) to optimise your self-awareness and function as a human.

To be clear: I'm not claiming that the **Two Worlds** concept is based in science or clinical evidence per se – there's no study in a lab proving we have two worlds. It's merely a concept – you may prefer a term like framework, tool, algorithm, or self-perspective – that I hit upon and used to get well, understand myself, and navigate my lived human experience, and still do. It is subjective, and the evidence for it is observations about the general lived experience of being human. All I'm saying is that it has worked for me and many of my patients over the years, and it may help you function better as a human too. It is also important to acknowledge that some people may experience more than two worlds. I am aware that some people report the experience of psychic and other influences, for instance. But most patients I see do not relate to these experiences. We all share the two worlds discussed below, and I believe the concept is useful for building self-awareness and achieving self-mastery.

Basically, the **Two Worlds** concept compartmentalises all our lived human experience – the stimuli, inputs, and influences of our lives, whether conscious or not – into two worlds, an **inner world** and an **external world**. These two worlds are inextricably linked: they constantly impact and affect each other – and, ultimately, the choices we make, our behaviours and our quality of life. The interplay between these two worlds makes up our experience of living and self. I hope this basic breakdown of being a human is helpful. It aims to be objective, matter of fact, and non-judgemental. Let's go over these two worlds, one at a time, outlining what they are made up of in a little more detail. Let's first look into the human inner world.

Our internal world

This is our private, hidden, intangible, personal experience of living. No-one knows how your internal world is for you, and you don't know how another person's internal world is for them. However, what we do know is that we all have this vibrant, secret and often chaotic inner experience, and that our internal worlds have shared elements, including thoughts, sensations, urges, and emotions. Although our individual experience of these things is variable, we all experience them in some form on a daily basis and they impact our function. Let's go through each of these individually.

- **Thoughts:** We all have a mind that generates thoughts. God only knows their origin. What is clear is that thoughts are relentless and involuntary – we can't control them. They can be conscious or unconscious, useful or useless, pleasant or unpleasant, fact or fiction. Thoughts can be in the form of language, movies or images: it's as if within us there's a chaotic and random news desk, radio station and film studio. Sometimes, the volume of the thoughts is super loud, and other times, not so much. We need to learn to live with our mind and all the millions of thoughts it produces for us, beyond our control, each and every day. (Did I mention thoughts are relentless?) A Google search quotes an average of 60,000 thoughts per day! As an overthinker, I may have even more.

    It's important to accept thoughts as a fact of being human but that not all thoughts as necessarily factual. Many thoughts are absolute nonsense. They're a part of your lived human experience but need not define you or determine your actions. The insight that you are not fully your thoughts is powerful when aiming for **real wellness**. You can learn to identify your thoughts through mindfulness and train yourself to focus less on unhelpful thinking; you can learn not to allow your thoughts to consume your awareness. If you identify that some thoughts are troubling you, you can seek help, use your mindfulness skills, and other strategies discussed in later chapters – like diffusion – to get some breathing space from your thinking (internal regulation).

You would not be alone if, some days, you felt that managing your thoughts seemed like a full-time job! Metacognition is the term used to describe this awareness of thinking. Mindfulness builds your capacity for metacognition, which as previously mentioned is helpful for self-awareness.

Consider your thoughts as a part of your inner world and something that we, as humans, must accept and learn to live with. Friend or foe, they are a part of our humanness and a major player in our lived experience of being. Simply becoming aware of your thoughts is the first step forward to mastering them.

- **Physical sensations:** The body has physical sensations, like heartbeats and muscle tension. Humans are sensate beings, meaning we feel a lot of this stuff! For starters, there are multiple biological processes going on in us all the time, so it stands to reason that we feel stuff every now and then. Like all inner-world elements, these experiences are private and subjective. It is often difficult to describe pain to another person, for example. In medicine, we have a lot of language around this. We classify physical sensations as somatic (from skin, bones, joints, muscles, mucosa, organ capsules), visceral (from solid or hollow organs, deep lymph nodes and large muscle groups) or neuropathic (from nerves and neural tissues). Physical sensations can be perceived as pleasant or unpleasant. They vary in intensity (obvious or subtle), region (limb, trunk or head), frequency (constant or intermittent), and character (sharp or dull).

Interoception is the term used to describe the experience of internal sensation. A lot of interoception is unconscious, thank gosh! Imagine if we directly felt all the subconscious changes within, like at the ever-changing cellular electrolyte levels. While we don't need such detailed awareness, tuning in to your body is valuable. Some people are detached from their body and unaware of their physical sensations, which means that tension can build up and go unattended; these people generally have poor self-care. They can be taught to tune in more to their physical sensation to better care for their needs. Other people may be overly focused on sensations, leading to a heightened experience of feeling. Some of my patients have chronic pain syndrome and fixate on their discomfort. Part of chronic pain management is distracting yourself and turning your attention away from sensation. Building your conscious capacity for interoception through mindfulness is helpful for self-awareness: through awareness of your sensations, you can get to know your body better and bring some balance to the mind.

Although there's always a 'reason' for physical sensations, you need not always know the cause or act on them: feelings aren't always internal alarms to be concerned about. Yes: sometimes they may be your body's way of communicating potential harm – like a burn pain, or a need, like thirst, which does require you to act. But they may also be random and minor fleeting experiences you need not worry about, like a twinge of pain in the tummy after eating a big meal (as long as we stop eating!).

Some of us have more sensations than others to accept and manage. Some of us are more connected to the feelings of our body. Because all of us have so many physical sensations, it can be distracting and challenging at times to discern what requires attention and action and what to ignore. It is masterful to check in with yourself and your body to notice what is going on, meet needs, and regulate tension. We need to work with our body to function optimally, and part of this is simply developing the self-awareness skill of noticing sensations within and developing some familiarity with them to build your mastery of them.

- **Urges:** These are intense inner-world experiences that grab our attention – 'It's urgent!' – and motivate action. Urges may be triggered by or associated with the experience of thoughts, emotions, and physical sensations or environmental factors. Biologically, urges may be linked to neurotransmitters and hormones in the brain, which play a significant role in regulating emotions, mood, and motivation. Whatever its underlying cause, you have an impulse to move towards a choice right now.

  Like the other elements of the inner world, urges can be rational or irrational, helpful or unhelpful, and benign or potentially harmful. They vary in strength and clarity, and, like ocean waves, they rise and fall regardless of how conscious you are of them or whether you act upon them. They don't last forever and will eventually pass. An urge may indicate a desire – like the urge to buy a new pair of shoes – or a need – like the urge to eat when peckish – but it might not be framed in an effective, healthy way if you have addictions or unhelpful habits. In order to best live with our urges, we must tune in to them, and learn to predict, and expect them.

  The first step towards mastery over this inner-world element is simply to build your awareness around your urges: when you are having them, and how they are manifesting within you. Understand and accept your human urges, their utility and relevance. Get familiar and comfy with urges by noticing them. Notice their place in your inner world.

- **Emotions:** These are complex inner-world states that have physiological and psychological dimensions and are often spontaneous. Common emotions are happiness, sadness, anger, excitement and fear, but it's impossible to say whether people experience them in the same way. An instance of emotion can be experienced as a combination of sensations, thoughts and urges. If you feel the physical sensation of pain, you may also notice an associated raised heartbeat, and worry thoughts around potential danger, culminating in a variant of fear.

While personal, individual and variable, emotions are also shaped by culture and language. In English-speaking culture, some researchers have identified that there are four core emotions: fear/surprise, guilt/shame, anger/disgust, happiness/joy. But these may be combined in numerous ways and experienced in varying degrees: there may be an endless number of emotional states all of us can experience. They can be complex and difficult to understand, but emotions are a normal and required part of being human. Like urges, emotions drive behaviour. They are essential for decision-making, for instance.

Emotions have a purpose, carry a message, and serve as a gateway to our ethics and value systems. Because we tend not to feel strongly about things that aren't meaningful to us, when emotions arise unexpectedly, they tell us that the matter at hand is important to us and help us realise what we care about. Emotions give us important information. For example, fear serves as a message to do something to protect yourself from a threat. It may be expressed with wide eyes and dilated pupils. Shame is a by-product of your instinctual need to be accepted and part of a tribe; it's triggered when you act against your or society's standards and can present with lowered eyes and deviated gaze. Anger indicates a violation of your rights and may look like a glare with tight lips. Happiness is triggered by meeting your values and enjoying your priorities and usually manifests as a smile.

Like thoughts and urges, emotions can be helpful or unhelpful, valid and rational or otherwise. Although emotions cannot directly harm us, depending on our relationship with and handling of them, they may lead to issues. Say you have a fight with a friend and become angry, that intense spontaneous response shows that you care about your friendship. You might use this insight to adaptively speak up and correct the situation to nurture your relationship. However, you could also allow the anger to overwhelm you, and impulsively manifest an aggressive response that makes matters worse. Some people fear such intensity: they live avoiding their emotions and use numbing out coping mechanisms like drugs and alcohol, which may give rise to problems.

Emotions are influenced by the state of your body, so if you optimise your nutrition, sleep, movement and stress levels and avoid drugs and alcohol use, you will be well placed to regulate your emotional state. Poor emotional regulation coupled with poor self-care is more likely to be characterised by extreme emotional highs and lows. Becoming aware of your emotions, understanding them, noticing them, and enquiring into the relationship you have with them is the first step in developing self-mastery for **real wellness**. The more emotionally literate you are, the higher the level of self-mastery you will enjoy.

- **Values, ethics and beliefs:** These elements of our inner world are like its invisible framework. They guide our perceptions, processing of data and events, decisions, actions, and interactions with others, often without our realising. For example, if you value generosity, then you may be more inclined to notice acts of generosity, feel inspired by them and experience thoughts around how generosity is a good thing. Your ethics influence your emotions and in turn your thoughts as well. When you act against your ethics, you're likely to notice the experience of guilt associated with judgemental thoughts around doing the wrong thing. Beliefs shape the stories that run through your mind and the quality of your emotions. For example, if you believe cats are not nice animals, then you're more likely to feel and think unpleasant things when you pass a cat compared to someone who believes cats are lovely.

Our values, ethics and beliefs may be expressed to our conscious mind via thoughts, sensations, urges, and emotions. They are shaped by things like our upbringing, culture, religion, personal experiences, education, and societal influence, but they can be modified.

Building your awareness of these parts of your inner world helps to develop your understanding of why you may respond to certain things in the ways you do. I discuss values in more detail in Chapter 6 and beliefs in Chapter 9. For now, simply see your values, ethics and beliefs as a part of your inner world to get to know, understand, and make space for to work on your self-mastery for **real wellness**.

Our external world

Cast your mind towards the second world we inhabit – the external world; everything that happens outside your body. Notice all you sense and consider what your external world is comprised of. It includes the weather, the environment, things, creatures, other people and also cultural, religious, and social norms. Others' judgements and expectations of us play a large role here.

We experience this external world through our five basic senses – taste, touch, smell, sound, and sight. In neuroscience, this is called exteroception (sensing things external of us, as opposed to interoception where we sense experiences within). We may attend to one sense more than others, which shapes our experience, perspective, and interactions. A neurolinguist would argue that if I use vivid, image-heavy descriptions when I speak to a 'visual person', they would be more likely to engage with my conversation than if I spoke to them without such visual detail. Empaths – individuals who are highly attuned to people's emotions – assert that they readily pick up on others' energy, allowing them to take on board others' feelings. A surprising number of patients tell me they have extra-sensory abilities and sensitivities, like getting nauseous when a storm is coming. Recently, a patient was adamant that whenever the barometer drops, he has a hypoglycaemic episode, so he uses weather reports to help decide his insulin doses! Although I found this medically concerning and did not condone the behaviour, it was an interesting perspective.

Whatever you believe, it's reasonable to assume we all have tendencies to attend more to certain external experiences. Meaning we will notice and focus more on these things. What's most important is understanding your own tendencies so you can balance out your perspective more completely.

The external world is a busy place with all manner of distractions. Unlike the internal world – which is ours alone, invisible, and difficult to articulate and share – the external world is shared, tangible and visible. The majority of us can touch it, see it, hear it, smell it and even taste it. Consequently, the external world is easier to talk about with other people and may seem more real than the inner world. For these and other reasons, we may end up with little awareness of the inner world. But both worlds contribute to our perceptions and behaviour. Being aware and noticing both is key to cultivating self-awareness and self-mastery.

Living in two worlds at once

Start using this **Two Worlds** concept to notice *all* that is happening for you. Think of these two worlds like compartments. Play around with placing your attention on your external compartment to notice all the things going on around you that may be impacting your lived human experience. Then look within at the internal world and see what you notice there. Simply noticing and accepting the experiences of both worlds to build familiarity and self-awareness is the first step towards mastery and allows a more complete perception of your reality.

Our inner and outer worlds are in constant dialogue with each other. Understanding this two-way connection is vital to self-awareness.

Firstly, our experience of the external world feeds through to our thoughts, sensations, and urges. These inner-world experiences then drive our decision-making, which manifests as actions that in turn affect our external world. For example, if you feel a cold breeze (processing of external data), you may become uncomfortably cold and have an urge to be warm (inner-world thoughts and urges are triggered). You decide to turn on a heater (action that alters your environment) and as a result, there's a rise in the temperature of the room (your external environment has been affected).

Secondly, our reactions, responses and behaviours influence and change both our inner-world experience and our outer world and environment. For example, say you see an advertisement selling chocolate (this is an external piece of data), and it triggers an urge within you to eat chocolate (inner-world experience). So, you head to the kitchen, where you've hidden your chocolate stash – which you think your partner doesn't know about. You act on this urge and eat some chocolate. Now you're left feeling regretful: you have a goal to lose weight and a plan to do this by cutting down on your discretionary calories; you've just done exactly the opposite. By acting on your urge, you've lessened your environmental supply of chocolate and created an uneasy internal-world experience for yourself. You were stimulated through your sense of sight to crave something and reacted by meeting that craving, which altered both your internal and external worlds.

Maybe you're now in a bad mood and poor company for those around you, affecting their moods too. You also now need to go to the shops and buy more chocolate.

At the interface between the internal world and our external world is our behaviour, which includes decisions we may make. Our capacity for equanimity, free will, and measured choice determines the inter-relationship between our two worlds. My lived experience suggests that, for the most part, it is comfortable and good for our two worlds to be connected and responding dynamically to each other, as our circumstances constantly evolve. However, not *every* stimulus requires a response: it's possible to experience events and choose simply to sit with them – rather than following them with words or actions. For example, something external to you may occur – like you find yourself in a traffic jam – and you choose not to act on its influence: no hand-wringing, cursing to yourself or aggressive lane changes. It exists without an impact on your behaviour. Likewise, something within you occurs that you notice – like a hankering to binge-watch the latest season of a show you are keen on rather than have an early dinner then attend your weekly toastmasters meeting – and you choose to notice it without reaction. It exists without an impact on you and your environment.

Realising you can manage this connection is a superpower. For example, if someone annoys you and it triggers some anger and an urge to yell or angrily react in some way, you can choose to do that or you can simply let the anger naturally pass without changing your behaviour at all (using mindfulness and your equanimity skills). No-one will ever know you were angry. However, if you allow your inner-world experience to affect your behaviour, then you've brought life to it and in some way allowed it to influence the world around you.

From time to time, it works better for us to choose not to respond – to simply cease all action and keep the interface at bay. By staying still, being, breathing, and refusing to give in to negative inner-world impulses, we prevent inner-world turbulence from affecting our external lives.

In encouraging you to stay still – not do, not react, and not allow the internal-world stuff to generate external-world change – I'm asking you to try something that will probably feel contrary. Consider that, for a human, it's often far more powerful to not-do than to get things done.

It's wise to acquire the insight and ability to choose what influences you. I for one like to aim for good vibes all around me, even when my inner world is full of self-loathing! I don't want to project my internal struggles and dramas onto others – especially at work, when I'm interacting with innocent patients, or at home with my loving family. The inner world can be as intense and overwhelming as a house on fire, but it cannot generate action or affect our external world unless we react to it.

Mastering the **Two Worlds** concept is about learning to tune in to the fleeting experiences of your inner world and remain unshaken – well, not too shaken, and at least able to sit with it all, rather than impulsively reacting and making your life more difficult.

When we re-engineer the connectivity of our two worlds – switch it from automatic to manual; give ourselves some control – we gift ourselves choice. Once you can experience without reacting mindlessly, you are asserting your mastery over your internal and external worlds. They don't have to be linked in a cause and effect way 24/7. Booyeh!

To recap, this basic **Two World** concept aims to help you simplify your lived human experience into compartments so you can more easily notice and understand your influences and develop your self-awareness as a stepping-stone towards self-mastery. Think of it as a tool to organise and declutter your humanness and self-perception.

It's helpful to consider these two worlds and all they are made up of separately. If your inner world is familiar to you, you understand its elements and become comfortable with them, you'll avoid it less and consequently notice more information to more accurately respond to life. You'll pick up on the predictable patterns contributing to your life choices and health behaviours. Once you see things more clearly, you'll learn where your power lies and develop the capacity to intervene and respond to life in ways that work well for you. You nail this, and you've nailed living as a human (it's a big call, I know). Behaviour self-mastery starts with allowing yourself to notice what's going on inside and around you, using mindfulness.

*

In my younger years, I was confused by my humanness and this intense world around me. I lacked a practical framework for living and being human and managing it all coherently – with a sense of understanding and order. I yearned for an algorithm or some visual text in my mind to help view myself and all the distractions within and around me in a way that brought comfort, understanding and peace.

Eventually, I worked out this framework. Once I adopted it, my lived human experience felt far more organised: things were in compartments and categories and felt less random. Stuff had a purpose, a role, and a place to live. It was less confusing. My life was less bewildering. My day-to-day experience of the world started to feel clear, neat, and tidy. I felt like I had some control over my experience. On reflection, it makes perfect sense that adopting a concept around my humanness that organised, tidied up and decluttered my self-percept would help me thrive: I hate being in a messy space. In fact, I thrive on decluttering my house, taking a haul of no longer needed items to an opportunity shop and living in a well-ordered, minimalistic environment.

The upshot was that slowly my inner world became less overwhelming and more pleasant to notice: my influences were less mysterious to me, my behaviours less confusing, and my life felt less complicated. I was able to look within with more peace and calm. As a result, I noticed my default modes of thinking and reacting. I learnt how my emotions served as helpful data and messages, not things to be ashamed of or that needed to be nipped in the bud. Once I picked up on my behaviour patterns, I could start to reshape them more to my liking.

I noticed how my environment played a huge role in my choices and wellbeing. I learnt how the elements of both worlds were related and affect each other. Eventually, I familiarised myself and became comfortable with the whole contents of my two worlds, and I learnt to manage them optimally.

The **Two Worlds** concept helped me to build my self-awareness but also my self-acceptance and self-management skills. I feel greater mastery over my humanness. Once I stopped avoiding certain parts of myself, I started to dive deeper within to notice and connect to the root causes of my challenges so I could respond and grow in ways I chose for my wellbeing. To manage it all more skilfully, I started to play with techniques and strategies such as diffusion and other tools outlined in Part 4. I don't think I could have made these **real wellness** gains without mindfulness and this **Two Worlds** concept.

I view the **Two Worlds** concept as essential for human-mastery and relevant to any human being keen to develop their self-awareness. You needn't have a certain faith, sense of spirituality or cultural background to benefit from this concept. Universal to all humans is the fact that we live with an internal world and an external world.

If you're a human being and want to better understand and manage yourself, then the **Two Worlds** concept is for you. I encourage you to invest the time to get to know your two worlds and their relationship with each other in order to gain insight into why you may do the things you do. Then you can assert some power over your impulses and actions. Hopefully, using this **Two Worlds** framework helps you break things down in a simple, digestible, tangible and practical way so you can view yourself with more clarity and then understand, accept and manage yourself with more skill. I hope it helps you cultivate compassion for your humanness and that it is as useful to you as it has been for me in my own quest for self-mastery.

Case study

Jenny really valued being a mum. She adored her kids. But for some reason she kept finding herself speaking and acting to her children in unkind ways. This pattern of behaviour was deeply wounding to both her kids and her own soul.

By diligently applying the **Two Worlds** concept, and making time each day to review what she observed, she was able to identify the influences contributing to her reactions. She found conceptually breaking down what she was experiencing in these moments into two sections helpful to build her self-awareness. She got into the habit of checking in with her inner world and started to notice the urges within that preceded her mean-spirited behaviour. She noticed how the urges occurred with strong emotions and predictable thoughts and beliefs. She also started to notice her external world and the expressions of hurt on the faces of her kids, the time pressure she was typically under, and even the irritating noises that were usually occurring when she lost her temper, like the TV being on at high volume in the background, which contributed to her stress levels. The concept provided her with a framework to notice what was going on for her in a balanced and systematic way, then to build her self-awareness.

With routine use of this concept, mindfulness and other therapy, Jenny was able to slowly grow her capacity for equanimity and change her habits. She learnt and became familiar with her triggers and developed skills to manage them in more effective ways. When triggered, rather than reacting angrily and losing her temper – making her children frightened of and disconnected from her – she used her breath and a time-out to calm down. Once regulated, she was able to explain to the kids why their behaviour was challenging and to effectively problem-solve, using reasonable consequences and rewards.

Take-home messages

- Concepts serve function. The **Two Worlds** concept is a simplified framework of the human experience designed to build self-awareness and mastery around your humanness.
- Humans all live with and manage two worlds: the internal world and the external world.
- Simply put, the internal world is comprised of thoughts, physical sensations, emotions, and urges, which we sense through metacognition and interoception.
- The external world is made of all the stuff outside our bodies that we sense via exteroception and our five senses. This includes other people, places, and things, as well as expectations and social norms.
- We need a balanced view of both worlds in order to thrive.
- These two worlds are inextricably linked and influence each other to drive our behaviour and, ultimately, our life outcomes.
- We have the power, in part, to control our responses and behaviour, breaking the link if needed.

Try this

Get comfy, take some deep breaths, and bring your attention to your body. Feel your body. Notice all the sensations of the physical self. Rest your attention on the experience of these sensations. Scan from the top of your head, through your whole body, and down to your toes to notice without judgement all the physical feelings manifesting.

Now shift your focus to the mind. Is your mind distracted with thoughts and stories of the day? Does it seem busy and restless, or is it calm and quiet? Notice thoughts, images, or other mental constructs as they arise. Notice how they exist within you and are yours alone to experience. Scan through your inner world and see if you can detect any urges – subtle or strong. Maybe you might be craving food or water, to use the toilet, or to get up and do something. Notice the physical nature of that urge. Where does it live? Can you describe the experience of feeling it?

Now tune into your emotions. How are you feeling emotionally in this moment? Is there any subtle experience of sadness or frustration? Maybe you're experiencing an unusual mix of things, with individual emotions difficult to tease out. Or maybe you feel as if you're emotionally flatlining. If you do experience an emotion, take the time to notice where it's coming from, its strength, its nature, and simply experience that. Your complete internal-world experience has just been acknowledged, and you've allowed yourself to be aware of your mind and body. Great job!

Now turn your conscious focus to your external-world experience. What can you see, feel, taste, hear, and smell?

Meditate on the idea that what you sense within yourself and what you sense externally are connected.

6
Values

When we talk about values, we are talking about traits, qualities or characteristics. Commonly held values include honesty, kindness, generosity, and fun: these are positive attributes, things we value. Your values are your internal anchor. They guide you on how to be, and how to carry yourself through your life. They are your purpose in life.

Values are your journey, not your destination. They create the architecture of your life path, the direction towards your end point. They inform the ways in which we fill our fleeting lives, our soul's expression. They are not a task to be achieved. Rather, they're how you're living your life while life is going along. Many people misunderstand the concept of values, seeing them as pastimes to take up or things to acquire. But they're neither. You cannot dabble in values or buy them from a shop – they are the way you conduct yourself as you shop and partake in activities.

All of us have values – we absorb them from society, culture, and family into our inner world. They may change over time, and we can choose them – your chosen values are how you wish to treat others and yourself – but we may not be conscious of this aspect of ourselves or even have considered it before. If you cannot name your values, then you don't fully know yourself, what you stand for, or how you hope to behave and treat others. Tuning in to your values is an important element of developing self-awareness.

Your values contribute to your experience of living. Living aligned to your values brings worth and purpose to your existence. Without an astute and current awareness of your values, you are more likely to find yourself lacking a sense of meaning to your life. So, I'm sure you can see why identifying your values is a huge part of **real wellness**.

Identifying your values takes conscious consideration and continual reflection. When I run wellness retreats, no matter the cohort, I always speak to this and dedicate time in the schedule for values reflection, as it is so beneficial to our wellbeing to do so. I find that people are often not able to name their values until they go to the effort, but are always grateful to discover what they might be.

We may have a surprising mixture of values across the various domains of our life and our different roles. A person's values as a parent may be completely different to those they have as a friend or partner. It's useful to list all the hats you wear and roles you play in your life and identify your top values for each of these. I value being a predictable and loving mum, a fun and supportive partner, and a calm, compassionate, humble and conscientious physician.

*

Once you've identified – and maybe added to – your values, you can focus on living in alignment with them. The biggest payoff is that living a value-fueled life – no matter what your circumstances are – is conducive to contentment, meaning and purpose.

The commitment to live in accordance with your values informs how you carry yourself in times of challenge. Even on a day that is derailed by unpleasantness, if I have shown up as the person I wish to be, then I can sleep at night content in the knowledge that I did my best and the day had value and meaning.

For inspiration on leaning into your values to create a life of meaning and purpose, I recommend reading the masterpiece *Man's Search For Meaning* by psychiatrist and holocaust survivor Professor Viktor Frankl. He endured extreme adversity and loss of rights and states, 'everything can be taken from a man but one thing: the last of the human freedoms – to choose one's attitude in any given set of circumstances, to choose one's own way.' His key message was that embodying your values is a birthright. No-one can rob you of your ability to choose how you respond to the world. Even though all control was taken from him and he endured years of unimaginable hardship, including witnessing horrific acts, Frankl was able to maintain a sense of meaning and purpose in his life by embodying his values and acting the way he chose for himself – with dignity, kindness, and respect. That power fuelled his determination to survive.

Another source of inspiration comes from traditional Japanese culture, where the concept of *ikigai* (pronounced ee-kee-guy) is taught to promote optimal wellbeing. *Ikigai* is regarded as a universal experience open to all humans. It is attained when a person's spiritual needs are met and they're living a life filled with purpose and meaning. Although the term is difficult to translate into English, and its definition is hard to pin down, most practitioners agree *ikigai* is our reason for existing, living and waking up each day. It may involve a particular hobby or activity, or time spent doing something.

For me, what shines through is that this state is attained when people live aligned with their values and their actions embody their values. Values-driven activity cultivates purpose and meaning to our life. And a life of purpose and meaning is a life of **real wellness**.

One of the hallmarks of *ikigai* is that to be well we must consider how we are – not just what we do. What a person does – apart from unethical choices – matters less to their wellbeing than the way they do it. If you focus a little energy on the way you make others feel, the way you carry yourself, and less on kicking goals for optimal wellbeing, and then behave in line with your desires, you may notice you feel proud of yourself.

As a junior doctor working in a hospital, there was a strong focus on task achievement and getting through the heavy daily workload. All day long, I flogged myself getting everything done. But I rarely felt rewarded by my efforts or proud of myself and the work I'd achieved. When I started to learn more about the influence of values on wellbeing, I realised that my workday was focused on task achievement, rather than the way in which I was completing work, treating others, and carrying myself.

I started to play with the idea of putting more effort into mindfully implementing my values at work. It was important to me to conduct myself in a calm, kind, caring, compassionate and loving way. Once this was clear to me, I noticed opportunities I'd previously missed to show up in these ways, such as gently holding a patient's hand during a ward round or spending an extra minute to properly hear their concerns. I took more time to look into people's eyes and ask them how they felt and whether they were coping with everything. I ensured that I wasn't breezing past patients in a rush to get jobs completed or focusing on my task list rather than their faces. Thanks to my mindfulness skills, I became better at noticing times when I wasn't behaving and feeling in alignment with my values so I could start to conduct myself differently.

The best part of this learning experience was discovering that, despite seemingly spending extra time embodying my chosen values, all my jobs still got done each day! I'd remained efficient, was a more content doctor, and I suspect I left my patients feeling better, too.

These days, I can still find myself busy, task-oriented and prone to forgetting to pay attention to my values. So, I've learnt to remind myself of my values regularly. I usually structure my days with a list of goals and things to get done. But at the very top of this list, I have my values written down. This prompts me to focus on how I'm treating others, carrying myself, and being, irrespective of how long my jobs list is or how stressed I may feel. Besides, if productivity has to be paused in order for me to be calm, kind, caring, and present, in my view, the outcome will have been worth that small sacrifice in productivity. If I can look back on my day knowing that I've lived it in tune with my values, then I'm proud and content regardless of whether it's been 'productive'. It's more beneficial to my soul that I live aligned with my values.

*

Values serve as an internal compass, or decision-making guide, pointing you in life directions that are most likely to work for you. In modern-day Western culture, we can be overwhelmed by options. Many 'First World' problems stem from too much choice. How do you decide on whether to spend an hour comforting your friend who's just broken up with their partner or going out with workmates for drinks, your career direction, or where to live? A young person may be unsure about whether to have kids, worried about whether they would cope with the sleep deprivation and doubting their abilities and competence as parents. But if they value family and value being in loving, nurturing relationships, then any stress, sacrifice or challenge that comes with the role will be counterbalanced by the fulfilment it brings them to embody these. If they're able to be loving as a parent, it will likely be a satisfying experience in the end, no matter how tired they may be.

For many people, myself included, indecisiveness can be paralysing. Having too much choice can contribute to a sense of uncertainty around the future. If you can learn to reflect on your values to help guide your choices and actions, then the path forward becomes clearer.

This approach to life problems also works well for getting through times of uncertainty. Whenever you're stuck or unsure, bring to mind your core values: you'll soon identify the choices that do and don't align with them. This is when you're happy that your internal world sparks action in the external world.

Years ago, I received a career offer that perplexed me. It was a year's contract and involved doing things I was bad at and had previously avoided. I hate doing things I'm bad at, so my first instinct was to decline the offer. But after super-deep reflective work on my values, I saw that taking the job was exactly what I wanted and needed. I realised my values of living courageously, with freedom from self-limiting beliefs, being a loving and available parent, and being of service aligned with this job opportunity and outweighed my fear of working beyond my comfort zone. In this instance, I skilfully used values awareness to steer me towards a path that ended up working well for me and allowed me to live authentically. I took the job, spent a year developing my skills and gaining priceless experience working as a physician locally while living at home and working part-time. It made me a better physician and mum and I spent the whole year embodying my values, relishing a career of deep meaning and purpose despite all the challenges – and there were plenty of them!

*

When we live misaligned with our values and we go off path, there will be consequences of some sort. We may develop mental or physical illness, or a sense of dis-ease. During these times we may feel 'unwell', stuck, trapped, unsure, and in a rut of sorts. When people come to me reporting that they feel off, even though their physical health is stable and as good as it can be, I have learnt to enquire into their connection to their values. Chances are, they're not living their life attuned to them.

Once I started to embody my values in my work as a doctor, there was a welcome drop in the pressure I previously felt to be a 'perfect' physician: to perform optimally, know it all, and meet the expectations of my seniors. From then on, my focus was more on being the way I wished to be when at work and less on my performance – and remains so to this day. With this change in attention and intention, my discontent with my work significantly reduced, and my anxiety lessened. Who knew my anxiety had links to living a life that was out of alignment with my values!

What I also experienced was a deeper connection to my spiritual self. If we accept our spiritual self to be something other than our physical form, and the human self as embodying this physical form living this life, that opens the possibility that our spiritual self is our heartfelt wishes and potential, our true essence, unaffected by the influences of others and all our conditioning. That is a massive sentence sorry – maybe read it a few times slowly.

I see my values as expressing something of this true essence and connecting my spiritual self with my human self. My values are the yearnings of my true essence, nudging me to become the best I can be. To me, values are an internal compass directing us towards living a human life that's spiritually authentic and deeply meaningful. When we embody our values, we actualise our spiritual self, our gifts and the energy we have to offer.

Don't get me wrong, I'm fallible: I'm certainly not constantly living aligned with my values: ask anyone who knows me well. Despite my desire to be Zen and loving, I do things like get stressed at work when the demands are high and the time pressure is on. On those occasions, I may speak a little abruptly to colleagues despite my best intentions. If I lived a life of spirituality and true essence, then things like that would never happen. But alas, I'm not just spirit, I'm also very human, so I miss the mark a little every day –

sometimes for the whole day, but we all have tough days. Living your life trying to express your values is obviously an imperfect process! But that's okay. Every human has moments when their behaviour is not what they're aiming for. Simply being aware of them and aiming to be this way is a desirable and healthy start.

Rest assured, we're all flawed and vulnerable human beings. But aiming for values-aligned living or simply being aware of your values is a great first step to achieving the goal of **real wellness**. I am acutely aware of my values and work towards embodying them each and every day. That is the best any of us can ever do, and there's meaning and purpose in that.

Case study

Mr Hill was ageing. Little by little, he was losing his faculties and physical abilities. He had always enjoyed driving and often took long car trips, exploring back roads according to his whim. On those drives, he felt free, excited, and immune to the world's stresses. These values were important to his wellbeing.

Sadly, we had to cancel his license because of his declining cognition and vision. It was a heart-wrenching process, and I felt awful for him. I knew it was for the greater good, and the mums of the world would thank me, but it didn't make it any easier to break the bad news to Mr Hill. His love affair with driving had to come to an end.

For some time, Mr Hill was devastated and lost. But, to his credit, he worked out different ways to meet his needs for freedom, excitement, and stress relief. He realised he could embody these values when being driven or going on group outings, and by watching travel and car shows. Using his imagination, he would relive the experience of driving freely without a care in the world. He was able to tap into that way of feeling, thinking and being. Sure, it wasn't quite the same as being at the wheel, but it was the next best thing that he could access, and by doing so, he was able to maintain his love of driving, his sense of identity and freedom when driving, and his wellbeing.

Take-home messages

- We all absorb values during our upbringing and are being guided by them, but often we are hard-pressed to name them.
- To build your self-awareness, take the time to consciously look inside and identify your values.
- Knowing your values helps you to understand what currently drives you and also who and how you wish to be in life.
- Values are traits you aim to embody. They are *how* you do the thing, not *what* you do.
- We may hold different values for different domains of our life, and we can choose new values.
- Being aware of your values helps you to stay true to yourself when challenged.
- Values serve as guides, an internal compass for when you feel lost or stuck or need to make life decisions.
- Wellbeing isn't cultivated exclusively by what you do; the way you go about doing something matters.
- We may view our values as the way our true essence yearns for us to be in life, and embodying them is an expression of our spirit, which is an important part of **real wellness**.
- Embodying our values is a birthright and something we can do no matter how dire our circumstances may be.
- In order to live well, whatever you choose to do, do it in line with your values. When you live in accordance with your values, you will feel well. Check in with them when you're not happy or feel unwell to find out where you have gone off your path.
- Living a life aligned with your values is part of the path to **real wellness** and brings deeper meaning and purpose to your life.

Try this

Develop the habit of keeping your values top of mind each day. Keep a journal where you jot down points on these probing questions every now and then to keep track of your progress. Regularly check in with yourself to see if you're living in accordance with your values, and if not, then work towards doing so. If you're exploring what values are important to you, some probing questions to ask yourself are:

- How do I want others to see me?
- How do I want to make others feel?
- How do I want to feel today?
- What is it about others' characters that I admire or am envious of?
- If I lived my best life today, how would I act?

Some examples of values: loving, honest, compassionate, kind, caring, fierce, independent, innovative, collaborative, outspoken, strong, creative, calm, introspective, considerate.

For a higher level of self-awareness, consider the domains in your life and the roles and responsibilities you have. Write the top 5 categories (parent, friend, teacher, artist, sister and so on), then list your top values for each.

7

Priorities

Being self-aware means knowing your likes, dislikes, desires, and preferences to help direct your choices and energy in ways that are most likely to satisfy you and meet your holistic needs. It sounds so obvious and simple for achieving for **real wellness**, yet so many of us live our lives without this awareness. Spending time consciously considering and working out your priorities is a key part of building your self-awareness.

When I use the term 'priorities', I'm talking about carving out time for the things that light up your life. For me, these things include quality time moving my body in nature or being with my friends and family having a laugh. Surprisingly, hosting my retreats and creating these weekends of beauty does too. Less surprisingly, sharing an instance of honest connection and emotion with my patients fills my soul; it leaves me feeling nothing short of privileged and blessed to witness these vulnerable and important moments.

Just as identifying and embodying your values is important to self-awareness, so is identifying your priorities to factor them into your life. Both are important to **real wellness**, yet they are two very different things. Values are *how* you wish to be when you do stuff (for instance, loving) and priorities are *what* you wish to be doing and spending your resources on (for instance, time with kids). If you had all the freedom in the world, you'd probably fill your days enjoying your priorities. Common priorities include nurturing your physical health with exercise, doing your best at work and producing quality work outcomes, spending time with family and loved ones, getting quality sleep, and travelling.

Priorities naturally change with time and context. One year, you may prioritise raising your children, and the next you might put time and resources into your residence; maybe there's a renovation to focus on. This is normal and appropriate, as new life events come and go with each passing season.

It's a useful practice to mindfully reflect on your priorities each new year or whenever you feel life veering off in ways that are not working for you. Be open to the idea of your priorities changing over time, and again, reserve judgement if it arises within you. Simply move fluidly with them and trust your intuition on where to place your focus each year. It is a lovely adaptive practice to ritualise this reflection.

Some people go by the moon calendar to timetable self-enquiry. I use my sense of wellbeing: when I feel uneasy, unsatisfied, or unwell, I schedule time to reflect on my values, intentions and priorities and check in on my life, habits and choices. I enquire whether it's all working in harmony, and if not, then why? Regularly checking in on what is most important to you is a clever practice to incorporate into your self-care routine. In my view, it's way more effective for fostering **real wellness** than spending a whack of money on the latest wellnessy trend. All it costs is 10 minutes of your time, a pen, and a piece of paper!

*

One caveat to identifying your priorities is that you need to be honest with yourself. To be honest with yourself, you need to take any self-judgement out of the identification process. There's no right or wrong priority. Your priorities don't necessarily reflect your worth. They don't make you 'good' or 'bad'. They're simply preferences that work for you. So, drop any shame and blame when getting to know your truth. It's all okay. For example, the raw truth may be that you prioritise your work and career over anything else, and that's perfectly acceptable. Some women may feel selfish or heartless if they prioritise their career over living as a domestic engineer. Because of perceived stigma about what a good mother does, many women suffer unnecessary guilt over preferring their work life to being a stay-at-home mum. If a parent who genuinely prefers their job to being a stay-at-home mum were to give up work to parent, they're likely to end up resentful and even depressed. Their life dissatisfaction may impact their ability to be a happy and healthy mum. These mums are more satisfied if they work, and they're even better mums for it.

Some men who prefer to parent than work may feel insecure about being a stay-at-home dad while their partner is the breadwinner. Sexism and gender stereotyping have no place when it comes to manifesting your unique lifestyle for ultimate wellbeing. Just tune into yourself and try to drop comparisons and concerns for what others may think about your choices.

If someone designed a life based on how they felt they *ought* to spend their time and energy, rather than how they really wished, then they'd risk feeling lost, unhappy, and unwell. Once we own our truth, no matter what it may be, we can make authentic choices that will work for us. If your priority is true for you, then spending time and energy on it will benefit your wellbeing. If you find yourself dedicating hours of your life to a false priority, you may notice a lack of wellbeing benefit. In this instance, reevaluate your priorities. Get into a safe space free of personal judgement and conditioning and ask yourself again, 'What is most important to me right now?' Stay honest and get real about your priorities for **real wellness**.

*

When you live a life with time for your priorities, you're more likely to feel content, satisfied, and well. Most people thrive when living a balanced life with adequate time for their priorities. If you find yourself feeling unwell, check in on your schedule – whether you keep a diary or just have it in your head. Are you allocating protected time to savour the things you love? I look back on stages of my life when I was unwell and can see I invested energy in things that weren't my true priorities. I was most unwell when my life choices reflected what I felt I *ought* to be doing. I became well once I knew my priorities and values and was able to carve out a life that enabled and embodied them.

Once your priorities are clear to you, it will be easier to notice if they take a back seat to other demands in your life, and you will have more opportunity to cultivate a balanced lifestyle of work and play.

In the previous chapter, we discussed how living in tune with your values is a birthright, and something possible for everybody despite their circumstances. In contrast, we can't expect to spend our life doing only the things we love (but it is a lovely idea to fantasise about). Annoyingly, more often than not, we aren't able to spend our days lovingly enmeshed in our priorities, due to other pressing responsibilities, such as meeting work deadlines or parenting a sick child. Take heart that a lifestyle that enables you to focus one hundred percent of your time and effort where you choose is a luxury not accessible to many. Living this way temporarily is not going to be detrimental to your wellbeing.

Be kind to yourself if you're not in the privileged position to choose how you spend your time. Let go of any envy or

PRIORITIES

comparisons. Rather, focus on what you can do and start to navigate towards a lifestyle where you have more autonomy over your time. Design a life that can accommodate your priorities a little more. Create for yourself a silver lining to survive stages of life when you feel deprived of opportunities to enjoy the things you love. By simply being aware of your priorities, you will be more likely to notice when an opportunity does present itself, then steer your lifestyle accordingly. This self-awareness is important.

*

Times where our priorities are unable to be nurtured are a fact of life, and that's okay. These periods won't cause illness unless they're protracted and extreme. Furthermore, there is always something you can do to change a situation – even if it's the smallest tweak to your schedule. With a little creativity, flexibility, and skill, you can optimise your ability to live aligned with your priorities. Say your key priority is family time, but you're required to work away from home. You could schedule video calls to your loved ones twice a day, send letters in the post and plan a reunion together that everyone could look forward to. Living away from family can be detrimental to wellbeing, but these small efforts may keep your family feeling connected (your priority) despite the challenge of being apart (the inconvenient reality at that time).

Look to reclaim time lost to procrastination. I, for one, could put my phone down in the evenings and turn to my husband for a chat on the couch or a cuddle! Consider small changes. Small changes are always possible.

Take back time that is frittered away on distractions and turn it towards your priorities. We all have some free time, whether it be after hours, on rostered days off, or when we're sitting in front of the TV. These moments are so easy to fill with meaningless activities – what's the weekly time spent on your phone, for example? Investigate opportunities to redirect any meaningless time consumption to your priorities. For example, going to bed earlier allows you to get up earlier and squeeze in that workout, or spend some time on a hobby.

But sometimes, small adjustments to your lifestyle may not be sufficient to maintain your health and wellbeing. Sometimes, big sacrifices or major life changes are called for. With self-awareness, you may discover that you're living a life that isn't sustainable or conducive to wellness and may even be costing your health. If this is the case, you need to be courageous and alter your commitments to make space for your priorities so you can live a life that meets your needs. This can be a scary position to be in and hard to grow through, but making major life changes in the pursuit of **real wellness** is likely to work out in the long run. As a young adult I recognised a need in me to live somewhere other than in a big city so I could spend time in nature, on a beach, and in a more relaxed environment. Relocating took a lot of time, hard work, planning and bravery. Today, everyone in my little family is thriving, and I suspect the move earned us an extra decade or two of longevity.

All doctors agree: prevention is the best treatment of all. Rather than finding yourself in a position where you must make big and challenging life changes to meet your needs, try to consider your priorities before taking on new commitments, roles and responsibilities. For example, before entering a contract, take the time to consider whether this new agreement is going to stop you from being able to prioritise putting time and energy into the things you love that contribute to your wellness. I have said no to amazing work offers because they would mean missing out on the things that matter most to me. Those decisions are hard at the time: I don't take lightly turning down chances for income that will support my family and take pressure off my husband, and I don't want to close the door on opportunities that might suit me in the future. But, in the end, making a decision in line with my priorities and values has always worked out for me. Being thoroughly aware of my priorities has always helped me when it comes to my planning and decision-making. As an indecisive Libran, I need all the help I can get!

Whether big or small life tweaks are required for you to enjoy more of what you love, the first step is to build your self-awareness and be aware of your holistic needs. Bringing insight to your priorities may be hard, and making all these life decisions and plans can be even tougher. You may find yourself needing professional support. Consider discussions with your doctor or engaging with a life coach or psychologist. Reaching out for help is a gift to yourself and those you love, and if you have the resources for it, do it and pat yourself on the back! It is a privilege to access that kind of guidance but also requires courage: kudos to you.

Remember that whereas embodying your values is a **real wellness** power that can never be taken from you, living according to your priorities is a matter of privilege. You may not always enjoy the freedom to focus on your priorities. If you manoeuvre through tough times embodying your values, you'll optimise your wellbeing by cultivating life meaning and purpose, come what may. If you are lucky enough to live a life aligned with both your values and your priorities, then you're truly a master of your lifestyle. Celebrate living freely and fully. Celebrate your balance, your wellbeing, and your feelings of contentment. Go you!

Case study

Xao was an entrepreneur. He was born to run a business and really enjoyed his thriving career until he became a single parent when his partner left him unexpectedly. Juggling work with one child was hard, but without a partner he found it wasn't possible. He was worried about his son's adjustment and did not want to leave him alone as he grieved the absence of his mum. Reluctantly, Xao took some time off work to raise his young child. Xao hated home life and missed being at work. He felt shame about this truth and kept it secret. He started drinking more alcohol to cope with the lack of stimulation. His discontent made him a grumpy father and his parenting deteriorated. One day, he decided he'd had enough of the situation, put his toddler in daycare and returned to work.

Although initially he felt guilty – he felt he was letting his kid down – once he was back at work, Xao's day-to-day level of satisfaction rose, life felt balanced, and he was a better dad for it. By being aware of and honest with himself about his priorities, and how he wanted to spend his time, he was able to make a life choice that worked for his wellbeing, which in turn rippled out to those around him and his family. He stopped the drinking, enjoyed the time after work that he shared with his son, and consequently was able to be a better dad.

Take-home messages

- Being aware of your priorities is key to building **real wellness**.
- Priorities are *what* you care most about, *what* you want to spend your time and energy on.
- Knowing your priorities is key to self-awareness and helps decision-making and life planning.
- Priorities will change over a lifetime.
- Spend time reflecting on yours at least annually.
- Be honest and non-judgemental when identifying your priorities. There's a lot of social pressure, expectation, and convention that may influence you. Stay true to yourself.
- Having time to enjoy your priorities keeps you feeling well.
- Not everyone has the privilege of always being able to focus on their priorities. Focus your efforts on living in line with your

PRIORITIES

values as you take small steps towards your priorities, and you will maximise your wellness.
- Get creative in finding ways to incorporate your priorities into your life.
- If it is the case that big life changes are needed in order to have time for your priorities, be courageous in acknowledging and addressing the situation.

Try this

Consciously identify some of your current priorities. Asking the following big questions may help:

- What is most important to me in my life?
- What do I wish I could spend more time doing?
- If I had one week to live, how would I spend it?
- On a perfect day, what would I have time to do?

8

Intentions

Understanding your intentions is another important part of developing your self-awareness for **real wellness**. We have discussed in the last two chapters that knowing your values and priorities is important for building self-awareness. Let's recap: values are *how* you wish to be, and priorities are *what* you wish to be doing and spending your time and resources on. Your intentions are your *why*.

An intention could be what a person hopes to bring about; for example, they might visit a friend whose beloved pet is sick to offer support. It may be to express a value they hold, like being a caring friend. In rehabilitation medicine, the intention behind the care we offer is to support each person we see to optimise their function and quality of life. Fundamentally, however, your intentions are about meeting your needs. As humans, we have all sorts of needs – emotional, physical, and spiritual. In medicine, I consider a patient's biological, psychological, spiritual and social health issues and needs, using the biopsychosocial spiritual framework of health.

Think of a time when your emotional, physical, and spiritual cup felt full and reflect on your lifestyle at the time. Chances are you were living in balance and meeting your holistic needs. By knowing your needs and intentions, you are more likely to meet them and feel well. Further, intentions that are conducive to **real wellness** align with your values and priorities. In my work, I view a patient's values and priorities as fundamental to their spiritual needs.

It is masterful to be clear on *why* you do all you do. This clarity keeps you in the driver's seat of your life and helps you to cruise along undistracted by the chaos of living and the influences within and around you. It helps you meet your needs and stay on your path during times of challenge – knowing your *why* fuels self-determination, self-agency, and measured action.

Your life is precious and fleeting, so if you are on a personal mission for **real wellness**, you want to be sure that what you fill your life with is working for you. You don't want to spend years inadvertently doing things to please others if they are not what you need and desire. You deserve a life that you choose. Ask yourself why you do stuff. Why are you making certain choices? What's driving your actions? Your answers to these questions should help you to clarify the intentions behind your efforts, and what's most meaningful to you in life.

It makes sense then that having some self-awareness around *why*, *what* and *how* you do what you do is a part of **real wellness** and self-mastery – yeah? Think of this work on self-awareness as the foundation on which to build and expand your efforts. Once you cultivate these insights, you will have a solid base of self-awareness to return to in times of decision-making, confusion and challenge. It will help you to stay on track and live your best life!

*

Intention awareness influences the outcome of your actions. If you are aware of your intention before and during a task, you will be more likely to meet it. In yoga, teachers often ask students why they have come to class and what their intentions are for the practice. This facilitates a student's insight into their needs for the practice, so they have a better chance of meeting such needs. I usually find myself showing up to yoga to be my best version. Yoga brings presence, calm, and grounding to my life and it just feels so good. So, my intentions for practice are usually to bring more presence, calm, grounding and good feelings. When I approach a class with these intentions top of mind, it helps me to ensure I cultivate these properties and leave feeling fulfilled.

Tasks you undertake will have a different effect on your wellbeing depending on the intention driving that activity. Your intentions directly impact how you feel and conduct yourself while doing something and once it is done. Doing yoga while consciously aware that I am doing so to become more calm means I may practise it more calmly and be more likely to leave the class calm. In contrast, if you practise yoga to tick 'move my body' off your to-do list, as opposed to striving to achieve a state of flow (this a term commonly used to describe the state of mind when you are deeply attuned to what you are doing, like mindfulness, you are fully engaged in the present) and relaxation, it will feel different at the time and you will have a different after-effect. You are most likely to feel accomplished having completed a goal but maybe less relaxed and Zen.

It is masterful to consider the intention behind a task before you start, to ensure you will reap the benefits of your efforts in the way you need. Have you ever done art with the intention of being creative but ended up doing it simply to get it done for completion's sake so you could get on to other activities? Maybe the intention of creativity left your awareness, and you became distracted by an urge to be finished? It's far less rewarding doing art this way when you need to be creative. My point is, to best fulfil a need, be aware of your intentions when you undertake the goal you set yourself. Otherwise, you can miss out on the benefits of whatever you're doing. What is the point in undertaking activities like that?

Note that it is perfectly okay to have more than one intention. Sticking with the artist example, you may hold both the intentions to be creative, productive and earn some cash to provide an income to support your family. In this instance, once you have creatively produced a piece to sell, you will feel great having completed your goal with conscious intentions that work for you.

*

If we lack conscious awareness of our intentions and values, we may go about our days pretty much following our noses. Then we're in danger of sleepwalking through life. Without clear principles to guide our actions, it's easy to respond to situations mindlessly, haphazardly or in ways that don't make us proud of ourselves and won't meet our needs. You are likely to miss out on, or misuse, opportunities for growth and fulfilment.

To take a small example, I value and need relaxation, mindfulness and self-care. I may book in to get my nails done to treat myself and relax but lose sight of *why* I have come to the salon and end up spending the time focused on my phone – checking and replying to emails, rather than mindfully relaxing and enjoying the pedicure. In this instance, my lack of self-awareness means I miss out on an opportunity to meet my needs. So, I have learnt to pause, remind myself of *why* I have come, and pop the phone away. By recalling my intention and values – my need for relaxation, mindfulness and self-care – I can gently remind myself to close my eyes, relax my body, and allow myself to reap the benefits of being pampered and groomed. Consequently, I will leave the salon richly rewarded in the way I needed. I have had the me-time I went for. Without awareness of my intention, I may have missed out on meeting my need.

*

If we are not aware of our intentions, we may inadvertently hold ones that are unhelpful. Not all intentions are going to work for you, so learn to question them. Becoming aware of my less-than-ideal intentions regarding my clinical work – to pass everything with the best possible marks without taking heed of any personal cost – was a starting point in my personal journey towards **real wellness**. By building this insight and self-awareness I was liberated to make choices in line with my needs and values that ended up working well for me. I was able to pick up on an intention behind my work ethic that was harming my wellbeing.

For many years I slogged away towards various goals, unaware that I was constantly trying to prove my worth. Eventually, I realised that intention wasn't working for me, and I chose other intentions that did. In a nutshell, my intentions switched from working to prove my abilities, to working to be of service and help others. I still work hard but now my efforts feed my soul. As a physician, I focus on my patient and how I can help them. I'm no longer distracted by concerns around my performance. My more authentic and healthier intention at work is to be a good physician and to be of service. I do this by embodying my values of being resourceful, compassionate, patient-centered, and caring. Adopting this mindset and adjusting my approach to my practice accordingly was a game changer. It freed me up to put energy into building my skills in areas of need, reduced the incidence of distracting inner judgement, and improved my ability to effectively tailor my consultations to what the patients required. My self-awareness allowed me to pick up on an unhelpful intention and switch it to better meet both my own and my patients' needs.

Learn from me and be mindful of the intentions behind your choices and actions. Be aware that sometimes your intentions may not be beneficial to you; they may actually prevent you from meeting your needs. Become aware of your intentions and adjust them to work for you using your mindfulness, and values, priorities and intention awareness skills, along with wise-minded discernment.

*

If you are aiming to fill your soul, then check in with yourself and enquire whether your intentions align with your values. When your intentions are in harmony with your values and meet this spiritual need, you will be on your path to **real wellness**. Say a person who values creativity and self-expression as paramount to their wellbeing decides to cultivate a garden. Their intention for this task is to meet their need of embodying these desired values (calm and connection to nature). When they undertake the task with this intention top of mind, they are most likely to be able to undertake it in this way (calmly and mindfully engaged in the gardening process, allowing it to foster a sense of connection to the natural world), and will be most likely to feel well once the artwork is complete (spiritual need has been met). However, if they rushed through the process to produce the garden quickly, then despite their impressive efficiency, they may be left feeling as needy for calm and connection as before the garden was formed. They will not have fulfilled their values-driven need to cultivate a sense of calm and connection to nature and, consequently, will be left feeling unsatisfied.

If you find yourself feeling unfulfilled despite achieving all your goals, ask yourself, 'What was my intention here? Was it in alignment with my values and soul? Or did I inadvertently miss the mark?' A surprisingly high number of people unknowingly design an entire life based on unclear intentions.

If you are discontent or unhappy, it may well be because the intentions driving your productivity are off track with your values. For example, someone may invest a lot of time and energy into their research role because they value learning and sharing information, leaving them feeling well despite the effort. However, another person may be expending a similar amount of effort on a role but doing so for a reason that doesn't resonate with their heart and soul. Maybe they're marking time while they try to figure out what career they would rather be doing? It's highly likely the work will leave them exhausted, depleted and unsatisfied.

I can rock up to work, see a bunch of clients, and finish on time, but by the end of the day be left feeling uneasy because I wasn't carrying myself in line with my values; in other words, inadvertently, my motivation that day was to *just get things done* and not my true intention of *healing and caring*. The reality is, I can achieve a million things in a day, but none of that will leave me feeling well or proud if I have done so in a way that is in conflict with my values and hasn't met my intention. A common trap is to work hard to please others or fit in and 'belong'. These intentions are not necessarily dysfunctional, but they are often at odds with people's real desires for their life.

It is useful to review the reasons behind why you do what you do. Check that you are the one in the driver's seat. Hopefully, you're not conforming to some old toxic belief and conditioning that is trapping you and holding you back from being truly yourself – in other words, really well. (Note that beliefs are relevant to intentions and are discussed in detail in Chapter 9.)

Your spirit's intention is always to embody your values. By asking yourself *why* you are doing something, you bring your intention into awareness, which consequently allows you to ascertain whether you are living in line with your values. This is an opportunity to make any necessary adjustments and ensure your outcome will be as you desire.

Sometimes our efforts are intended to be practical and functional. We need to pay bills, feed our kids, and keep some

INTENTIONS

measure of daily hygiene. Associated with those needs are essential daily tasks, which typically feel unenjoyable. Inviting your values into the intention behind them reframes them as rewarding and can even prompt you to perform them more effectively and efficiently. I can complete the laundry and smash out the house cleaning with a 'just get it done' mindset, or I can do the same with the conscious intention of being loving, mindful, and present. Ironically, this usually takes the same amount of time or *less*, as I'm less frustrated, more aware, and make fewer mistakes (accidentally spill less crap and smash fewer glasses). Have you ever noticed that when you approach a task mindfully, you tend to complete it more easily and with fewer errors?

*

When you have made the effort to set your intentions, it can be powerful to remind yourself of them, especially when you are engaging in challenging or painful activities. Intentions serve as the justification behind your actions and highlight your hopes for the outcome. Recalling your intentions can help increase your willingness to do something and overcome low motivation.

Even though I really disliked partaking in my son's swimming lessons when he was tiny, I showed up and did it with him because I want to be a responsible and giving parent. My intention in signing up with swim school was to equip him with the skills to keep safe in and around water. As a mum, showing up to swim school was also an opportunity to be a responsible and giving parent, which are strong values and priorities for me. When it was hard to find the motivation to turn up, get into a swimming costume post-partum, during winter and jump into that urine-filled chlorinated pool, I recalled my intentions and values. Although I was always tempted to give swim school a miss, I got there each week.

Intention awareness provides the power to drive and manage behaviour. The clearer you are on your intentions at the outset of an activity, the easier it is to remind yourself why you are doing something, combat internal resistance and get into action.

*

Once you develop your self-awareness and cultivate a practice of routinely checking in on your intentions and needs, you may notice that *what* you do with your days can be seen as a medium to serve your values (your *how*).

In Chapter 6, we discussed how your values set the meaning and purpose of your life. It is my view that, in the long run, *what* you do with your time here on earth matters less than *how* you do it. I know that people can be of service, compassionate, and care for others in countless ways. We don't all need to work in the health industry to meet these values. The other day, my carpet cleaner completed his annual visit. As he went about restoring our home carpet and couch to mint condition, I was inspired and touched by his approach and service. He was able to do his work with integrity, kindness, respect, and care. I suspect his intentions behind his work are top of mind.

I, for one, can get caught up in my inner-world stories around the importance of my day-to-day productivity on the home front. I can easily fall into the trap of taking my to-do list too seriously at the expense of what matters most to me. All of a sudden, my *what* has become more important than my *why* – I'm kicking goals in terms of productivity but at the expense of my values, and operating like a maniac who no-one enjoys being around. When this happens, I'm not striving for personal wellness or embodying any of my values. When living this way, I usually end up clashing with my husband, ignoring my son, and experiencing a lot of neck pain. However, if I plan my day with the intention that these tasks and errands are opportunities to live out my values, then my perspective shifts to one of ease: there is less pressure, and even a sense of freedom.

I can fall into this trap at work too. Still to this day, I feel like I can present as either of two types of doctor. Both are highly professional, helpful, well-meaning, and competent. One is calm, carries herself like someone who's got it together, is enjoyable to be around, and holds space for patients with the intention of healing and connection, while the other is markedly serious, frowns a good deal, and comes across as short on time – she talks very fast. The second version of Dr Ward has somehow lost sight of the intention behind her practice and allowed her *what* (task completion) to get in the way of her *why* (compassionately caring for others). Ironically, both versions of Dr Ward usually get the same amount of work done – but they do so with different outcomes. The former leaves her patients feeling heard and supported, while the latter may leave them feeling rushed. Also, one leaves me feeling fulfilled and the other feeling bad about myself (no prizes for guessing which one is which).

When I notice I'm lost in busyness, I try to gently remind myself of what matters most (my values and *why*) in order to get a grip and ground my efforts. I reconnect to my intentions. Usually this means getting all my tasks done but in a more considerate and compassionate way. Keeping my intention top of mind throughout my workday reminds me to be aligned with my values as I plod along through all the jobs. I remember not to take my task list so seriously at the expense of what matters most. This self-awareness is an opportunity for fresh insight – to see life from a different perspective.

*

Cultivating a conscious intention for the things you do each day leads to **real wellness**. Asking yourself, 'Why do I want this?'

and 'Why am I doing this?' will help clarify your motivation. Developing self-awareness around your intentions maximises your chance of fulfilling those intentions. It is also an opportunity to return to your internal compass as a guide to wellbeing. A conscious intention brings your values into awareness so that you can implement them.

Living with this level of self-awareness facilitates self-mastery and a life conducive to wellbeing. When you live with **real wellness**, you are in good control of your choices and take the opportunity to check in and ensure you are living in ways that serve you well.

Case study

Mel was in her 20s when she suffered a spinal cord injury that left her in a wheelchair with significant functional limitations. She had always been a driven person and a high achiever. At the time of the accident, she was in third-year medical school. Mel had plenty of motivation, did well in her recovery and predictably achieved all her rehab goals. But when she returned to her demanding studies and living in the community, things got messy for her. Studying was a full-time job, but so was caring for herself with a spinal cord injury. Mel struggled to keep up with all the demands and started becoming less well.

We talked about her drivers and motivators and how important it was to her to pursue medicine. After some soul-searching, her honest self-appraisal was that she was hard on herself, had enrolled in medicine partly to please her parents, and that she was drawn to working in information technology. With an IT role, she'd be able to express her creativity yet still enjoy problem-solving, which was something in medicine she enjoyed. This was an exciting realisation as IT work is highly wheelchair-friendly and many roles can be done part-time from home, which would be conducive to managing life with a spinal cord injury.

While it was hard for Mel to let go of her goal of a career in medicine, thanks to her insight into her intentions, she switched to IT. She started reaping the rewards of the lifestyle change: she had more time for appointments and started to get on top of her health issues. Her parents were very relieved, impressed, and proud of her.

I'm confident she will continue to thrive in her new career, which better suits her needs and intentions. Mel's self-awareness and self-honesty was inspiring.

Take-home messages

- Intentions meet needs and values.
- Intention awareness influences our actions, the outcomes of our endeavours, and how we feel during and after a task.
- Intention awareness means we are most likely to fulfil our intention. By keeping top of mind the intention behind a task, we are best placed to meet that need and embody the value as we desire.
- Try to be aware of your intentions before creating a to-do list; that way, you'll be more likely to achieve both the tasks and intention.
- When engaging in self-care, without conscious awareness of your intentions, you may inadvertently miss out on meeting your self-care needs.
- When your intention aligns with your values and needs, this fosters wellbeing.
- Without realising it, we may hold unhelpful intentions, but with awareness, we can modify them so they contribute to our wellbeing.
- When engaging in something challenging or painful, reminding yourself of your intentions can help to motivate you. Tasks may be viewed as opportunities to live out your values and meet your needs.

Try this

Next time you have a task to complete, before you start it, ask yourself why you are doing it (your intention) and how you wish to complete it (your values). Then, notice if this self-awareness alters your experience and outcome. For example, doing the laundry is a mundane and relentless task that is nevertheless essential for daily living. We do it to care for ourselves and our families, to live healthily and with hygiene, and to feel good in cosy, clean, nice-smelling clothes. The values here are to care, love, protect, be healthy, and to feel good. All of a sudden, doing the laundry seems virtuous and of paramount importance.

9
Beliefs

Taking some time to consider your beliefs, and how yours play out in your life is fundamental to self-awareness. If you want to understand and know why you tend to perceive yourself and life in certain ways and habitually respond to contexts as you do, then you need to do the inner work of enquiring into your beliefs. They affect our actions, reactions and mood, colouring our perception of life. Your core beliefs impact the relationship you hold with yourself and thus play an integral role in wellbeing. Being well-acquainted with your beliefs builds self-awareness for **real wellness**.

I view beliefs as thought presets ('Here's a thought on this topic that I prepared earlier') – like opinions people adopt consciously or not (more often unconsciously) that affect their processing and interpretation of things. Others define beliefs as repeated thoughts we take on board as true. When reflecting on a belief, the mind may create visions or retrieve memories, and we may notice some associated thoughts, sensations, emotions, and urges.

Like all the elements of your inner world, beliefs are invisible, intangible, and intrinsic to you, but are also influenced by your external world. Beliefs are formed by experiences and stem from stored data throughout the networks of the brain. We may or may not be aware of them and their influence. They are cognitive fathoms that our brain creates to find meaning in things and protect us from harm, so we can survive and function.

Neuroscience suggests our brains are spontaneously active and efficiently designed to make predictions about reality by referencing prior experiences. It seems that all we perceive as real is simply a best guess based on our past experiences. The sensory inputs that we receive – both from within and external to us – error-correct or reinforce our predictions. Beliefs alter your perception of data.

Beliefs are based on the facts available to you in your life so far, including the influence of others and the society around you. If the facts change, to an extent, you can upgrade to new beliefs that reflect your broader lived experience, freeing yourself to live with more opportunity and a little more in line with reality.

As previously highlighted, beliefs are a part of your inner world. As is true of all the elements of your inner world, your beliefs don't necessarily define you. You're more than your beliefs. They're not necessarily accurate or reflective of reality. Although beliefs can be adaptive – like 'I can do hard things' (helpful, flexible, and useful to function and have exciting growth) – they may also be maladaptive and unhelpful long-term – like 'This will be a disaster' (may cause problems and prevent optimal function and personal growth).

We may not realise how much our beliefs influence us; we may be unaware of those that drive our habits and behaviours. For too many years, my achievements were, in part, motivated by a toxic belief that I wasn't smart! I was always pushing myself to prove my abilities. Once I realised this ridiculous belief was hidden within me, influencing my life choices, I was able to challenge it, lessen its grip on me, and choose other mindsets with more freedom. I now hold a healthier belief that intelligence is complex and diverse. I now believe I have high creative intelligence and a unique thinking style that is a strength as a physician. Whatever I am, I have adopted the adaptive belief that I am enough just as I am, independent of my achievements. This is a lovely and comforting way to live.

If you can chip away at the task of identifying your influencing beliefs, it will facilitate freedom from self-limiting or toxic beliefs and propel your personal growth. Having the ability to notice and disregard maladaptive beliefs and choose alternatives is liberating.

Beliefs can be well hidden, secret, and tricky beasts, making conscious awareness of them challenging. But once revealed and conscious, unhelpful beliefs can be challenged and even debunked. With awareness you'll start to notice the relationship between your beliefs and your choices. Further, you'll gain an opportunity to lessen the grip of those beliefs that have been proven untrue or just plain unhelpful. We may not be able to eliminate certain beliefs entirely, but we can certainly learn to lessen their impact on our perception, behaviour and wellbeing.

*

A core belief is a thought about yourself – it could be positive, neutral or negative – that you consider to be true. It influences your identity and the relationship you hold with yourself. For example, if during childhood your needs were consistently left unmet, then growing up you may have formed the negative core belief that you are not worthy or lovable. Many people suffer from the core belief that they're not good enough, which is toxic to wellbeing. I would say 99.9% of the population have this core belief, whether they realise it or not. Note that a characteristic of beliefs is they exist on a continuum of intensity: strong ones typically are harder to modify than weaker ones. The people who strongly believe they're not good enough suffer a great deal.

Some psychotherapists theorise that it's our experience of life during our first four years that's most crucial to the formation of core beliefs, and that the nurturing you receive during this time will determine how you perceive yourself. I'm sure early childhood experiences play a role in the formation of core beliefs, but it's also true that at all ages, life experiences influence us and our identity. In yoga there's a word for life impressions that impact our perceptions: *samskaras*. These *samskaras* create mental imprints that impact how we react and view our human experience. But yoga teaches it is possible to free ourselves of our *samskaras*, using certain yogic strategies.

In the world of mainstream psychology, core beliefs are called schemas, and we all have them. Schema therapy aims to identify a patient's core beliefs to help them understand their inner worlds and perceptions. Because core beliefs are formed when we're so young, we may not have any memory of the experiences that imprinted our core belief because our capacity for memory develops later in life. We are often not consciously aware of them or where they came from and may need professional support to unmask them and dissect their influence on our wellbeing.

Although we may not be able to entirely erase unhelpful, or self-limiting, core beliefs (you may notice them rear their ugly head at times), with insight and self-mastery skills, we can manage their influence on us and flick to more adaptive mindsets that we choose.

Excitingly, we can develop the ability to challenge our core beliefs and thus change our relationship with ourselves. Self-limiting beliefs can markedly hold us back. They serve as an obstacle to self-determination and asserting our personal power over our human experience and life. Self-limiting beliefs can stop people from initiating steps towards embodying their values and living aligned with their priorities. They can prevent us from creating our dream life and way of living.

BELIEFS

A rather toxic core belief of mine that is quite sticky and distracting is that things will go wrong (rather than well). It tends to manifest as self-talk (things I 'tell' myself in my internal world) like, 'This is never going to work.' This isn't helpful at all, and I have become skilful at picking up when it's influencing my perceptions, interpretations, and behaviour. Then I choose an alternative statement to myself that's more functional. It's not rocket science but the 'This may work' adult adaptive statement that I choose to adopt with my conscious attention serves me well in comparison. Suddenly, I give things a try, and usually things do work out AOK.

*

You can try the Downward Arrow technique, developed by David Burns in 1990, to help identify your core values. Note that these can be tricky to unmask without psychology or health professional support, but it's worth a shot. You work through a series of self-questioning statements. For example, someone may feel a piece of work needs to be perfect. They may enquire into why – asking themself what would happen if it weren't (downward arrow) and realise they would be worried what their boss thought of their capability. If again they self-enquired why that would be an issue to them (downward arrow) they may uncover the underlying core belief that they are worthless. Once uncovered, the belief can be dismissed and/or challenged. In this example, by acknowledging that perfection doesn't exist, hopefully, the person frees themself from the pressure to perform in an impossible way.

Are your core beliefs holding you back from value-driven action? In my experience, new beliefs can be imprinted on the mind or existing ones that work for us can be reinforced using skills like visualisation, affirmation, meditations (discussed in Chapter 22, other holistic skills) and mantras. A mantra I love is, 'I can do hard things.'

Because beliefs are internal, they're ours, and we have the power to modify them. We can use our conscious awareness to choose the beliefs we engage with and then, over time, override those we don't. I'm not going to lie: you're looking at the work of a lifetime of continuous effort. But don't let that put you off making a start. We have every right and every ability to choose our beliefs. Every day and in every moment, you can choose to override any nonsense you've somehow taken on. The alternative is to live as a slave to toxic beliefs; for instance, that deep down, you're a miserable failure.

With mindful awareness, we can exercise positive choices. I choose functional beliefs that aim to serve my own **real wellness** and the health of others. With mindfulness and self-reflection, all of us can chip away at our beliefs wisely so that we live contentedly, with more peace and ease. We may not be able to fully undo the conditioning of our minds or eradicate negative core beliefs completely from the networks of our brain, but thanks to neuronal plasticity (discussed in Chapter 21, Habit autonomy) we can modify our brain activity.

*

We've all heard the saying 'rose-coloured glasses', meaning that a person perceives things with a positive bias. Negative thinking and biases can be termed 'blue-coloured'. While rose – pink – is a colour associated with positivity, softness and lovingness, blue is associated with sadness, and a grim way of thinking and interpreting events. The biases these coloured glasses symbolise are strongly connected to our beliefs.

Consider the blue glasses: we all have a pair of these that we wear on occasion. These blue glasses turn everything into a worst case scenario. People with a disproportionate number of negative beliefs – like 'I'm a failure' and 'most people are mean' – often wear the blue ones. If you're less of a negative Nelly – maybe your temperament is more Pollyanna, with beliefs like, 'I can do anything' and 'most people are nice' – you might wear the pink glasses most of the time. Think of pink glasses as representing the underlying belief that even in the worst adversity, there's always an opportunity. When you wear the pink glasses, you see things as achievable. These glasses allow you to see possibilities rather than just obstacles that in your way.

Using this analogy of coloured glasses, you can learn to check in with biases and also choose which pair to wear if the ones you seem to be wearing don't really suit your needs for the day. Simply building some self-awareness around your perspective and what glasses you may be wearing is a significant and helpful first step towards self-mastery.

Your beliefs are powerful. They shape all your choices and reactions, including the way you process and interpret your reality. Beliefs can bring people together or divide them entirely. Could you imagine a version of you with the skill to adapt your core beliefs to optimally serve you? If that seems overly ambitious, what about a version that is alert to the specific beliefs behind your perceptions and behaviour? When you develop the insight and self-awareness to notice your beliefs, you can identify those that work for you and those that are likely stifling your growth. With self-awareness, attachment to belief is ultimately a choice. So, get noticing, practise that mindfulness, and aim to wisely choose your mindset to live freely and fully.

*

We all have blind spots that alter our perception of reality and affect our awareness, insight, discernment, reactions, and responses to life. Common blind spots include: people pleasing ('I must please everyone') and fear of rejection ('I won't be wanted');

perfectionism and unrelenting standards ('I have to be perfect'); conflict avoidance ('conflict is bad'); fear of failure and being judged ('I will do badly'); fear of needing help and feeling you must cope alone ('I need to be independent'); arrogance, ignorance and thinking you know it all; playing the victim and refusing responsibility ('I am never wrong'); overanalysing, catastrophising ('the worst will happen'), rumination, chronic worry; low self-worth and never feeling good enough; imposter syndrome ('I don't deserve to be here'); and addiction to doing and task completion ('I must achieve to be worthy').

Now take a deep breath: it's a lot, I know. It's all fine. We all have some of these, and yes, you may relate to a good many on this list: I know I did when I first came across these concepts. But it doesn't mean you're deeply character-flawed, broken, in need of healing, unethical or 'bad' in some way. It simply means you are human. We all have a variant of these.

Blind spots are a subset of beliefs. They seem to be formed from underlying beliefs that we, as humans, hold about ourselves. When they're in play, they can limit our ability to see things fully and clearly, alter our behaviour and choices, and hold us back from new ways of being and growth. Most people go about their days in blissful ignorance of these shadow tendencies, yet slaves to their impulses. But if we are aware of these, we can use them to our advantage.

It's exciting and empowering to identify your blind spots because as soon as you do, they needn't determine your behaviour or cause suffering at all! They only have power over you when you don't see them. So, shedding light on these shadows through self-awareness, identifying them, getting familiar with when and how they play out in your worlds is an incredible wellness investment – it offers a far better return on investment than buying an infrared sauna, believe me. Lots of high-achieving and successful people live with perfectionism and, if it's managed, can use this tendency to their advantage. They can challenge their trait, inviting in high-quality outcomes, as opposed to perfection, which is impossible and can be paralysing.

Our blind spots are often the root cause of our stress and distress. You read it right: blind spots can be the underlying cause of our stress. We may think our life is stressful, but the truth is that we are the ones creating the stress. Stress is a human construct produced by our *interpretation* of life and stuff (let that soak in a little).

Depending on the lens through which you view things, you will experience them differently. For example, it is common for spouses to hold different beliefs about money. One partner may stress about finances while the other not at all. They share finances, so why are their experiences so fundamentally different? It is, in part, because of their beliefs and blind spots. One may be a chronic worrier, raised with little access to money and influenced by the belief they don't and/or won't have enough money to survive, with the result that personal finances are a source of stress. The other may have been raised with enough wealth that no-one ever mentioned the possibility of losing the roof over their head, and consequently, they have never been stressed by the topic.

A little stress is normal, healthy and adaptive. But during times when we feel unwell, underlying excessive or chronic stress may be the true culprit, and we need to check for blind spots.

The wellness industry sells gadgets, clothes, supplements, activities, and rituals geared to reduce stress in people and make them feel more 'well'. Wellness is marketed as some elusive state of being – a better version of you – when **real wellness** boils down to living as a self-aware and self-accepting human, able to mitigate stress and manage life in adaptive ways that cultivate pride, safety, and the self-appraisal of feeling relatively 'well'. A cheaper and more masterful approach to your stress management than indulging in the latest wellness fad may well be to simply get to know your blind spots and the role they play in your stress response so you can start to challenge these traits and grow beyond them. It may sound like the tougher of the two options – and yeah, it certainly is a bit of effort – and less sexy than taking a supplement, but it may just lead to the breakthrough you're hoping for, and need, to start feeling good.

An ice bath may seem like a hard thing to do, but undertaking this kind of inner work is far more challenging. The difference is that the effects of an ice bath are transitory and don't address the root cause of stress. I psych myself up and force myself to jump in an ice bath (yikes) after a training session or if I'm stuck in a maladaptive mind or emotional state because I know it helps recovery and has a refreshing, feel-good effect as soon as I jump out. But it is a quick fix and, ultimately, an adjunct to this deeper and wise inner work.

Despite the effort required to delve into your blind spots, once you've identified them, you only ever build on this self-awareness and ability to overcome them, which can change your stress response forever! At work, I notice when my Type A personality is coming to the fore: suddenly I'm stressed because my clinic letters seem to be 'not good enough'. I'm able to recognise this blind spot, let it go, and take the pressure off my performance. Then, I get to the end of the day without the accumulation of stress I used to experience commonly. When I overcome the potentially stressful effect of my filters, then I feel more at peace, calm, masterful, and well. I'm left less desperate for hot power yoga and massages in order to relax, and I don't feel the need to spend money on stress-relieving supplements or vitamins that allegedly assist me to avoid any stress-associated depletion of internal resources. Rather than taking the supplements to make up for any negative physical impact from stress, I am tackling the root cause and reducing the stress in the first place. It's wonderful to implement wellness skills and tools for relaxation, but it's far more effective and efficient to prevent the stress build-up by sorting out your blind spots as soon as you can.

*

We have discussed why knowing your beliefs is masterful. But what do you do if you struggle to identify them? One clue is your behaviour and reactions. Our responses to situations can shed light on our underlying beliefs and biases. For example, if you have a core belief that you're unlovable, you may become quite hurt and upset if, say, one day your friend cancels coffee on you. Your reaction is likely to be more intense than that of someone who does not hold this belief. You may take the cancellation personally, believing it has something to do with your worth and the value your mate places on your friendship. However, it could be that the friend had a hangover and was too embarrassed to say this. You may assume the worst, that it's about you, feel hurt and rejected and consequently become defensive. Perhaps you distance yourself from the friend in order to prevent further hurt. If something like this was a pattern of behaviour that you noticed, you might start to see the underlying belief.

Do you regularly get triggered by your partner or another person in your life? Chances are there's a core belief driving that trigger.

If this work is tricky and your beliefs remain unclear, and you have the resources, I encourage you to consider health professional assistance to unmask your blind spots and core beliefs.

Getting to know your core beliefs is a powerful part of the process of building your self-awareness for self-mastery, and being able to live a life of **real wellness** because beliefs filter our perception of life. Don't be disheartened if this skill seems out of reach. This is a high-level skill for self-awareness and one that many never fully form. The truth is, you've done amazingly well even to read this chapter. Read it over and over until the words sink in and come to life. With repetition, understanding and actualisation is created. Having self-awareness of your beliefs and building mastery around them takes time to develop. It is an ability that often requires professional assistance to build. But it is worth the effort for the liberation and growth it enables.

Understanding your core beliefs and how they affect your interpretation of life, and being able to identify when they are filtering your perception is human-mastery at its best. It's a skill to be used lifelong as we are constantly forming beliefs and constantly vulnerable to bias. We may not be able to grow out of our core beliefs or eliminate unhelpful filtering entirely. But we can always aim to be mindful of our beliefs and intentional around choosing alternatives that better suit us.

Case study

Mr Lee was in his 60s and had managed an amputation for most of his adult life. On first impression, he seemed to be coping well. In terms of his amputation and physical health, there wasn't much I needed to do. What bothered me was Mr Lee's social isolation. It didn't make sense. He could drive, had good cognition, seemed a delightful man, and lived in a social part of town. On deeper enquiry, I discovered Mr Hill self-isolated out of a fear of attaching to and loving other people. He had lost both his son and wife to illness. When I met him, what was upsetting him was that his dog had just died from old age. Mr Lee shared with me that he didn't want to make friends or enter a new relationship as it was too painful to attach and then lose. He didn't even want a new dog. He believed that he would lose what he loved, and the pain of loss was not worth the experience of love.

It's well known that social isolation and lack of connection and comfort pose risks to a person's wellbeing, and I was really worried about how Mr Lee would cope moving forward. I was determined to intervene and help him change his belief around love and connections. I tried to persuade him that having relationships was worth it and that we're better to have loved and lost than never to have loved at all. But Mr Lee's heart was closed. I suspect losing his 16-year-old dog had been the last straw. Within a year of that clinic appointment, Mr Lee went into care following marked deterioration and multiple presentations to hospital.

It haunted me that I hadn't been able to support Mr Lee to change his mindset and detach from his belief. But I reminded myself that beliefs can be so deeply ingrained that, by the end of our lives, it may not be possible to loosen their grip. If there is a chance of that happening, the determination must come from the person attached to the belief. All I could do was reflect on myself and be mindful of the beliefs I feed as I age. I am conscious that that the longer I attach to beliefs, the more likely they are to stay in my brain and colour my perspective.

Take-home messages

- Beliefs play an important role in our wellbeing.
- Developing some insight into the beliefs you carry is a high-level and incredibly powerful self-mastery skill that builds self-awareness and fosters **real wellness**.
- Beliefs are like opinions you've adopted, consciously or unconsciously.
- They are based on past experience and conditioning.
- Beliefs affect your perception of life and your mindset; they can be helpful or unhelpful.
- You can separate yourself from your beliefs.
- Core beliefs concern your perception of self.

Try this

- Use the Downward Arrow technique to identify your core beliefs and any dysfunctional schemata.
- Get to know your blind spots without judgement. We all have them. But a master of them has the insight and flexibility to loosen their grip.
- Be mindful of how you're perceiving situations. Are you wearing rose-coloured glasses or blue-coloured glasses? Whichever ones you regularly choose, it's possible to develop your ability for awareness and adaptability.
- Use your mindfulness skills to notice any unhelpful beliefs, loosen their grip, and adopt new, healthier beliefs.
- Keep a beginner's mind when it comes to beliefs. Remember that a lot of what drives you is inaccessible – it belongs to the world of the unconscious mind.
- Be flexible with your beliefs. Aim to engage those that work for you.

Consider these questions:
- What's the usual tint of your glasses?
- What colour glasses are you wearing right now?
- At what point in your life do you think you started to wear these? Were you born this way, or did you become conditioned to it?
- Can you recall a time when this tint worked for you? Can you recall other times when it has caused you to suffer?
- Now choose the ideal tint for your current circumstance. Put them on, then fake it till you make it. If you've got a lot of work to do, then rose-coloured glasses will assist you to overcome any inhibiting thoughts and help you get that work started and completed.

PART 3

Pillar 2 – Self-acceptance

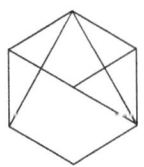

10
Acceptance

The second pillar of **real wellness** is self-acceptance. Rather than going straight into it, this chapter starts by focusing on cultivating the general skill of acceptance. That's because it tends to be hard to accept challenging realities about yourself, so it makes sense to first develop the general skill of acceptance. Practising minor challenges not directly relating to you is a stepping stone to being able to address sensitive and personal matters when required.

After years of practice, I'm pretty good at adaptively accepting unexpected change – even when I may have had something planned to the nth degree – and turning my resources towards what's relevant and useful. Now that I'm facing the ageing process, my skills in acceptance are coming in handy.

Being flexible and accepting is key to living with disease and disability and plays a major role in rehabilitation medicine. As the saying goes, the only constant in life is change: regardless of your circumstances, developing your ability to accept whatever life throws at you will help your pursuit of living with **real wellness**.

The skill of acceptance is masterful. Some pain in life is inevitable, and when faced with discomfort, acceptance is key to limiting suffering. Having a capacity for wise acceptance allows for open awareness and focus on what is going on. With acceptance, you have a chance to see situations with clarity. Acceptance promotes efficient and effective problem solving and growth. You can't effectively solve problems and deal with reality without acceptance. If, for example, the company you work for goes into receivership and you find yourself unemployed, the sooner you accept it, the sooner you can access services and start hunting for a new job. By surrendering to what is genuine, you can appraise your reality with accuracy, and effectively move forward to deal with whatever it is you are facing. Being able to accept losses, pain, and other unpleasant events that come up is a vital skill for living a life of contentment and **real wellness**.

The opposite of acceptance is denial. If you approach your life and reality with denial, how can you ever expect yourself to properly address issues that come up? A lack of acceptance creates an internal state of physical, energetic, and cognitive struggle and strain. This tension is exhausting and stressful for all concerned. Living this way also makes it hard to focus on other things and may further narrow a person's focus and amplify any pain.

Death, our inevitable human fate, is the ultimate example. If we go through life in denial of our mortality and fragility, we're liable to make harmful choices, which is likely to then set us up for negative consequences: unnecessary suffering.

While working in palliative care medicine, I observed the enormous difference acceptance could make, and how much peacefulness and tranquility it contributed to people in that terminal phase of life. Compared to patients who remain in denial, those who are accepting of their fate seem more settled, less agitated, and their loved ones are less distressed by the process. Generally, those who appear to have fought or denied their reality require more sedative medications, seem to suffer more pain and complications, and their families and supporters suffer observing it all. This experience taught me that accepting irreversible health circumstances not only limits people's suffering, but it's a gift for those who love them and feel their suffering too. Having the capacity for acceptance in this context not only benefits the patients and their families but also the numerous caregivers involved in their final days and passing, who care too.

*

I agree with the basic tenet that non-acceptance is the root cause of suffering. At the heart of the branch of psychotherapy known as dialectical behavioural therapy (DBT) – an evidence-based intervention for numerous mental health conditions and a powerhouse toolkit of human-mastery skills – is its polar opposite: 'radical acceptance'. This is when you stop wishing things were different and instead focus on how things are. DBT teaches it as a core skill to help regulate emotions. With radical acceptance, rather than fighting reality, you radically accept – in other words surrender to – what is and turn your resources towards what's most effective and efficient to problem-solve where able, while avoiding any unnecessary suffering and protracted drama around avoidance of reality.

This skill of radical acceptance is all about:

- Noticing the problem.
- Acknowledging it's present.
- Realising that wishing it wasn't so, spending time complaining about whether it's fair or wondering why it's happened to you is a choice but also a waste of your time and energy. Non-acceptance is suffering: what do you choose?
- Redirecting your focus to what you can do, and needs to be done, while limiting the drama.

- Cycling through these steps as many times as you need until your emotional wave naturally subsides or you're able to move on.

The classic example given in DBT is coming home to find your painter has painted your house pink when you wanted coastal white. Could you imagine! Spending time and energy arguing, lamenting, and ruminating over the error is futile. You could do that, sure, but you're only creating your own suffering and using up your own resources. With radical acceptance, you wholly accept the house is pink and then do something about it. If something occurs that you're powerless to control, you use your radical acceptance to connect to the facts, let go of rumination and, instead, turn your attention to what you can control. A mother may not be able to control the outcome of her IVF treatment and magically form a second child, but she could radically accept her fate of having one child and turn her energy, focus, and spare time to nurturing and enjoying them. In this way, she has not only avoided a world of suffering but also created more beauty and bliss in her and her child's life. It may be hard to accept painful truths that we don't want, but it may also be helpful, freeing up energy, time and focus to enjoy the things we do have and are real.

Radical acceptance limits suffering and drama and sets a more efficient – and less draining – path forward for solutions, recovery and restoration. It isn't about forgiveness, understanding, or empathy. It isn't saying that whatever has occurred is just, fair, or okay by you. It is not about lying to yourself and trying to embrace and want what you are accepting. It is a mindset of allowing what is to be – despite any pain, disappointment, fear, and frustration. It facilitates your capacity to address your reality rather than waste precious resources, time and energy on rumination. It is a tool you can turn to in order to limit misery and rumination and deal with your reality.

ACCEPTANCE

*

Inherent to life is pain and loss. Tough things happen around us and to us that cause pain. Unfortunately, there may be times in your life where grave injustices occur, causing immense suffering and disruption. We may accept the losses around us but can we also accept the secondary pain within us?

Losing a loved one can be exquisitely painful. That pain cannot be avoided and needs to be processed. Counterintuitively, accepting and making space for pain limits your suffering. This ability allows us to survive a shared human experience that could otherwise destroy us. Whether your raw, debilitating suffering is ongoing is determined by your response to this hurt. By pushing away pain, avoiding it or numbing out to it, you heighten its grip on you. But with acceptance, time, and compassion it will naturally fade into the background of your life. You may be able to reconnect with certain pains when triggered – it may always be there – but with acceptance you can again make space for it when needed. To limit self-harm, you can turn to this skill to manage challenging inner-world experiences time and time again.

Sustaining debilitating injury and illness that changes your functional independence is another extremely painful reality to endure and process adaptively. As a clinician, I aim to support others to adjust to painful struggles they have with themselves, whether that be cognitive changes post brain injury or physical disability from injury or illness. I believe the first step to optimising a patient's wellbeing is supporting them to accept their reality – pain and all.

An acceptance mindset does not mean feeling apathetic about reality or not caring. It isn't intended to avoid emotional processing. Rather, being accepting allows you to manage emotions more effectively and with more ease. You can practise acceptance while fuming and grieving. Taking an acceptance approach means nurturing yourself through whatever discomfort you are carrying by acknowledging your predicament until the time comes that you can move on. Rather than wasting time and energy fighting your predicament, you can turn your attention to what is and focus on self-care as you naturally work through the challenge, with all the emotions that come and pass. Developing the ability to grieve and process emotions but also accept outcomes is hard and takes practice, but once cultivated, it helps prevent burnout, mental illness, and disability. To put it another way, what's called for is to accept the reality, feel the feelings, and simply aim not to make matters worse.

*

Some stress is healthy and required to thrive. But when chronic, stress may cause health problems. I'm sure you have read and/or heard about how chronic stress can contribute to physiological inflammation, and how inflammation seems to cause all sorts of health issues. Geriatricians (doctors of the elderly) speak of inflammatory brain changes as associated with cognitive decline and neurodegenerative illness. Cardiologists are now promoting an anti-inflammatory lifestyle – with regular exercise; sufficient sleep; a Mediterranean, plant-based diet; and adaptive stress coping – in order to prevent vascular illness.

Inflammation from chronic stress can be caused by both external and lifestyle factors as well as internal and psychological factors. Living in a state of suffering is stressful and, when chronic, may impact your overall health and wellbeing and prevent you from living your best life. The body cannot discern between types and origins of stress. All stress endured by the body is cumulative and sooner or later has an impact on our health.

As someone who lives with anxiety and is frequently stressed – and I consider myself well – I attribute my good bill of health to the combined effect of my internal mastery skills, such as acceptance, and living a healthy lifestyle. If I were chronically suffering from a lack of acceptance, I might live with higher levels of distress, suffer from secondary avoidant harmful behaviours, and consequently experience more health issues.

People living in a state of suffering are often tempted to use avoidant coping mechanisms – things like alcohol, food, and other potentially harmful strategies – that they hope will numb their pain. The trouble is that each brings its own new drama, set of consequences and potentially a fresh dose of suffering and pain. There are negative impacts to their overall health and wellbeing and they are further prevented from living their best life. Most people can relate to drinking their sorrows away, paying the price with a hangover the next day, and then finding themselves in the same predicament that triggered the binge but with extra challenges to deal with. Does drowning our sorrows solve any problems or just create new ones? Accepting a painful reality is much harder with a hangover.

To manage my tendency to worry and be stressed, I have adopted adaptive lifestyle and psychological coping mechanisms that work for me to shake off the day, release built-up tension, and let go of worries. My yogic lifestyle lends itself to health. It's possible that the tonne of vegetables I eat daily, my regular outdoor Zone 1 and 2 exercise (the Zones are shorthand for the level of intensity: 1 and 2 are both pretty light), yoga practice, and commitment to sleep, are helping to relieve the accumulation of stress-induced inflammation in my body enough to keep related diseases at bay. I do believe exercise, to an extent, can undo a lot of sins. But really, if you can combine an anti-inflammatory lifestyle with the masterful skill of acceptance, you will limit stress and suffering and benefit from external and internal peace.

A wise person once wrote what's known as the 'Serenity Prayer', which more or less gives this advice: change what you can, accept what you can't, and have the wisdom to know the difference.

Discerning when to practise acceptance – as opposed to when to attempt to change matters – is a skill to be mindfully developed over a lifetime. Useful questions to consider are: What is really happening? What are the facts? What can I modify or control here and what must I accept? What are my options moving forward?

One could argue that an element of acceptance is required for change. Acceptance is how you create a clear vision. By accepting what truly is, you can see the truth, assess the reality, and then make plans for change based on what is happening. If change is called for, a situation must first be assessed truthfully and accepted in order to see clearly the best route forward. With a lack of acknowledgement, problems may drag on and evolve into bigger problems. The acknowledgement of truth (even if painful) is what precedes the action necessary to solve a problem. Without this, problems further evolve and increase.

*

Let's narrow the focus to the self now. In my work, I see patients who don't feel well, are living with unpleasant chronic symptoms that are difficult to explain and possibly don't have a conclusive diagnosis. The people in this category who cultivate profound wellness despite these unexplained and unpleasant experiences are those who adopt an acceptance mindset to their health. These people are able to live full lives by accepting their struggles and aiming to make the most of who they are. They focus on other things that bring meaning and purpose to their existence and by using self-care to cope, they avoid making things worse for themselves. They haven't necessarily given up on the hope that their symptoms will go, or the pursuit of a diagnosis, but if they're not suffering unduly from their symptoms, it's because they've accepted them as a part of their world and have learnt to adaptively live with them.

ACCEPTANCE

Even if we long for a cure and live in hope of one, we can still radically accept symptoms and place our efforts on optimising ourselves. This might look like increasing rest and pacing activities to lessen fatigue, or starting a new hobby for diversion therapy when living with chronic pain. It seems to me that people who succeed in doing this have knowingly or otherwise discarded the stigma of living with imperfect health. To me, they embrace their humanness and understand themselves (Pillar 1), accept themselves (Pillar 2) and are managing their unique selves as best they can, and doing this successfully most of the time (Pillar 3). The irony is that people who endure a life of chronic illness can be the most masterful at living a life of **real wellness**. Rather than losing their lives to the pursuit of diagnosis and cure, or their mindset to one of victim and patient, they turn their time and energy to living their best life, in keeping with their values and true priorities.

At the other end of the spectrum of **real wellness** are the many people I've met who may be considered 'the worried well'. These are people who spend exorbitant amounts of time and money on 'self-care' in the pursuit of 'wellness'. Often, these people seem to lack a sense of self-acceptance and holistic self-mastery. Instead, they seem compelled to aspire to be something they're not or to change in some way. From my perspective they end up as slaves to an expensive and time-consuming lifestyle of 'self-care' that distracts them from pursuits that would bring more meaning and value to their lives. Going to the gym, shopping for all the latest wellness super foods and lycra, scheduling in a yoga, sauna, ice bath, massage and meditation session, *and* capturing it all on Instagram to make it real – if it's not on Insta, it didn't happen, right? – is hectic and not at all necessary for **real wellness**. Thank heavens.

Eventually, aches and pains become part of everyday reality for all humans, but we can nurture our bodies in order to lessen their impact. We can focus our time and energy on other aspects of our life, making necessary adaptations in our behaviour and modifications in our environment to do so. I like to discuss with clients how, yes, they may live with significant health issues, and a certain body system or part is affected: that is real and their reality. But there is a lot more to them. I bring focus to the functional parts of people and aim to nurture what is working for them. I try to get patients to leverage their strengths and functions. With time, what doesn't work has less impact on their lives, even if it remains a chronic health complaint. If restoration is not an option, in rehabilitation medicine, we focus on compensation and prevention to maintain value-driven functions. This journey requires acceptance.

It's useful to remember that we are complex beings with multiple facets to our existence. Even if a bit of us isn't functioning optimally, it's probable that a large majority of our bits still are, and we can focus on and celebrate that. I often chat with elderly who have their brains intact but their bodies are failing them, and vice versa. The ones who make the most of their lives don't take this for granted and keep top of mind what does work and what they still can do. 'Well, at least I still have my mind,' they may say. This approach requires self-acceptance and acknowledgement of what is really going on. I am deeply in awe of some patients and feel blessed to cross paths with those who have embraced living their best life with disability. It's entirely inspiring to meet amputees who engage in wheelchair sports and do things like mentoring other amputees who are adjusting to their new impairments. This role-modelling helps me to be my best person too. I see so many patients as role models.

But similarly, I've also met wonderful people who sadly choose a life of suffering by not accepting their circumstances. It's tough to watch these patients predictably encounter the additional problems and pain this approach invites into their lives. These are the complacent cohort. The ones who, rather than surrendering to their realities, have surrendered to harmful avoidance behaviours. They have given up on themselves and their life instead of acknowledging change, accepting it, and making the most of what is. Don't let that be you! (Don't let that be me, either!)

I'll bravely disclose that I have lost significant stretches of time to non-acceptance and avoidant living. I have been there, done that. Now, I use mindfulness and self-compassion to radically accept myself while making the most of whatever comes my way.

We are all vulnerable to this life trap. When stuck with pain and challenge that you can see is inevitable, breathe and be kind to yourself. Exert self-care and nurture yourself through your journey of radical acceptance.

The skill of acceptance comes into **real wellness** when it's applied to ourselves. Self-acceptance is coming to terms with the specific facts of who we are and what we must acknowledge and manage. Accepting a painful truth about your identity and character may feel impossible at times but with self-compassion and self-honesty – the skills covered in the next two chapters respectively – and maybe with a bit of trial and error, it is entirely possible.

Case study

I met Sally as a patient on a dementia ward. Sally fought reality her whole life. She never got over the ending of her marriage and never made peace with her former husband. Because she refused to let it go and move on, her everyday life was weighed down with toxic distress and suffering. To her credit, she didn't fall prey to drugs and alcohol as a means to numb her pain. But she aged alone, and she chose to hate her ex until she lost her mind to dementia in her 60s.

Because that was quite young, I can't help but wonder whether Sally's lifestyle of hate and distress contributed to her declining brain health. Maybe if she had been more accepting and found some peace following her separation, she might have delayed her neurodegenerative process a few years? Maybe that chronic non-acceptance and stress did cause inflammatory brain disease?

The silver lining to this sad story is that once Sally became demented, she no longer remembered or had the brainpower to struggle with her story and fight her truth. In her muddled thinking, for the first time in decades, she found contentment and peace. Maybe her brain mushed itself to survive and end the pain? Or maybe a lifetime of suffering from non-acceptance caused inflammatory brain changes? I will never know.

Take-home messages

- The second pillar of self-mastery for **real wellness** is self-acceptance.
- To build your ability for self-acceptance you need to first cultivate the general skill of acceptance.
- Acceptance allows problems to be solved and change to happen effectively and efficiently.
- Suffering is non-acceptance of reality that cannot be changed.
- Radically accept even the most unfair and painful realities in order to move forward in healthy ways that work for you and limit suffering.
- Use radical acceptance as a tool to help you accept truth, even when it's hard.
- Use adaptive self-care and self-soothing to cope with hard things that need acceptance.
- Don't fall into the trap of avoidance and pain numbing with things like alcohol: those strategies only cause more problems. Instead, accept what is to make the most of all you have and are in this precious life.

Reflection

Use this version of the 'Serenity Prayer' as a mantra for meditation during challenging times. Find a comfortable, safe, and quiet place to position yourself. Settle your body and breathe. Slowly repeat the following words:

'I accept the things I cannot change, take courage to change the things I can, and have the wisdom to know the difference.'

Lightly hold this mantra in your awareness. Without judgement, notice any changes to your internal world from reciting the mantra. Simply and gently rest this concept in your awareness as you sit and breathe. Allow the words to flow through you and naturally connect with your mind, body, and soul without thinking or striving.

11

Self-compassion

In order to accept every aspect of your complete, imperfect and vulnerable human self – including any 'bad', disappointing, impermanent, ageing/declining, ugly and painful aspects – you need self-compassion. A basic definition of self-compassion is mindful self-care – the practice of treating yourself with kindness and understanding, fostering a sense of emotional self-support. In practice, this may look like having an early night when tired or making yourself a wholesome meal when you need it – and even if it is just for you.

Self-compassion is a tough skill for many of us and has certainly challenged me over the years. If I'm to be frank, it continues to do so, and far more often than I would like. Being kind to ourselves and treating ourselves with wise-minded and supportive care may not come naturally to us all. But cultivating this skill is possible and important. It is a much-needed tool for self-acceptance and self-mastery. Self-compassion is essential to a healthy relationship with yourself, and even a work-in-progress version of self-compassion will bring you considerable wellbeing benefits.

Our ability for self-compassion is defined by our capacity for:

1. Mindfulness
2. Self-kindness, and
3. A sense of connectedness to others.

Understanding self-compassion and the role it plays in your ability for self-acceptance is key. Developing this skill and some tools for it serves all three pillars of self-mastery for **real wellness**.

Mindfulness skills for self-compassion

To be kind to ourselves and recognise that our perceived failings or difficult experiences are indeed human and shared, we first need mindfulness skills. It's crucial that we notice when we're beating ourselves up, judging ourselves, and feeling down. Mindfulness allows us to be open and curious about our experiences and to pick up on opportunities for self-compassion. If we're not mindful, then we may not even notice when we're being hard on ourselves. If we do not notice we are being hard on ourselves, we may treat ourselves poorly – whether in the form of conscious punishment or to avoid our discomfort. Chronic poor self-care results in low self-worth and fosters a negative self-image, not to mention unhealthy behaviours and poor health outcomes.

It's amazing how many patients report experiencing depression, anxiety, overwhelm, and unhealthy habits yet are unaware of the inner critic screaming at them contributing to these issues. Frankly, it's also amazing that I still get tripped up by this tendency, despite knowing all I know. In fact, during the writing of this book I have felt completely overwhelmed multiple times and have had to fight the urge to pack it all in. But, I'm aware that these moments of overwhelm are associated with inner judgements about how long writing a book like this should take, self-imposed time pressure, along with unrealistic expectations around consistent quality and perfection. I use my mindfulness skills to notice and let go of these unhelpful triggers and simply turn my attention back to the task at hand with tolerance and patience with my flawed and imperfect writing ability. Rather than quitting and falling into a withering heap of critical self-loathing, my mindfulness helps me be kind and self-compassionate, and get on with what I need and truly want – to thoughtfully complete this book to the best of my ability while maintaining my nurturing self-care.

When patients begin to cultivate and apply their mindfulness skills, they are typically gobsmacked by the high number of strong opinions and negative self-judgements happening inside them. But with mindfulness they can do something about it. Rather than becoming fused to them and getting down and out, they can be self-compassionate around their experiences. In this way they will feel empowered and masterful improving their self-worth and self-view. These states are conducive to healthy and helpful self-care.

If you're stumbling through your days mindlessly, it's difficult to apply self-compassion when you need it. When the going gets tough, those habits can intensify and make matters worse. Rather than providing yourself with the loving kindness you need to cope, which acts as a critical circuit-breaker, you can end up acting out to punish yourself or escape the harsh judgements.

If you lack mindfulness skills, it may be only after you've eaten the entire box of chocolates that you realise you're feeling down on yourself. The kicker is that consuming a whole box of chocolate is most likely to make you feel worse. Have you ever devoured a whole box of chocolates? If you have, you may remember feeling poorly shortly after and regretting your choices. While relishing, in moderation, the joy of tasting chocolate may be an act of self-kindness, mindlessly finishing a whole box of it certainly is not.

To avoid poor self-care, and fusion with negative mind states, use your mindfulness skills to adaptively address any inner-world discontent.

Self-kindness skills for self-compassion

The kindness aspect of self-compassion is cutting yourself some slack, forgiving yourself for your imperfections, accepting the limitations of being human and recognising that, although you may try, you may not always achieve your desired outcomes. It is kindly recognising that part of being human is being a work in progress, and that there are certain experiences you may not be able to control or change, such as unpleasant thoughts and emotions or difficult urges.

Continuing with the chocolate-eating example: operating with self-compassion, a person may notice they're feeling low *before* they hit the choccies, and offer themself some loving support — encouraging themself to recognise that what they're experiencing is tough and what they're feeling is perfectly human. Once they fully accept and embrace their experience, they may kindly look into what they need and choose to care for themself, all while recognising how hard that moment is. Rather than distracting from the pain using chocolate, maybe that person has a quiet lie-down or seeks out a cuddle from someone they love. Maybe they just enjoy a few of the chocolates mindfully in a self-caring way.

Connecting with others for self-compassion

The connection aspect of self-compassion starts with the awareness that humans are social animals and we all experience suffering. Yet all too often, people remain isolated and alone in their struggles. For instance, on some workdays, I think I must be the least 'together' doctor in the hospital as I plod along wearing my professional mask as best I can, terrified of being found out as human. Shame thrives in isolation, so it's a terrible pity we don't connect more during our challenges – that I could safely and effectively debrief with a trusted colleague, for example. A lot of suffering from shame would be avoided if we could be braver and more vulnerable about who and how we are.

The truth is that all humans (including doctors) struggle, and none of us is 'together' – whether we acknowledge this or not. No-one has it all, can be it all, or does it all. As humans, we are fundamentally flawed, and that is okay. We are not perfect. We are all just human beings, being human.

Further, some of the most successful and high-functioning people on this planet are the most unwell (I'm thinking of several white, male, overweight world leaders). The pursuit of power and money may be considered humanity's greatest and most disabling illness.

Being human can be difficult to manage. We all make slips, stuff up, let ourselves down and misbehave. Why? Because we aren't gods or robots. Being human is unavoidably painful. Life is impermanent. Loss is a given: we're constantly faced with a need to let go of people, things or situations as we go through life, and this can be deeply painful when we're attached. It's a human thing to attach to stuff we care about. Remembering you're not alone in your struggle, pain, and humanness is key to self-compassion and cultivates a sense of connectedness, acceptance, forgiveness, and peace, all of which help us to cope during tough times. We're all in this together, and we're all only – and only ever going to be – wholly human.

A simple self-compassion practice I turn to as a tool to cope during moments of pain is to recite to myself:

'This is a moment of pain' (I recognise with mindfulness the moment of pain).

'We all have this' (I remember that pain is a shared human experience).

'I will be kind to myself' (I commit to an act of self-kindness).

*

Practising self-compassion entails connecting to others and our shared humanness. But it also means you're teaching yourself to stand mostly on your own two feet – to cope autonomously. If we develop the skills to turn to ourselves for kindness, understanding, forgiveness, and comfort and to reach out to connect with others on our own terms, as needed, then we can learn to trust ourselves and to think and act for ourselves. Being independent in this way is rewarding. It fosters a safe and peaceful relationship with ourself, where we trust we can care for ourself and therefore can look to the future with confidence and enjoy living as us – which is synonymous with living a life of **real wellness**.

Dependence on others in the form of inappropriate behaviour (like dumping or taking up too much of a certain individual's time and space) or over-reliance in order to manage distress can be disempowering. It can also exhaust the goodwill of those caring for you and consequently you may find yourself without support during tough times. We need to respect the personal limitations and boundaries other people have and to be able to manage without relying on supports to avoid imposition and projection ('seeing' in others the characteristics they don't want to acknowledge within themselves). It is also deeply empowering and fosters the development of self-agency to know you can cope alone when needed. When you can be kind to yourself, meet your needs and self-compassionately self-care, you feel safe and at ease living as you.

Note the difference between nurturing self-care and commonly used external coping tools like alcohol, food, other drugs, achievements and weight control. If a person leans on and starts to rely on these external ways of managing their pain and loss and, over time, the usage becomes extreme, it may result in mental illness and behavioural disorders. What I am talking about here is an inside job. Being able to rely on your own mindful, kind and connected self for comfort during challenge is masterful and healthy.

*

Being self-compassionate does not mean taking the easy option regarding action and behaviour. It does not mean copping out, living a hedonistic life or staying in your comfort zone, unchallenged. Neither does self-compassion necessarily mean choosing the more appealing option. Often the kindest and best courses of action for us are hard, maybe downright painful. Some people have an aversion to eating vegetables but do so because it's what their body needs, and they want to treat themselves well. Self-compassion is doing the things you genuinely need to do to be well, and doing so in a mindful, kind and connected way.

Using mindfulness, kindness and connectedness to work through the barriers, you can self-compassionately move out of your comfort zone, do hard things, challenge yourself and grow. In my opinion, the kinder your approach to your personal growth, the more effective it will be. I believe it's a complete misunderstanding that 'tough love' is what gets the results. Doing the kind thing is what helps you be well.

Self-compassion is being able to skilfully navigate your way through challenges to treat yourself well. Inevitably, if you act beyond what is easy and get out of your comfort zone then you face challenge, stress, and fear. This is normal. Use your self-compassion skills to remember that to get you through in a loving and connected way.

*

When attempting to recognise, process, and acknowledge a distressing event or painful fact, you're better able to accept and address your reality – whether you welcome it or not – with a self-compassionate approach.

SELF-COMPASSION

In yoga, *ahimsa* (loving kindness) is synonymous with *satya* (truth). Yogis are taught they go together. Without loving kindness, it's hard to imagine we coul adequately see and process truths that may be painful and challenging in some way. It may be a struggle to face and connect with consciously truths about ourselves thatare shameful, for example.

Some inescapable and painful facts are that we all die, we all experience loss and pain, and we're all imperfect. It's worlds easier to face such truths with a sense of mindfulness, self-kindness, and shared human connectedness, isn't it?

Self-compassion facilitates self-enquiry and personal development. Consider operating without self-compassion: why would you want to confront your flaws and inadequacies if you knew it meant a whole lot of beating up on yourself? Not to mention that once you start to become self-critical, you lose objectivity about yourself. On the other hand, if for instance you have let someone down and are feeling bad about yourself, then self-compassion will allow you to process that painful truth to learn from it and troubleshoot. Without self-kindness, you may go through life denying truth in order to avoid pain, leading to a life of delusion and retraction as opposed to growth and courage.

Our egos are wired for survival. If we subconsciously believe facing a truth will be too painful and potentially harmful and even lethal, then our ego will come up with all sorts of defense and denial tactics to keep us safe from the perceived risk of death. The remedy is loving self-kindness to lessen the painful impact facing a truth may have. With this self-kindness, the ego will settle and step back, allowing you to consciously connect to the truth you need to process.

A classic example is the defensive dance so many couples get stuck in. During a confrontation, rather than objectively hearing your partner's concern and putting in effort to empathise and understand why they're perceiving what they are so it can be remedied, we may get lost in ego, defending ourselves – maybe even robustly and angrily – in order to avoid any pain associated with acknowledging we may have done something 'wrong' or hurtful to our partner. We can get carried away in the pursuit of shutting down criticism so we feel okay, even if it is at the expense of connection and growth with your partner.

*

Self-compassion is the buffer needed to cope with our ordinary human flaws and weaknesses, which we all have and need to manage. Individually, much of our behaviour is driven by subconscious triggers that we may never understand or have control over. Some philosophers argue that, as humans, we do not have free will or that we have it only to a limited extent. Kindly reminding yourself that, as a human, you're naturally limited in your self-control and habits is helpful.

More often than not, our behavioural issues are deeply painful because we believe they're ours alone, and we misperceive them as evidence of our character flaws, that we are failures or unlovable or [insert your core belief and schema wounds here]. But the administration of self-kindness alongside an acknowledgement that you are human can break that negative loop, and allow you to pause, reset and adjust your behaviour. This self-compassionate approach permits us to step aside long enough from our shame to look at what's painful so we can address it head on.

Whether you have a habit you've been unsuccessful in kicking or there's an ability you long to possess but can't seem to acquire or improve on, there are a host of opportunities on any given day to negatively judge ourselves. If you struggle with self-compassion, following a day's worth of relentless criticism, you can be left feeling depleted and then find yourself vulnerable to poor or inadequate self-care.

It's easy to highlight the need to be self-compassionate when life throws you a crisis, but it is a lot more difficult to notice the subtle opportunities to show yourself a little compassion each day. One red flag – a sign you need to increase your use of self-compassion – is feeling shit at the end of the day or overwhelmed at the start of the day. These states may indicate that you're judging yourself harshly – perhaps in a series of unconscious moments – or perhaps you're putting yourself into unfair or unrealistic situations. If you have something new and planned for your day which is generating uncertainty, then without realising it you may be setting yourself up to be flooded with negative self-talk in the form of pessimistic predictions about your performance and catastrophising.

If you can switch on your self-compassion and tread mindfully, kindly, and connectedly through all the psychological smog of your day, you may manage yourself a whole lot better than you would otherwise and thus may end up feeling proud of yourself by the close of the day, as opposed to depleted and burnt out. In other words, if you're wise to the subtle self-criticism that vetoes self-compassionate mental states, you can use your mindfulness, self-kindness, and sense of connectedness to take the pressure off yourself a little.

*

It may be surprisingly difficult to implement self-compassion when you need it most. It's a smart idea to train yourself to be more self-compassionate when you're feeling receptive to self-kindness and can access it easier, so you're more likely to draw on self-compassion when it's seriously needed.

Self-compassionately plan for tough times ahead by increasing your supports and resources. In the months leading up to my final medical exams, I planned for a supportive and nurturing home life. I moved to a regional beach town, worked part-time in a super supportive department, and got two extremely affectionate shih tzu puppies. Home had never been such a soothing and lovely environment, which I appreciated during those hours I spent studying in the lead-up to the most terrifying exam of my life – and I'd done over ten years of exams, so that's saying a lot. All that self-care and self-compassion allowed me to face my fears, show up, do the work, and I ended up doing extremely well! I attribute that growth and success to the fact that I'd planned things skilfully and self-compassionately.

If you can preempt tough times ahead, you can navigate challenges with planned self-compassion to get you through with more ease and less drama. Say you have an elective surgical procedure planned which is going to place strain on your physical abilities post-operatively and impact your everyday efficiency and function. You could predict that this will be frustrating, and that you're likely going to feel pain and unpleasant emotions. In this situation, you can use foresight and up your self-compassion efforts. This might look like increasing your regular mindfulness practice, booking in with a psychologist, reading some books on managing pain, or scheduling time for acts of self-kindness like gentle massage.

*

Remember, there's not too much we have to do in our lifetime other than get by, limit harm and be of service. If you want to add more, then go for it! But grow at your own rate. You need not be rich, popular, or 'beautiful', and you certainly do not need to be perfect – in fact you can't be perfect, sorry. There's only so much one person can achieve in their lifetime, and some days are a complete write-off. You're much more likely to have a meaningful and positive impact on the planet with small, consistent and daily acts of kindness towards yourself and others than with any big career moves or great inventions.

The difference between someone who suffers through life versus someone who navigates it successfully is, in part, self-compassion. Don't underestimate the power of leading by example. If we could all model self-compassion for those around us, the world would be a more peaceful place.

Case study

Joe's dad had smoked since the age of 14 and, sadly, died of emphysema. Joe also smoked from a young age. He knew he had to quit, but his addiction was strong. Also, he tended to beat himself up about his habit. Every time he finished a packet of smokes, Joe punished himself with internal judgements and criticism, which made him more down. When he spiralled into self-loathing, he chain-smoked, telling himself the story, 'I don't care anyway', as if his health and wellness did not matter to him, even though it did.

When Joe read about self-compassion, he connected to a new self-view. He was able to forgive himself for being human and being hooked on a predictably highly addictive drug. To cope with his tendency to hate himself, he started using self-kindness strategies. Plus, he found judo, the unarmed martial art. Judo taught him about the breath and self-compassionate discipline. In judo, he developed a new identity which he was proud of. Not only did Joe's respiratory function improve with his smoking cessation but his entire wellbeing did too, thanks to his skill in self-compassion.

Take-home messages

- Self-compassion supports self-acceptance for **real wellness**.
- Self-compassion requires mindfulness, self-kindness, and connection to humanity.
- Mindfulness enables us to notice judgements and opportunities for self-compassion.

- Kindness is what helps us to see our reality despite pain.
- Connection is the shared human experience of pain, limitation, and impermanence.
- An awareness of the connection between us all breeds a sense of inclusion, comfort, understanding, acceptance, and forgiveness.
- Self-compassion facilitates self-enquiry, self-development, and behaviour change.
- Self-compassion allows us to live fully and freely alongside the pain, fear, and loss.

Reflection

Look for opportunities throughout your day to be self-compassionate. Use unpleasant feelings as the red flags to notice your inner criticism. Ask yourself, Am I being unfairly harsh here? Am I denying my humanness? Is this something many people experience? How can I be kind to myself to cope and avoid doing something to make this worse? What is the kind thing to do right now?

12

Self-honesty

Being honest with yourself is fundamental to achieving **real wellness**. Understanding the importance of self-honesty and ramping up how honest you are with yourself – making it an iron-clad habit – will turbocharge your capacity for self-acceptance and **real wellness**. If the prospect of that scares you, don't worry because this skill is a struggle for pretty much everybody. People lie to each other all the time, from the most dramatic fabrications down to the smallest fibs. But it's the white lies we tell ourselves that trip us up on our health journey and hold us back from our personal development.

Without the ability to accept ourselves and this life as it is, we can't expect to live with **real wellness**. It all comes down to the role self-honesty plays in self-acceptance. If we can't be honest with ourselves, it's impossible for us to see the truth we need to accept.

Reality is already complex enough without the compounding, confusing, distorting effect of dishonesty. To accept and connect with your reality, you need to be honest with yourself and about yourself. It requires you to let go of what you may want, dream of, wish to be true, feel is only fair and just or rightfully yours to claim or reclaim. Rather, you need to see exactly what's there, how you are, who you are, and what you need.

Maybe this means confronting your vulnerability and flaws. Maybe it means coming to terms with your age and acknowledging that you're coming to your likely last decade. Maybe it means facing the truth that you're never going to be that famous cricket player you'd so wanted to be. Or maybe it means acknowledging that your chronic health symptoms don't have a clear diagnosis and you may never get the diagnostic answers and cure-all you've been holding out for. Whatever your honest truth, you must face it in order to accept it.

If you want to be well and enjoy a healthy relationship with yourself, then you must learn to accept every aspect of how you are. Self-acceptance sows the seeds for inner peace, calm, and self-compassion. With self-acceptance, you can focus effectively on your true needs, and cultivate a non-striving mindset, which is conducive to living with **real wellness**.

Being honest with yourself not only allows you to work on your self-acceptance but it also enables you to make the most of yourself and grow in strength and character, where and when needed. For as long as you deceive yourself about what you're doing, how you are, and what you could be doing differently, you'll never get ground on change. To improve any aspect of yourself and grow, it's essential to be honest with yourself about the status quo, the starting point. You have to be able to see precisely how things stand and what to amend. You have to be able to turn the spotlight on yourself and your actions and face the consequences.

To effectively resolve problems, you need to deal with the problem honestly. You need to be able to let your guard and defenses down, soften and relax your body, and enquire within: what's really going on here?

*

So, how is a person to be honest with themself when the truth hurts like a thousand paper cuts? The answer is to face it, accept it and pair it with loving kindness. Use your self-compassion skills to forgive yourself for your humanness. As previously mentioned, you pair the yogic wisdom of *ahimsa* (loving kindness) with *satya* (ultimate truth).

The truth is, every one of us can be selfish at times and driven to please ourselves. All of us have moments of weakness and temptation; all of us are susceptible to ageing, disease and disability, and all of us wane occasionally in our discipline and self-control. Don't be fooled by virtuous appearances or professional masks. Behind the scenes, yogis can be argumentative and obnoxious, and professionals can lack ethics and discipline: I've witnessed abominable behaviour from people who are revered by those who come to them for help. In a different vein, plenty of high-functioning adults are silently managing significant mental and physical impairments day in and day out with never a misstep: you'd never guess.

My point is, try not to beat yourself up too much when you notice your standards slip. Don't expect yourself to be a saint when most of us are anything but, and don't expect yourself to be immune to making mistakes.

Do accept the truth that whatever has happened in the past has happened, and whatever or whoever you are, is what it is. Whether you want to admit it or not, deep down you know your truth, and being honest with yourself can bring unexpected and immense relief once you begin to accept it all.

If you have acted horribly to someone, self-compassionately own it, bravely look at it, courageously face and feel the shame and pain, and breathe into it. It's okay to make mistakes; that's only human. But what redeems you is your ability to honestly take stock, repair any damage as best you can, and learn from your mistakes and failures. In fact, these moments need not be a point of shame and personal condemnation; rather, they can catapult your personal growth and be your best teachers. You won't know what damage there is without facing the truth of it first, and you won't be able to come to terms with that truth without self-compassion.

Next time you notice you're lying about something or denying your truth, try to forgive your-human-self, or at least remind yourself of your humility, and then get real.

Self-love doesn't seem to come easily to me, but I do love life. It follows that I can access the concept of loving my humanness when I view it as part of the gift of being alive. When I find myself struggling to accept some truth about me and my world, I come back to the reassuring reality that I'm only a human, that I'm grateful to be alive and consequently I love my humanness. With this human love, I can forgive myself for my imperfections and face the truth.

This self-honesty helps me deal directly with personal problems and to manage them most effectively and efficiently. It's not always possible to solve problems – there's nothing I can do about my short stature, for example – but with self-honesty I can work through them to the best of my ability to enjoy **real wellness**.

What are you lying about? The truth is painful, and that's why we lie. Use your self-compassion and radical acceptance skills to stop being avoidant. The sooner you can lovingly accept the truth, the sooner you will reduce your suffering.

Case study

In his early adult life and beyond, Roger took a lot of drugs while partying. By his late 40s he was noticing significantly reduced attention and concentration. He was forgetting things, struggling to complete work, and getting into arguments with his wife. When Roger read a book about adult ADHD, he suspected that might be his issue. After obtaining a positive diagnosis, he tried some medication, but the meds only made his symptoms worse.

On reflection, he wondered whether the diagnosis was correct. He had performed well at school and had not had problems with concentration when growing up. Gradually, Roger realised that he had wanted the diagnosis to explain his struggles. Accepting a diagnosis of adult ADHD – something out of his control – was less painful than the idea that he had acquired his brain dysfunction through his own lifestyle choices.

Once Roger faced the truth – that his brain injury could have been avoided, and that it had probably resulted from his own actions – he was able to process the emotion and come to a place of acceptance. He resolved that he couldn't be 100% certain what had caused his impairments but that was okay because knowing the cause wouldn't change things. Besides, even if his behaviour was the cause, it wasn't a reason to shame himself.

After this process of self-acceptance, Roger was able to focus on self-masterful management. He stopped the meds and explored non-pharmacological strategies to optimise his function: he cut down on his screen time and phone use, started making lists and keeping a calendar, decluttered his office and home, and optimised his sleep, nutrition and exercise.

Luckily, Roger's symptoms weren't progressive, and the strategies he implemented made his symptoms manageable. Regardless of the root cause of his loss of focus, he and his wife agreed he suffered ADHD symptoms; this helped her to understand him, and their fighting reduced.

Occasionally, Roger still wonders to what extent his drug use contributed to his concentration issues, but it's no longer a topic he has to avoid. He's processed the potential truth and the pain that comes along with it. When the question arises, he turns his attention elsewhere, knowing that any answer cannot change matters and that self-blame won't help him. Today Roger rates himself as being very well and enjoys a healthy self-relationship.

Take-home messages

- You need honesty to adequately appraise reality and thus effectively deal with it.
- Self-honesty is hard when the truth hurts.
- Pair self-honesty with self-compassion and acceptance to enable self-acceptance.

Reflection

Here's one technique that helps develop the skill of self-honesty. At the end of a day, write out any lies you told or truths you didn't face. Then sit with this and reflect.

- What are you not being honest with yourself about in terms of your health, relationships, work, and other relevant life domains?
- Accept your humanness with loving kindness.
- Breathe into the pain of the truth. You will be okay.
- Imagine a forgiving parent or compassionate friend is present. Treat your true and flawed self with this loving kindness, non-judgement, understanding, and forgiveness.

PART 4

Pillar 3 – Self-management

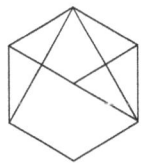

13

Ideal You

The **Ideal You** skill – you may find it helpful to substitute the phrase **Ideal Me** as you read – is a simple but fabulous tool to have in your self-management toolkit for self-mastery and **real wellness**. The **Ideal You** skill is a decision-making tool I use almost daily that helps me manage myself.

The **Ideal You** skill is when you ask yourself:

- 'If I were to behave now as the best version of myself, without any limiting beliefs or restraint, what would I do?'
- 'In this moment, what are my needs, values, and priorities and how can I meet them in a loving, healthy, and sustainable way?'
- 'What could I do right now to help me feel well, safe, and proud?'
- 'In my fantasy, I next do ...'

In a nutshell, you ask your ideal self a direct question requiring a concrete answer. The simplicity and matter-of-fact nature of this question facilitates honest deliberation. Rather than overthinking all the options, you're forced to come straight to your truth. The **Ideal You** tool forces you to enquire as to your best path forward. Use this when you feel unsure about how to get through your day or what will serve you best. It helps with decision-making, triaging your to-do list, dealing with urges and self-limiting beliefs, and getting out of your comfort zone. You can use this skill during any time of self-reflection to guide growth. It's a simple technique you can turn to when in moments of self-care deliberation. Not sure what to eat? Not sure how to navigate a hectic workday? Not sure how to best utilise a few idle hours? Try this hack.

I call it the **Ideal You** skill because you use a future-focused vision of a highly evolved version of yourself to guide you to action. This skill brings your attention towards your dreams and desires for your health and wellbeing and points you towards action that facilitates that direction. Sometimes our mind and environment can sabotage our decision-making capacity by throwing us distractions, self-limiting beliefs and thoughts, and urges or tempting influences. All of these can shift us off course, thereby derailing our wellbeing efforts. Having a skill to draw on during these times can help avoid moments of confusion, overwhelm, self-harm, self-sabotage, and keep us focused and moving towards what we need for ourselves.

The word 'ideal' seems to encapsulate qualities like realistic, objective, non-judgemental, honest and easygoing. If the idea of an 'ideal' doesn't resonate, substitute language that works better for you. Other adjectives could be: 'fantasy', 'wise', 'healthy', 'highest', 'kindest', or even 'parent'.

It isn't about aiming for perfect or best or even better. This skill aims to shoot you *towards* ideal – and that can be far from perfection, depending on the day and what you're working with. The ideal version of you lives aligned with your chosen values and priorities, meets your holistic health needs and is self-compassionately disciplined. **Ideal You** is your highest self: who your soul yearns for you to be, the self that carries you through your human life optimally, lives fully and freely, truly making the most of their worlds. **Ideal You** is firmly based in reality and your truth: you know who you are, how you are and what you need, and you can manage all that as best you can ideally.

It doesn't matter who you may think you are today or what you may think you're capable of, or how hard you may think you'll find carrying out the thing **Ideal You** would do. Instead of all that worry, simply reach an authentic conclusion as to what **Ideal You** would do. How would **Ideal You** respond right now? This skill removes paralysis by overanalysis and negative filtering.

*

Answering the question, 'How would **Ideal You** respond now?' may make it just that little bit easier to let go of any inhibiting internal resistance and urges that may be interfering with your clarity. Imagine being presented with a new work project that's big and scary. Maybe you notice there's a part of you excited by this prospect, but other loud bits are focused on all the 'what ifs' regarding potential failure and other negative worries. If the work venture aligned with your values and priorities and was within your abilities, then the **Ideal You** would go for it. Wouldn't they? I suspect **Ideal You** would seize the day!

Currently, you may have a billion and one reasons why rising to the occasion feels hard and unappealing. But **Ideal You** wouldn't languish in self-doubt or risk concern but rather would tread carefully towards this opportunity, knowing they'd use self-care along the way. By removing your current self from the predicament and instead imagining what **Ideal You** would do, you've gained clarity on what you need to do.

Mental imagery is an effective way to cultivate a sense of what an ideal version of you would do. Generally, it can be hard to simply answer a question in your head and especially when overwhelmed by options or urges towards unhelpful habits. Accessing an image in your mind of what you could choose to do is likely to be an easier way to answer your question. The imagery also serves as a blueprint for the next steps moving forward. By picturing your actions, you see what you need to do and how to go about it, making it that little bit easier to take the leap from idea to action.

Say you have a free afternoon at home all to yourself (if this is rare or unrealistic, please use your imagination here). How would you use this special free time? You could fill it watching TV or eating junk, or you could choose to use it to move your body, enjoy a hobby, or get on with a project that aligns with your values and priorities. When reflecting, you may get a little lost with all the options and various urges in unhelpful directions. If you were to employ some imagery and use the **Ideal You** skill to visualise what **Ideal You** would do, then – in my experience – you are likely to get clearer on how to best use your precious time to yourself in order to feel proud, cared for, free and well. You may see yourself taking a nap and once rejuvenated doing the washing then having a walk.

The next step towards action is best kept simple. Pick up a notepad and pen and list each tiny step you would need to take to do the thing **Ideal You** would do. Staying on the nap idea, you might write: lock front door, turn off lights, go to toilet, get water, put dog on bed, turn phone on silent, get ear plugs, draw blinds, etc. Then, using self-compassionate discipline, just do it! Start with that first bit. Then go on to the next bit. Cross off each step as you go to notice how you are doing the ideal thing. The more you do, the more you will be left feeling fab and full of pride. You will be **Ideal You** in no time. Often, I can skip this last step. The actioning part is easy for me once I have committed to doing it. I simply do the thing. But where I get stuck is the initial working out what to do bit.

*

I love this skill and use it all the time. Sometimes, if overwhelmed or stuck when I need to make an 'either/or' decision, I do 'scissors, paper, rock'; I'm also a fan of picking a hand – usually the smallest and insignificant decisions stump me the most. As I've already mentioned, I'm a Libran, and decision-making can be hard for me. This skill helps me work out my next step and path that will leave me feeling well and proud. It helps me decide stuff when I'm distracted by my internal world, my demons, fatigue, and the influences of others and the world around me. It helps me connect back to my higher self, what I need and what will work for me. It allows me to decide beyond self-doubt, worry, and self-limiting belief as the **Ideal Me** does not have those things, or at least doesn't allow them to hold back her virtuous actions. **Ideal Me** is a bloody superstar, and I love being her. The funny thing is I am her. But sometimes I don't feel that way. This skill brings us back together.

The purpose of the **Ideal You** skill is to connect you with your soul's desire – your needs, values and priorities – so that you can perceive beyond any immediate internal inhibitions and other distractions that may lead you astray from your wellness path.

Case study

Mikayla had done a full day's work and covered her income-producing jobs for the day. She had an hour spare until school pick-up, and ways to fill it started coming into his mind. The idea of snacking in front of the TV had some appeal, and she pictured the blue cheese and quince paste in the kitchen and thought about what a delicious combination that would be. But she wasn't hungry and felt she should walk the dog. Then again, it was a while since she'd gone for a run, she thought. Was that a better option? Way too much effort for the afternoon, she decided. There was also the washing to bring in and dinner to think about preparing.

Soon, Mikayla was overwhelmed and unsure how to use her precious spare hour. Although she noticed urges to eat and vege out in front of the TV, she knew this was not what she needed, and there was a tiny part of her that didn't want that for herself.

Then she remembered the **Ideal You** skill! She checked in and identified that ideal Mikayla would bring in the washing, defrost some sausages and walk the dog to the shops to buy some salad to go with dinner. With commitment, she did not think twice and actioned the ideal outcome. At the shops, she bought a cold drink as a special treat to reward her ideal efforts.

That evening, Mikayla had a lot to feel proud about: everyone in the family enjoyed dinner, the dog was happy, and her wife was grateful the washing had been taken off the line because it started raining 5 minutes before she arrived home. Mikayla was a winner that night and felt very well indeed.

Take-home messages

- **Ideal You** is a skill for making a decision when you're confused, overwhelmed, and unsure what to do.
- Use mental imagery and probing questions to identify what you need to do.
- This skill allows you to bypass any self-limiting assumptions and beliefs. It ignores your transient feelings and thoughts and brings to conscious awareness what you truly want for yourself. It allows you to see past all the psychological fog that can act as a barrier to efficient and effective action.
- By acting on what the **Ideal You** would do, you *become* the **Ideal You**!

Reflection

Next time you're not sure what to do with yourself, take the time to write out what the **Ideal You** would do. Enjoy this process. Remember that the **Ideal You** is self-compassionate, self-honest, and self-disciplined. Remind yourself of your holistic needs, your values, and your priorities. Make a list of steps and then simply start undertaking them. Commit to the list, discard internal-world distractions and off-putting experiences, and turn your focus to the first step. Then just keep going through that list. Give it your best shot.

Before you know it, you'll be on a roll and proud of your efforts. You may even find yourself completing your list.

Now, evaluate the outcome. Did you find this empowering to do?

14

Goals

Being present and having gratitude for what you are and have right now is a powerfully healthy way to be and live. So why throw goals into the mix? Being able to effectively set and meet your goals is a skill to build for self-management and **real wellness**. It is an aspect of self-care that is easy to underestimate, but goal setting will help you live your best life; it will guide your focus and help keep up the momentum when putting in place new behaviours.

It is a skill to live accepting of yourself, with gratitude for what you have, while working towards positive change. There is also absolutely nothing harmful about doing this while also dreaming and working towards positive change, if you do so in a self-compassionate, mindful and values-driven way. Being goal-focused does not necessarily mean you are not accepting of reality or grateful. It can mean you are simply aiming to make the most of who you can be and the life you are living.

Many of us set and tackle our goals without forethought and planning: whether or not you do this is not an issue. But if you – like 99.9% of people – struggle to reach your goals, then having some skills in goal setting and goals achievement is going to help your wellbeing. Admittedly, goal setting is a bit of an art form, but there are some skills you can learn and use to help achieve your goals optimally.

*

In rehabilitation medicine we are trained in supporting patients to set achievable goals. We use the SMART goals (Specific, Measurable, Attainable, Relevant, and Time-based) algorithm to best ensure goals will be completed. I think I have already mentioned how I love an algorithm, and this one really works. I see patients with SMART goals progressing along their rehabilitation path, making the most of their healing and recovery potential. Using the SMART goals approach to care means patients can track their progress and remain engaged and encouraged.

For a person who has had a stroke and cannot walk but wishes to walk again, setting SMART goals will help make this seemingly insurmountable task less overwhelming by breaking it down into little achievable steps that can be taken slowly, one at a time. The patient may first need to relearn how to simply sit up out of bed; from there, they develop balance and core strength over graded amounts of time. They may then need specific retraining in strengthening and coordinating their legs as they slowly work towards taking a few small steps, with an aid for support, as they rebuild their walking abilities. Breaking down a large, multifaceted goal like this makes the process less intimidating and more conducive to committed action. If a patient has a supportive, encouraging experience where they set goals and complete them successfully, a sense of competence, mastery, and self-trust is formed.

Next time you identify a goal for yourself, check that it is specific, measurable, attainable, relevant and time based. For example, a broad goal of 'I want to be a runner' could be expanded into the following SMART goal:

'I want to run for 2 minutes straight during a morning walk (specific and time-based)

five days of this week (measurable and attainable)

in order to increase my cardiovascular health, which will help me live a long and healthy life with my loved ones (relevant to values and priorities).'

If you have a long-term or substantial life goal you wish to achieve that feels impossible, try using the 'small SMART' goal-setting approach, using smaller goals that build towards the overall task. For example, many people dream of moving to live somewhere completely different. But relocating to an unfamiliar place is a lot to undertake. It might entail taking financial risks, having to source employment, selling up and buying another house and cultivating a new circle of friends, not to mention making a host of lifestyle changes. To avoid overwhelm and make progress towards this dream, break this big goal down into a series of smaller SMART goals.

To start, your first small SMART goal could simply be to write a list of all the things required to move. Setting out a small SMART goal to simply write out this list is not an intimidating task and will help the process of working towards actioning it. Your next goal may be to break the news to friends and family. The next day you may decide to see a real-estate agent or investigate the job market in the area you want to move to. The next week you might set yourself SMART goals around applying for jobs. You see how this works. There's an enormous amount of life-overhaul to be sorted when relocating but all the tiny steps towards it are entirely achievable when done one or two at a time.

This small SMART goal approach enables humans to work with any internal resistance around tasks being scary, too big or that seem almost impossible to achieve. It turns the universal human thought of 'I can't do it' to '*This* I can do today.' Slow your journey of achievement down, take away the urgent pressure to achieve something massive, and enjoy taking tiny steps towards your desired end point. It is each little step that will get you there.

*

Another technique you can employ on long-term or intimidatingly large goals that you struggle to imagine ever achieving is to spend time daily doing exactly that: imagining it. Sit down and meditate on your goal. Use your mind's eye to visualise yourself doing and completing this goal. Picture how you look, act and feel as you achieve the goal. Make the mental image as detailed, specific and heartfelt as you can. Notice any internal resistance that comes up for you, breathe through it and commit to the visualisation.

Allowing those inner-world messages to come up is rehearsing for real life – when you are literally working towards your intimidating goal and inevitably such feelings and thoughts will emerge. The fact that you had dedicated a practice to experiencing this will mean you're more likely to stay focused on the task rather than be discouraged or halted by unpleasant or discouraging internal stories and experiences.

When you start your goal, in the moment, if you become stressed by doing the work, you can gently comfort yourself knowing you've done all the work already in your mind. You've been there before, you know what to expect and you know how and what to do to get through.

Visual imagery allows your subconscious mind to see how things could work and how you could cope. Your visualisations seep into your subconscious. Somehow this simple practice has a powerful effect on the mind. Visualisation may seem too simple to be useful. It may even come across as 'woo-woo' hot air. But don't underestimate how effective this simple and free skill is for overcoming anticipatory anxiety around new and unfamiliar futures.

In rehab, we use mental imagery to rewire the brain after injury. As a physician, I've had success using mental imagery with patients to start their neural and psychological rehab even before they physically begin. If a patient fears falling, while they are lying safely in bed, I ask them to visualise getting up, which exposes them to their fear and encourages them to develop resilience. It helps them to prepare for actually doing the work.

In my private life, I use visualisation to foster courage and resilience and to prepare for new roles and responsibilities. For instance, I imagine myself showing up to a new place of work then visualise what I would do and how I would do it. If I can picture myself doing something, it seems more doable, and when it comes to action that thing, it seems more familiar. If I can picture it, it feels possible. Visualisation helps to cultivate the confidence I need to start something unfamiliar. If in my mind's eye I can see myself kicking goals, then I tend to be able to do so in real life.

Visions can motivate action. If you wanted to be a runner, you might use visualisation to picture yourself running with your kids and envision yourself enjoying being fit and able to engage with your loved ones in that way. Visualisations also ingrain into your awareness your desires and intentions, so you're less likely to talk yourself out of getting on with achieving your goals and avoiding any hard work required. Visualisations help you stay focused and accountable about your goals.

*

Another tool to put in place when struggling with your goals is using sheer commitment. Committed action in the face of waxing and waning motivation is your friend when it comes to being successful at kicking goals. Successful people do what they do even when they don't want or feel like it. If you want to be an expert in something, you just do it, spend time on it and consistently.

Consistency is another key to success. More often than not, the path towards achieving a challenging but rewarding goal is on the unpleasant side – hard, painful and, well, unappealing. Has anything really great in your life not required a bit of hard work? Some days, every cell in your being may feel like *not* doing the work. If you commit to action regardless of how your body feels or any impulse not to do it, then by the end of the day the work will be done, you will be fine and the goal will be achieved or just that little bit closer to being done. I am not saying achieve your goals through brutal means to the detriment to your health. Rather, relate your goals to your values and priorities to bring the relevance of the goal and your 'why' top of mind. Then self-compassionately discipline yourself to act. Committed action need not be violent or abrasive; it can be nurturing and supportive self-care. Committed action need not be restricted or strained; it can be freeing and flowing. Annoyingly hard and painful things may be self-care and acts of self-love (I find saying no to things that don't align with my spirit painful at times; so is putting my phone down when I need to enforce sleep rather than scrolling on social media). What would **Ideal You** do?

Because achieving things feels good – it's empowering and rewarding – striving for goals can be a means of expanding your motivation and competence generally. It could be argued that we all need goals to function and cope. Goals can create daily purpose, direction, structure, and a sense of control that is functional.

Goal achievement is also a great way to manage anxiety. I think everyone relates to those overwhelming moments when you feel you have too much to get done. Setting a task list and kicking goals may help lower your anxiety and provide a sense of control over your circumstances. I have seen patients start to thrive just from setting and completing the tiniest of goals. This experience for them opens a world of new potential and possibility that they seemed unable to access before.

Larger goals that require significant shifts in our lives and identity can feel impossible. But they rarely are (unless yours is to stay alive as a human forever: some things are fixed). Don't hold yourself back from working towards your big life dreams. Once you live the experience of achieving a huge life goal for yourself, one that you had only ever dreamt of, this can kick off a wonderfully liberating domino effect. You may be lucky enough to form the empowering belief that whatever you put your mind and energy into is possible. In turn, this is helpful in reducing self-limiting beliefs so it can work to optimise your potential and develop self-actualisation. The power of goals is not lost on me.

Don't hold yourself back from working towards your big life dreams. They are possible (unless yours is to stay alive as a human forever: some things are fixed).

*

Now, having said all that, to advocate the use of goals for self-mastery and **real wellness**, it is important to recognise that the desire to achieve goals can also potentially derail you from your wellness journey. If you believe all the happiness in the world will be yours if only you could smash out a particular goal, then you are likely to be left disheartened once it is achieved. Goals attainment is not the answer for everlasting joy. If you cannot enjoy the *process* of goals achievement, then you are unlikely to suddenly enjoy your life once you have your achievement.

Achieving goals can give your brain a lovely – and addictive – little hit of dopamine that is short lived. Before you know it, you may be chasing your next goal, seeking that bliss. You can spend your whole life this way if you're not careful and forever be looking to the future with a deprivation mindset and missing out on the joys and gifts of the present. Be aware that achieving goals can be addictive, and we may become dependent on achievement to feel good and valid. Do you believe that completing your set tasks will validate your worth?

If you rely on external achievements to feel good, you miss out on the self-permission to experience your worth just as you are. We love our kids unconditionally, imperfections and all. This same love is possible for us and our own self-view. Self-love is not cultivated by goals, achievement and external validation. It comes from within and is possible just as you are. Once you see that there is not any person, thing, experience, or completed task that determines your emotional experience, you are free to be as you choose, regardless of circumstance. Not to mention, you have now freed yourself from your tyrannical to-do list and may now conduct yourself in a way that fulfills your wellbeing, with potential for more time to relax on the couch!

Be wary of the 'tyranny of shoulds' and know that there is little you really need to do. Truly, other than meeting your and your dependents' basic needs and keeping your actions within the law, there's not a lot you must do on any given day. The truth is, our 'busy-ness' is often self-created to fill time and provide the ego with a story of self-importance (ouch, such a harsh truth relevant to me). It may be hard to see and feel that. If you feel you need to set and achieve many goals to feel valid and worthy, then you may have lost your path, and I would recommend seeking guidance from a professional.

Goals completion may even be harmful when set and completed without conscious intention at the expense of your values and priorities. I admit there have been times when I was blind to how my achievements came at the expense of my values. In other words, I got a lot done in a day, but I was pretty reckless about it. It was only once I took time to meditate, reflect, and put a stop to the 'busy-ness' that I saw clearly how my relentless pursuit to get through my daily tasks was negatively affecting my relationships, health and sometimes, ironically, my productivity. I was so determined to achieve the goals I had willingly set for myself each day, but at the expense of being warm, approachable, forgiving and loving. As a driven, Type A person, it was fear, people pleasing, and perfectionism driving my actions, and I was embodying a version of me I don't wish for myself and others. Though I like to set a good number of goals for myself for structure, productivity, and anxiety management, at the same time, deep down, my true self does not want to be ruthless, rushed, self-absorbed and insanely busy. It took me noticing this and remedying my behaviour to begin feeling well again.

Imagine staying present with how you are carrying yourself as you proceed through your daily tasks, ensuring that everything you do is aligned with who and how you want to be. Now reconsider the same day lived out mindlessly, where the pursuit of tasks was top of mind instead. You may finish the day with your jobs done, but you are unlikely to feel proud of the way in which you did them if you jeopardised your values in the pursuit of achievement.

*

Keeping your intention top of mind will help combat the potential for harm when being goal-focused. Consider what it is you're hoping to achieve. What will it *feel* like to kick this goal? Are you holding a belief that achieving this goal will facilitate inner peace, contentment, self-acceptance, or a sense of self-mastery and freedom? If this is the case, see if you can embody those things *now* as you work towards the goal. Give yourself permission to have those things now, and then go forth, enjoy the process of achieving your goals!

Would you want to dedicate yourself to building a healthy superannuation fund to make retirement carefree and easy if, thanks to what that process required, you ended up unable to live a carefree and easy life? While I would never wish it on anybody, what if after living a stressful, busy, and unpleasant life, you get hit by a bus just before retirement. On a brighter note, there's no reason why you cannot harness a carefree and easy mindset as you save and progress towards this goal. The future is now: be who you wish to be.

Don't do something to become the person you wish to be. For example, if you want to lose weight to be healthy, don't wait until you've lost a bit of weight to start exercising. Eat well, rest and train now in a balanced way and the body will naturally follow. In the meantime, you haven't had to wait for health: you have been healthy the whole journey. When achieving goals as part of a higher aspiration, whether it be to work hard and build super for a carefree retirement or relocate to a rural area to live more simply, see if you can work towards achieving those goals while embodying the outcome you desire.

Case study

Bob was super-competitive with himself. He didn't realise this – or at least chose not to. It was a trait that worked for him as he was driven and excelled at all he did. When Bob took up cycling as an interest, he became obsessed – not that he saw it this way. But Bob's family experienced him as obsessed, and his kids wished he spent less time cycling and more time with them.

Unexpectedly, after Bob made A grade – a significant goal that he'd worked towards for five years – the thrill ended. Once he noticed it had ceased to be rewarding, he took a break from cycling and started to spend more time with his kids. He realised that he felt healthier cycling less and was able to be more present as a dad, which was something he valued and prioritised.

While Bob still cycles each week, he no longer does so for hours on end. Some weeks he gives it a miss and instead goes for a quick run so he can be home with his family. These days, Bob is more settled and calm. His wife would say he's generally more well since toning down his competitive cycling and spending more time at home, not that he would admit it.

Take-home messages

- With a healthy balance of present contentment and ambition – which is where goals come in – you are well placed to live at your full potential and be really well.
- Use the SMART (Specific, Measurable, Attainable, Relevant, and Time-based) algorithm to best ensure goals will be completed. Relevant goals keep your intention, values and priorities top of mind, so that your path is realistic, sustainable, healthy, limits overwhelm, and you stay motivated and faithful to your dreams.
- Setting a series of small SMART goals helps break down intimidating tasks so that they can be achieved.
- Mental imagery (visualisation) and commitment are useful tools when working towards goals.
- Achieving goals can help alleviate anxiety, show competence, and breed confidence. Striving for goals can bring structure to your days.
- Achieving goals can be addictive, and mindless achievements can even be harmful to your wellbeing. It is the way in which you get through your day that determines your sense of **real wellness**, not the goals you kick.
- There's no goal that will bring you everlasting contentment. This comes from embodying your values and acting with conscious intention. In order to enjoy the journey of your life, be wary of any relentless pursuit of goals and ensure your committed action aligns with your values and priorities.

Reflections

- What were your goals in the last 24 hours?
- Was the way you achieved these goals in line with your values?
- Did you have a conscious intention as to why you set them?
- What are your goals for tomorrow, and why?
- How would you like to carry yourself while achieving your future goals?

15

Attention Regulation

Attention is the cognitive process of focusing and placing your awareness on something. Attention regulation is the ability to notice, change, pick, and choose where you place your attention. Being able to regulate your attention and place your attention where you choose and need is a fundamental skill for self-management and **real wellness**.

There are different terms used to describe types of attention. We need a variety of ways to attend to our present moment to function. Focused attention occurs when doing a fixed task, like studying. Sustained attention is when your focus is fixed for a long period of time, like when you are lost in a good book. Selective attention is when you focus on one activity amid others, like holding a conversation in a busy café environment with lots of potential distractions. Alternating attention is required to go between tasks, like cooking while referring to a recipe. Divided attention occurs when you 'multitask', such as looking after a toddler and shopping.

I find it helpful to use the **Two Worlds** framework (see Chapter 5) to consider all the places we can hold our attention. Internally, we may focus on thoughts or sensations, emotions, and urges. While externally, we have the five senses to draw on. Having the ability to hone in on one or all of the spaces for attention is a skill that needs practice. Open awareness – where you're most aware of stuff going on within and around you – is a state that allows you to be more connected to the present. Being this way means you notice more rather than being narrowly focused and potentially missing out on useful data and things happening around and within you.

Practising mindfulness is the best way to develop your attention regulation skills. Using screen time (social media such as, X, Instagram, Facebook and so on) is probably the best way to negatively impact your ability for attention.

If you cultivate the ability to pick and choose where you focus your attention, you create for yourself the flexibility to function optimally. There are times when it is useful and productive to purposely place your attention on one aspect of your human experience, like focusing on the mind when wanting to manifest creative ideas. If I have time to kill, I may choose to reflect on my day, review my productivity and ensure I haven't forgotten certain tasks. In this instance, I am purposely using my capacity for thinking to my advantage and keeping my attention on my thoughts. At other times, such as when trying to sleep, I may choose to attend to my body sensations, focus on the experience of consciously relaxing my muscles, and use my attention skills to switch from thinking to a more feeling state of being. I purposely focus my attention on the sensations of softening myself into the bed, and it helps me get sleepy.

Being able to place your conscious attention where you choose, and when you choose is a superpower. Imagine performing in an examination of some sort. If your focus is fixed on the task at hand rather than being derailed by negative thinking or emotions, you are most likely to perform optimally. I attribute my success in my rehab training exams to my mindfulness and yoga skills. Although they came at it in different ways, in both practices I had learnt how to notice distraction, let it go, and refocus my attention where I chose. When sitting the exams, I was able to keep a steely focus on my examination tasks and minimise attention lost to worry.

We gain an ability for focused attention when we commit to and practise holding a single point of focus. By placing our awareness on the reception of sensory data from one source, our attention is channelled into one point of focus. Mindfulness of breath is a great example of this.

*

There is something that you need to watch out for, however; it's known as fusion. This is when your attention is placed on something so much that your experience is overly narrowed – as if you are fused to the focus of your attention. With fusion, you become completely absorbed by the object of your focus, making it near impossible to notice any other stuff. If fusion sits on a continuum, at one end, we would call it a state of flow, a functional and helpful state for someone absorbed in a restorative and empowering adaptive activity. Think of a pianist playing a piece of music. At the opposite end, we might call it dangerous, bordering on obsession. In the context of someone experiencing a depressive state, fusion can cause problems like negative thinking.

Fusing our attention on one thing means we may miss out on other data. If you are stuck in your head, you may be physically present but not switched on emotionally and mentally for precious moments of life, like watching your kids play. Many times, I have been lost in thought and later realised that I failed to register the beautiful world around me – the singing birds, fresh air, and the sunshine kissing my skin. Even if there is a gorgeous sunset right in front of me, I find it hard to notice when I'm fused with my thoughts.

It is very easy to become fused to thoughts or feelings. No doubt you can recall a time where you were overcome by frustration or anger, unable to see beyond it for a while. This is a fusion state. Maybe you can remember ruminating over a loaded verbal exchange or even a casual remark someone made to you. This is fusion. The other day my husband was playing the piano and his food burnt on the stove. His fused focus meant he missed noticing the burnt smell. Luckily, I came home!

Use the **Two Worlds** framework to notice and practise playing with where you can hold your attention. Is your attention usually more inwardly focused – in other words, on thoughts, physical sensations, urges, and/or emotions or externally focused – in other words, on the influences of the world around you? Or do you have the ability to attend in a balanced way to both your worlds – the internal and external? There is no right or wrong here. What is relevant is whether your tendency works for you. Just start by noticing. When I have idle time, I might consciously choose to use my mind to creatively brainstorm ideas for the future. In this instance I am purposely focused on thinking as it suits me to in the moment.

Do you have good neuronal fitness and can flexibly switch your attention to alternate elements as it suits you? If you find yourself too focused on elements of your internal world, you can learn to consciously attend to the external and vice versa. For example, if you tend to be fused with the thoughts of your mind then you may miss out on things going on around you. In this instance you can draw on your senses like sound to attend to the external to cultivate a more balanced state of awareness. I find the sound of birds such an effective cue to remind me to bring my awareness away from thinking and into the world around me. Or if you notice a slight disconnect from your physical sensations you can try body scans to build more physical body awareness. After years of deliberate practice I have developed that cognitive flexibility to switch my attention where I choose.

The opposite of fusion is diffusion. One way to reverse the needle and pull back from the internal world is to take a moment to connect with nature. Watch the ocean; listen to the lapping of water or the rustling of leaves on a tree. Allow yourself to become fully immersed in that external data; it will allow you to get some space from the internal inputs that may be overwhelming you. Our ability to notice stuff and our capacity for perception is limited by our neurology, but the more we try to be openly aware, the more we optimise our ability to pick up more information.

Being able to maintain your awareness of all elements of our two worlds offers us the opportunity to notice more at any one time, so we miss less of life. I make it a routine practice to scan my inner world and the world around me throughout the day, to balance my sensory awareness and remind myself not to be too stuck in my head. Using the **Two World** framework (internal – thoughts, physical sensations, urges, emotions; and external – sights, sounds, touch, smells and tastes) as a checklist to run through all the spots you may choose to hold your attention is a skilful way of keeping a balanced awareness of your body and your environment. Rather than getting stuck and fused onto just one stimulus, try to remain relatively receptive to all experiences to build your ability for open awareness. The exception is if that fusion is exactly what you are after like being totally in the moment during a tai chi session.

*

Having the capacity to regulate your attention so that you notice things going on within and around you helps with decision-making, problem-solving and dealing with drama. At work, a balanced and aware person will not only deal with the demands of their role and the needs of their colleagues or clients, but they may also be aware of their own needs and the cues of their body. Their awareness means they are better able to manage their internal world and external world. This is about noticing more in order to manage situations in a holistic and connected way, taking on board all the aspects and needs. This is an essential – though sadly rare – skill of managers and leaders.

Having balanced and regulated attention may also help prevent the projection of stress onto others. When I'm at work and find myself in a heated moment or needing to manage a stressful situation, I use my internal stress as a cue to tune in to how others are feeling and responding. I use mindfulness to take a pause and check through all the data I can notice both inside and out; only then do I respond to the situation. This balanced awareness means I am more able to effectively solve problems without creating more of them! I create an opportunity for myself to better respond to the complete and holistic needs of my situation rather than simply reacting to it based on impulse or a biased single cue, such as an emotional experience inside me (think raising my voice because I'm overwhelmed by the feeling of being pissed off). If you can notice stress accumulating within you, you are able to then regulate it rather than allowing it to filter out into your environment onto others. People may inadvertently bully others if they lack skill around internal attention.

Our inner and outer worlds can seem overwhelming at times – it's like we operate at their whim, have no say over our responses and urges. Yet overwhelm is purely attention trickery. Next time you are overwhelmed, breathe, notice where your attention is, and place it on something useful in that moment. Avoid thoughts like, 'I'm not coping well' or 'I can't handle this.' They can come up, sure; you can't stop them, unfortunately. But you always have a choice. If you fuse with them, you are choosing overwhelm. But you can focus on something else and dissipate the grip these thoughts may have on you. It is normal for your mind to pump out these sorts of thoughts, but you need to use your developed capacity for attention to choose to ignore them if you want mastery over them and an exit from any distress they may be causing you. Don't try to stop them. That's never going to work. Rather, use your attention regulation skills to choose a different point of focus. Gently remind yourself that all things pass, and that you are so much more than this moment of overwhelm.

When I find myself overwhelmed by a big list of things to do or rattled by an overly busy day, I turn my focus towards my body and consciously ground and settle it. Once able to end the day, I choose not to worry, knowing that attending to thoughts in this instance is not masterful. Rather, if I sleep, I will get rest, recover and be in optimum condition to get on with my jobs the next day. In these situations, I hold my attention away from thinking and toward relaxation. It is all too tempting and easy to fall into the trap of rumination and scanning through your mind for solutions to problems. But I know that by holding my attention elsewhere, I will calm myself, sleep sooner, and have more chance of solving all those problems the next day. I accept the worry, the overwhelm, the thinking, and over and over and over again, turn my attention to rest until I wake up the next day.

It is futile to try to stop inner-world experiences or things in our external world that are outside of our control, but it is useful to be able to choose your focus. When you are stressed or experiencing something unpleasant, you needn't try to stop it or avoid it, but rather accept it and turn your awareness to something of value to you. This may mean doing something soothing, like breathing, having some thoughts of gratitude or picturing someone you love. If you wake up one day in a bad mood with a particularly evil monkey mind, let that go; let the thoughts flow, but rest your attention outside of yourself for a break. Rather than fixating on how shitty you feel, choose to notice the world around you. You may not be able to choose all your thoughts, but you can at least attend to something else. This way, it is also more likely your mood and thoughts will naturally lighten with a change in attention.

*

The brain and its pathways are plastic and modify with use. If you start training yourself to be more attentive and focused, your brain strengthens its abilities for this, and with time, attention and focus can feel easier. Conversely, due to the plastic nature of the brain, if you are someone who welcomes distraction, multitasking, and screen time, and does not practise mindfulness or yoga, then you're essentially training your brain to be easily distracted. The good news is that the more work you do to sustain your attention where you choose, the easier it gets. The bad news is that our society is increasingly geared to destroying our attention: it can take years to rewire your brain, and no-one, nor any pill, can do the work for you. I suspect the increase in ADHD diagnoses we are seeing in adults is, in part, acquired due to our modern lifestyle and distracting way of living.

Neuronal plasticity is the significant rate-limiting factor for internal-world change. But don't be disheartened or fooled into giving up on improving your self-mastery. If you are practising this work, then there will certainly be benefits, even if on a level that is not noticeable to you. Those neurons are pruning and growing every moment of the day.

Be warned, just like muscle mass, our ability for optimal and autonomous attention must be maintained with regular use. It really is all in the reps! A daily practice of some kind needs to be incorporated into your routine. Some people practise mindful walking, others engage in seated meditation or do yoga. What might work for you? If you are time poor and struggling fit in a meditation practice, find a way to integrate attention training into an existing part of your daily life. Pair some attention training with a routine you enjoy or can rely on doing, like washing your hair. For me, I find it easy to focus fully on my patients' faces, feelings, and stories during clinics. I enjoy fully immersing myself in these interactions. I also mindfully sip cups of coffee or hot chocolate, and practise open awareness during walks along the beach and time spent in beautiful nature. These savoured moments of my day serve as a reminder to notice where I am holding focus and to be attentive to things external to me. They are my opportunities to practise focused, sustained attention and/or open attention. I also do yoga most days for both the physical and internal-world attention benefits.

*

Most people have suboptimal capacity for sustained attention; this is revealed at times when tasks are hard, and it's tricky to stay focused. However, with the help of attention training, the human mind's ability to attend to something may be optimised. The practice of mindfulness is a useful means of attention training. In my opinion, practising mindfulness is the best way to start playing with attention training. Practising mindfulness builds our ability to keep our attention where we choose, regardless of all the other distracting things going on within and outside of us (including those pesky thoughts). If you find seated practices hard, experiment with yoga, try mindfulness of breath while running or walking, or you can incorporate mindfulness into your daily functions like mindfulness of making dinner. You can turn any act into a mindfulness practice. Do this by staying present, noticing what's going on with a sense of openness and curiosity, reserving judgement and holding your attention as best you can on the task; then, when you are inevitably distracted, simply turning your attention back to the object of your focus. I hope you are seeing why mindfulness was introduced at the start of this book and how it is a foundational skill that serves all elements of mastery for **real wellness**.

It could be argued that, in any one moment, we become what we attend to, and the focus of our conscious attention determines our reality and even our identity. So be careful where your attention habitually lies. Where you place your attention is the equivalent of sun and water to a plant. Be selective of the plants you grow, and that become prominent in your life.

The trick is to do something small each day to grow your brain's capacity for all types of attention and develop the awareness to attend to all the elements of both your worlds. That way, you may choose your reality and alter your focus to suit the needs of any given situation.

Case study

Suzie was under the pump. She had a strict deadline to meet and the task ahead of her was daunting. When she started to panic, Suzie realised she was in a state of overwhelm; as someone who regularly practised mindfulness, she could pick up on her inner world quickly. Also, Suzie was familiar enough with anxiety to know that when she was overwhelmed, it was usually because of underlying unhelpful thoughts and beliefs.

To ground herself, Suzie turned her attention to her external senses – finding things to touch, taste, smell, listen to, and look at. She reminded herself that, in this moment, she was safe. Then she used her mindfulness skill to notice the thoughts floating through her mind without being fazed or getting attached to them. Like leaves on a stream, one by one, she noticed them, and let them flow by. Thoughts like, 'You won't get through it all', 'You can't do it', 'What's the point in trying?', 'You won't be able to work this out', 'How can you do this when you haven't done it before?', 'It won't be perfect' came to her attention.

Once the thoughts started to flow with less intensity, she was able to focus on her breath and body. When Suzie noticed her breathing was shallow and her neck tense, she deepened her breath and relaxed her muscles. Then she took on the role of cheerleader, reassuring herself that she could do hard things – as she had many times before – that the work would all be done; it didn't have to be perfect; and all she could do was her best. The overwhelm subsided and she felt skilful and powerful.

A week later Suzie had achieved her goal: she handed in the work on time, having found that it was easier and more rewarding than she had feared. Her ability to manage her stress with such self-mastery was the result of years of self-taught mindfulness practice. Despite the fact that Suzie chose a highly stressful job, often under time pressure, she remained well thanks to her skills in self-management.

Take-home messages

- Attention is where you place your awareness. It can be fixed on one thing (sustained) divided, alternating, or selective.
- Our attention and mindfulness abilities improve with time and practice, as our brains are plastic and constantly rewiring.
- Use fusion for focused efforts and work.
- Use diffusion to escape suffering and overwhelm.
- Once you have the ability to focus wherever you choose, you have the opportunity to manipulate your experience and identity. When you attend to something, you feed it, and it becomes part of you.
- These skills need constant use to be maintained, so create a daily habit around them.
- Mindfulness is attention training.
- Learn to focus your attention within and outside of you – as best suits your functioning but also for solace and peace of mind!

Reflection

Next time you notice you're overwhelmed, check in with the focus of your attention. Are there other things happening inside and around you? Focus on something else for 2 minutes and notice the overwhelm become more manageable.

16

Internal-world Regulation

Our inner world has a lot of control over our lives and may even be more influential on us than the outer world. Yet we tend to place more importance on the external world and all its excitements and distractions. Because the inner world demands reflection – a certain amount of work, if you will – it tends to be neglected in favour of our obsession with the outer world. Consequently, many of us misunderstand and mismanage all our inner world's power.

Internal regulation is all about noticing, familiarising, understanding, accepting and being able to adaptively manage your inner landscape. It is essential for **real wellness**. With introspection (internal reflection for feeling), emotional intelligence (noticing and understanding the role of emotions) and metacognition (awareness of thinking), we tune in to thoughts, physical sensations and emotions. They are the senses of our private inner world. Together they make up our internal experience and have a colossal impact on our mood, relationship with ourselves, and behaviour. Use the **Two World** concept (see Chapter 5) to familiarise yourself with the elements of the internal world and the external world and how they interact to affect our lived human experience.

The first step when cultivating internal regulation skills is simply noticing what's going on within you. If we turn inwards and notice the internal-world influences on our choices, then our human behaviour may be more understandable. There are patterns to be seen and predicted; interventions can then be applied if needed.

This is why incorporating reflective practices into your recipe for **real wellness** is so relevant. You may be sick of being told by your health professional to meditate or to download and use mindfulness apps (I think my patients are). But the reason we professionals harp on about doing so is to enable you to bring some balanced awareness to your two worlds and create opportunity to learn about them, their relationship, and how they are affecting your health and life outcomes. You need not meditate, but do find a way that works for you to reflect on what's happening within, to focus your attention less on all the distractions of the external world and more on the goings on inside. Notice in order to learn the influences of your inner world and thereby to cultivate self-mastery.

All of the sensed internal elements are fleeting. Thoughts, urges, sensations, and emotions come and go, rise and fall. We may be quite detached from them, or at other times overwhelmed by their experience. What you feel within is constantly changing. It need not be acted upon, but it usually does need to be felt, validated, acknowledged, and noticed to be processed.

A common trap for us humans is to be unfamiliar with and disconnected from our inner world. A lack of familiarity breeds unease, and unease can trigger fear and avoidance, which can be the root cause of a lot of human suffering, such as addictions. Have you noticed that uncertainty, change and the arrival in your life of anything familiar can be unpleasant and even scary? If you haven't met your inner world, I suggest you do, so you can foster a harmonious and close relationship with it that feels known, safe, cosy and eventually like your home (which it is).

Over my career, I've met countless patients whose health was stolen from them by the long-term health effects of avoidant behaviours, which they adopted to cope with internal experiences (emotional pain and somatic manifestations of unprocessed life trauma). If we're comfy with our internal-world experiences, we're less likely to run from them and use unhealthy escapist behaviours to block them out or change them. Most self-destructive habits form from this pattern of avoidance. So, it's a superpower to be able to notice all that is going on within you (especially when it is unpleasant and unfamiliar), so you can start to get used to it.

*

Equanimity is the wise ability to sit with your inner-world experiences and respond in a measured way as opposed to being impulsively reactive to them. If you master the ability for equanimity, you are no longer a slave to your inner world. Rather, you choose if, how and when to respond. With equanimity, you are able to sit with these naturally fleeting experiences and notice them – choosing whether or not to react to them, something that is frequently unnecessary – until they pass. This self-mastery comes from noticing and accepting the existence of these inevitable components of our inner world, understanding their utility and developing the ability to sit with them and practise diffusing their impact on you.

Connect to and get comfortable with internal-world feelings and senses. Sure, they may feel entirely unenjoyable at times, but this unpleasantness is simply a fleeting internal experience. Building a healthy level of connection and awareness along with

INTERNAL-WORLD REGULATION

distress tolerance is useful. For example, in yoga you may hold challenging poses to build strength, and competence. These holds may be unpleasant at the time, but a yogi's ability to tolerate that distress enables them to process the experience to reap the benefits of the practice. The ability to notice, familiarise with, and tolerate your inner world is internal-world regulation.

Human-mastery in general, requires self-awareness, self-acceptance and self-care, so it will come as no surprise that the path to internal-world mastery is the same. The first step is to develop your inner-world noticing skills using mindfulness. We need to then accept our inner-world experiences as an inevitable part of living as a human. We need to care for them by acknowledging them, validating their existence, and spending enough time with them to be processed healthily. That is about building a healthy and functional relationship with your inner world, understanding its utility and relevance to your function as a human and caring for it so it works optimally for you.

We cannot eliminate internal-world experiences – our fleeting and invisible sensations, thoughts, urges, and emotions. Those aspects of our lived human experience are inevitable and here to stay. So, we must make space for them. We can ignore or be constantly rattled by and reactive to them or anything in between, but we can also modify our relationship with them. Learn to trust that they are serving a purpose for us: urging us to keep ourselves safe, for example.

It's up to us to choose where we place our attention. We can learn to use the mind, body and spirit to our advantage and limit suffering. This could be described as manipulating our humanness. But really, it's simply having some skill around managing your internal world, being able to make it work for you as best you can, using it to your advantage when you can – for example as an important source of information – and when you can't, at least having some ability to tolerate it.

It's less about manipulating and aiming to change your internal world and more about radically accepting it as it is for you now, while staying grounded and exercising autonomy over your responses and behaviours. Having the knowledge and skills for internal-world regulation is key to **real wellness**.

Managing thinking

No one really knows what thoughts are. But what is true is our thoughts form a central part of our lived human experience – they are happening in our inner world 24/7, the by-product of billions of neurons in our brain exchanging information, and shaped by genetics, environment and individual experiences. The thing about thoughts is that they are not always true and they are not always rational or comfortable. For many people, what goes through the mind can be a major source of suffering.

As already mentioned (this is a point that warrants regular reminders), while they are very much a part of our reality, we are not our thoughts, and we need to learn to live with them. How we think about things affects how we feel and behave. Our thoughts can powerfully impact our reactions in situations. It is important to examine your habitual reactions and underlying thinking styles (self-awareness), accept the thoughts (self-acceptance) and cultivate some ability to manage them (self-mastery) so you are not a slave to your thinking.

Relentless though the mind may be at times, we absolutely need our thoughts to function. Higher level cognitive skills – which are called executive skills – are the human's evolutionary power. We need this sort of thinking to organise, plan, problem-solve, create, innovate, collaborate, survive, and grow into our full potential. This is how we are able to run families, plan our finances, work as doctors, teachers, baristas, delivery drivers, and artists. The mind allows us to use our imagination, dream big, and invent. We are so blessed to have the cognitive functions we do. It is heartbreaking at times to witness the loss of these skills in my elderly patients as they age it is a reminder to me to be grateful for my mind while I still have all my faculties.

All this goes to show that, despite any inner critic or predisposition for negative thinking you may have, the mind is to be cherished and cared for. Unfortunately, negative thought styles seem an inevitable part of the deal of having cognition. By the way, this is evolutionary: *our* ancestors expected the worst and survived; their peers with the 'she'll be right' attitude were the ones eaten by sabre-tooth tigers. We need to accept, predict and manage this reality. Developing a healthy relationship with your mind means accepting the inevitable fate of thinking – and experiencing painful inner-world negativity – and having some ability to diffuse thoughts in order to achieve balanced awareness. With balanced awareness, you are tuned in to the potential utility of your thoughts but can take or leave them. Maybe next time you engage with negative self-talk, remind yourself how great it is that your mind can also plan your upcoming holiday … and then turn your focus to thinking about that. In other words, use your attention skills.

There's a time and place for all parts of us. There's a time to be fused with certain thoughts, swept away by all their glory, letting them take you wherever they may choose. But there are also times when this isn't helpful or timely and may even cause harm. Say you're bored while waiting for a train to arrive and you have nothing to do. You could dive into cognitive fantasy for entertainment; it could be argued that this was a masterful use of what would otherwise be meaningless time. However, if you had some reading to get through while waiting for your train and your thoughts were distracting you from your focus, then letting them go for the moment and refocusing your attention on your reading would be more masterful. Maybe if you smashed out the reading, you could later enjoy your thoughts as a reward for getting what you needed to do done. To be able to do that when we choose is truly a personal power. For this skill, you need mindfulness and insight in order to pick and choose how you use your mind to suit your situation, placing your attention where you choose and dropping it from what does not suit you.

It is masterful to be able to diffuse and separate yourself and your attention from unhelpful thoughts, to help let thoughts go and reduce your engagement with them to minimise any distress caused by them. One diffusion strategy is to sing a thought out loud to make it sound less stern and overwhelming. (Maybe use your auditory imagery and imagine yourself doing this if you're sitting on a train, lol.) You can also use mental imagery to turn a thought or sentence into a whimsical cartoon or a headline in goofy bold font to lessen its seriousness and any judgemental impact it may have on you. I like to label my habitual thinking themes as my usual 'stories', citing them to myself internally 'Oh, there I go again thinking that story.'

If you want to learn more tools for diffusion, seek out books on Acceptance Commitment Therapy, which go through this in detail. My favourite is *The Happiness Trap* by Dr Russ Harris.

Another approach to managing thinking is to challenge thoughts and replace unhelpful ones with thinking styles that work for you. Cognitive Behavioural Therapy teaches skills in labelling and challenging dysfunctional assumptions and thoughts so you can develop the ability to reframe your thinking. Cognitive reframing is a way to tweak your perspective and potentially see a more positive or helpful side to your reality.

It's helpful to identify when you're fused with classic negative thought styles such as: catastrophising (assuming the worst outcome); overgeneralising and discounting the positive (rejecting good things as if they did not count, and focusing on the bad); mind reading and fortune telling (assuming what others think about you, with limited evidence to support your thoughts, and predicting the future); labelling (identifying your shortcomings – "I'm a failure"); personalisation and blame (taking responsibility when it's not yours); demanding (putting yourself or others under pressure by thinking what you/they should do); and all or nothing thinking (thinking in extremes).

For example, you could say to yourself, 'I notice I'm thinking in a black and white way.' You can challenge thoughts by asking yourself certain questions:

- 'Is there another way to view this situation or person that is not so extreme?
- Are there any facts to back up an alternative explanation?'
- 'What is the worst-case scenario here and am I underestimating my abilities and resources?'
- 'What might another person's perspective be? What would I say to a friend in this situation to help them through?'

After decades of living with imposter syndrome, these days I can catch my negative thought styles and unhelpful stories around practising as a doctor and reframe them. Instead of being engulfed by my worries about whether certain things at work will be ok or not, I now know that regardless, I cope. I remind myself how I am a master problem solver and highly trained in being resourceful to cope when the shit inevitably hits the fan. In this instance, to manage my thinking, I use my noticing and labelling skills, and insert some extra thoughts to make the internal sentence more useful to me: 'I'll be fine, I always am. I know it will be hard and things will go wrong but I will work it out. I'm very resourceful and there is yet to be a problem I can't resolve!' Adopting a self-compassionate growth mindset allows us to gently learn and develop without punishment, harsh self-judgement and striving.

Sometimes allowing thoughts to be and flow, without putting in effort to challenge or diffuse them, can be helpful – not to mention a lot less draining. This is probably the most masterful strategy for manage thinking. Essentially, it is meditation. Simply allow your awareness to serve as a host. Your thoughts are invited to the party. They may be an offensive guest, less wanted than the rest, but as an accommodating host your role is to hold a safe space for them. You don't have to engage or focus on them but rather allow them to be present, knowing they will leave when they're done.

I am proud to write that I have mastered the ability to reassure myself during occasions of internal discontent. My messaging is that I know there are underlying cognitive reasons for the discontent but I don't need to waste my energy figuring them all out because I know my state will change and, right now, I'm safe. In other words, I can park the self-enquiry and enjoy the moment regardless of my suboptimal inner landscape. I don't expect myself to think positively all the time or feel 100% in every moment. What I do expect is self-compassion and the inevitable highs and lows of living as a human being.

Managing physical sensations

Forming a respectful and understanding relationship with your physical body is required to live peacefully in it, whatever its challenges, or where you are in the inevitable ageing and change process that occurs over time. This means learning to live with all the physical sensations we experience, and this can be equally as challenging as learning to peacefully cohabit with our mind. Just as some thoughts can be unpleasant and difficult to live with, so can our physical sensations. Headache is the most common presentation in neurology outpatient clinics. Body pain is the number one health concern most of my patients want to focus on. Be assured that you're not alone if you suffer from physical sensations within. Like thoughts, they serve a purpose, and must be noticed, accepted and cared for. It goes without saying, however, that you need to consult your medical doctor for advice when it comes to managing your pain.

Whatever the circumstance of our health and body, we all inevitably face physical pain and unpleasant sensations. Having some awareness and skills to manage it is pivotal to self-management for **real wellness**. The same skills you may apply to diffuse, challenge, and tolerate thoughts can be used to manage your physical sensations in general. For chronic inner discomfort, mindfulness, acceptance, and self-compassion skills are all very helpful.

If you live with neuropathic chronic pain (pain from nerve injury that is ongoing more than three months), your body's neural wiring for pain is abnormal, and stimuli that don't usually cause pain may become painful. Even the light touch of bed sheets can be excruciating for some people with nerve pain. Understanding chronic pain and learning to compassionately live with it is the cornerstone of optimal chronic pain management. In chronic pain medicine we teach patients skills around sitting with their chronic discomfort, reassuring themselves they are safe, and making space for the sensation as they direct their attention elsewhere. There are many wonderful books outlining in detail the evidence-based strategies for this. My favourite is *Manage Your Pain*, by Dr Michael Nicholas, Dr Alan Molloy, Lois Tonkin, and Lee Beeston.

I understand what it is like to live in a body you don't trust or that may scare you at times. When I am sleep deprived, I feel all sorts of crazy within. I feel vulnerable and weird, as if I am liable to have a seizure (in my defense, I did have one at 14 years, in the context of a lot of social stress and poor sleep, so I think I'm conditioned to believing this could happen again). When I feel this way, I use my inner adult to reassure my inner child that I will be okay; I just need some sleep and an early night tonight. I up my self-care by ensuring adequate hydration, protein, fruit and breaks. I limit my tasks for the day, clear my evening, and I wear my favourite colours and cosy clothes (I probably also have an extra strong coffee!).

*

Sensations within can be unnerving, especially when you are unsure of their etiology. When you experience unusual and uncomfortable sensations, you may worry that they could mean something sinister. You may have an urge to access reassurance that you are safe. Some people have vague unexplained medical symptoms that lead them to worry they have cancer or some fatal condition. The tough news, medically speaking, is that many sensations within cannot be fully explained. Some days, depending on countless variables, your body may signal sensations that – as far as a medical professional can interpret – could indicate imbalance or illness. But sometimes these signals are also meaningless, making discerning what's what very confusing! When you're worried, see your GP. It is okay to seek that reassurance from your trusted doctor.

But once the big scaries have been excluded after the appropriate evidence-based investigations, if your symptoms are chronic, then it's time to radically accept them as yours to house and learn to live with. The more you can care for yourself and live in a balanced way, meeting your holistic needs, the better your body sensations will be. They may never go away but at least they will be minimised.

*

Managing stress means managing physical feelings. Getting to know these sensations and being able to care for them helps to mitigate the risk of secondary aches and pains from built-up tension and unmet needs. Stress can be signaled to you in your body by muscle tension, headaches or migraines, fatigue or lethargy, digestive symptoms, racing heartbeat, shallow breathing, feeling flushed, and brain fog (to name a few – this is not exhaustive, and varies from one person to the next).

When I notice stress in my body, I use physical diffusion strategies to release the building energy. I know to consciously relax my neck tension and lower my hunched shoulders. I notice and send some love to any pain in my tummy or heart space and imagine opening up the channels of energy there to soften and settle the sensation. I keep hydrated if thirsty and rest my thinking if my head feels full or foggy. I often go for a long brisk walk or slow jog to shake off the energy and to settle all my body's sensory cues of building stress.

Experiment with ways of managing your body's hints of stress – indicated to you by your body's feeling state. Laughter or a rest may work for you. If you notice unmet needs, try your best to attend to them in helpful ways that work for you.

Managing emotions

Typical of our inner world elements, emotions can be a mystery to us. Sometimes, we need to reflect and take time to figure out what we're feeling. Whether obvious or mysterious, big or small, comfortable or otherwise, it is our relationship with our emotions that determines their impact on us. Emotions can be helpful or unhelpful, and they may or may not cause suffering: it all depends on how we manage and interact with them. Regrettably, many people don't manage their emotions effectively, which I attribute to a lack of familiarity and skills (this stuff should be in school curriculums). Those who do manage their emotions welcome them into their awareness, investigate their potential purpose and respond to them wisely – which in some cases means not at all. For those of us working towards **real wellness**, our goal is to accept emotions, use them as helpful messengers, and know how to care for ourselves as we move through them, so we may live with them adaptively (even when, thanks to our emotions, we feel shit).

Understanding that your emotions have a reason and message is important in order to accept them and learn to tolerate them. If people dismiss the relevance and utility of emotions – perhaps viewing them as juvenile, unreasonable or inconvenient – it's like they are flying a jet plane without the aid of all the engines. But emotions are a needed and inevitable part of our adult survival toolkit, and they should be seen and used as helpful messages.

Emotions drive motivation and behaviour. Advertisers know this, so they might do things like arouse fear to sell certain brands of car, for example.

Emotions are required for rational decision-making. The immediate unpleasant internal reaction we have to incoherence helps drive our decisions towards the rational. For example, it would be irrational to choose to buy your life home based purely on financial return and ignore your emotions. What if you hated it? It would be illogical to live in a home you hated living in just because it was a good deal.

We need to use emotions as guides, even the challenging ones, or we can end up creating a lot of unnecessary chaos and stress in our lives. Say someone you've known since childhood unfriends you on social media, and you experience a range of emotions such as upset and anger. One option would be to avoid feeling and thinking about possible causes and solutions and instead hit the [insert vice here]. This may make you feel even worse and mean missing out on an opportunity to resolve the issue at hand. Another option might be to notice your pain as an indicator that you care for your friend and plan how to respond in a helpful way to create space for your friendship to continue. This might look like having an early night and planning a call to your friend in the morning to chat it through once your emotional wave of upset has settled a little.

Pleasant or unpleasant, emotion shows us what we care about. It shows us we care! For example, grieving the loss of someone deeply important to you may be hard and exceedingly painful, but the emotions that come with it are a valid and super important part of processing your loss.

Emotions bring light and colour to life. How much more fun is eating something you passionately enjoy than something you are impartial to? What about that feeling of attuned love we can cultivate with someone or something we are deeply connected to? It's the best! And, as annoying as it may be, we need to experience the dark to acknowledge the light. After excitement, boredom may follow. Sometimes I find myself overwhelmed by how much I love my son and then equally terrified I could lose him.

Emotions help regulate our ethics and shape our identity. Guilty feelings about our actions, for example, prompt apologies and behaviour modification. Sometimes I feel a general sense of discontent when I am not fully showing up in my life, if I'm acting out, or holding back in some way. In these times, I am forced to dig deep and work out what needs change to optimise my wellbeing. It is as if my soul is speaking to me. This is when I journal and return to my values, priorities and intentions to get perspective on the issue and clear up why I am feeling that way.

*

To build your emotional fitness, firstly get familiar with your emotions. Notice when they arise and how they manifest. Are there associated beliefs, thoughts, physical sensations, urges? If you are safe, lean into the emotional experience and enquire what those feelings may be saying. Practise sitting with them, regardless of whether they are pleasant or unpleasant. Practise desensitising yourself to them to accustom yourself to their presence. This is so they don't freak you out: the alternative is that you inadvertently live your life avoiding them and consequently remain detached from their wisdom. In the past, I have gotten to know some pretty deep, dark and gloomy inner-world states. I learnt that simply lying down with a tea, a hot water bottle, and my dog by my side and taking the time to settle and process those big feelings was often the most masterful way to manage myself when in that state. It was not to problem-solve, 'do' or 'move on'. Instead, I needed to lie low and simply feel myself. Once those big feels had passed, then I had the resilience and reserve to fix or improve things where needed. It bears repeating that, sometimes, not doing and just feeling is what you need to do to be well.

Taking time to notice and feel your emotions is part of human-mastery. Without noticing, you cannot make much of a situation! Naming emotions is a helpful way of noticing what is going on for you internally. If you notice a big feeling, try to name it to get a handle on what is going on: it may be anger, jealousy, love, for example. Once you notice and label an episode of an emotion, you can internally say to yourself, 'I notice I am experiencing the emotion of …' This brings distance and highlights your awareness of it, so you have more opportunity to mindfully respond to it rather than avoid or carelessly react to it. This is an emotion diffusion strategy.

Take advantage of your emotions by learning from them. Ask yourself why they may be happening. What's their message and purpose? Are you feeling guilt because you acted against your values? Are you feeling anxious because you have not completed a task that needs doing? Are you feeling joy because you are doing something you truly love? There may not be an enlightening message behind your experience (so don't stress if you cannot see any helpful message) but if you find one, it may be useful to you and to your advantage to notice.

Lastly, accept the emotion and relax into it, knowing that feelings don't last all that long. Remind yourself you do not need to act or respond in any way to your emotions. You can simply turn your awareness to something else. You can make space for it, and once it has naturally passed, you can choose how to respond.

The internal fathom – which is my word for deep inner-world sensation or data – need not cause any harm. It's your action and response to fathoms that can. Your actions and response are your choice and may be within your control.

Whatever the emotion, try to welcome it into your awareness without judgement and leave any fear at the door. Don't be scared; remind yourself your actions and responses are the only way any emotion can turn from a human experience to a life consequence. If you freak out from an emotion, you'll panic and kick into fight/flight mode. This will cause secondary stress on the body. If you remain chill bro through emotions, you will be more likely to manage them with reason and control. They will be less amplified and more likely to settle quickly.

Remind yourself that emotions are messengers, and you can look after yourself while you process them. Like a wave, they pass eventually. It is your adult job to nurture yourself and make space for your emotions as you work out how to respond with measure, consideration and care. Worst case scenario: have a nap or go to sleep. It's the most effective way of processing big feelings. If your feelings become chronic and disabling, talk to your loved ones and please see your doctor to get the professional support you need and deserve.

Be aware that sometimes, to build your human-mastery, you may need to do the opposite of what an emotion urges you to do or, better still, nothing at all. We needn't be stuck in emotion or at their mercy when experiencing them.

Let's consider the natural and healthy experience of grief. If intense, a grief period can interfere with your life participation in an unhealthy way. Intense grief can feel all-encompassing, making basic self-care feel impossible. Intense grief may urge you to stay in bed, and isolate. But maintaining your nutrition, sleep, warmth, social connections, and self-care is super important to survive a period of intense grief. In this instance, you would benefit from being able to make healthier choices as you nurture your grief process. To do so, you can simply turn your focus elsewhere while allowing the grief to do its thing and naturally pass. It is not that you are ignoring, avoiding or repressing the grief, but simply allowing it to be a part of your existence while maintaining your self-care and looking after yourself.

When processing painful emotions, try to view yourself as injured and nursing an acute pain. Look after yourself as you would another person recovering from an acutely painful injury.

Check in with your thinking when an emotion arises. Your interpretation of your emotion affects your experience. Are anxiety and excitement different? They both tend to leave you feeling ungrounded, with an increase in the physical manifestations of the sympathetic nervous system like a fast heart rate, more frequent and shallow breathing, and an urge to flee. But the underlying belief attached to the experience differs and it is this underlying belief that, in part, determines your perception of the experience. You can choose to consider another line of thinking and belief to interpret your internal experience. When anxious, if you know you are safe, try flipping your view of fear and interpret it as excitement. See fear as a thrill. Progress with care and welcome novelty, growth and living an exciting life.

It is not only awareness of the purpose and utility of the emotion that enables you to effectively manage your experience, but also your awareness of the underlying belief carried along with it. With that awareness, you gain the ability to choose a belief that works for you in order to change your perception and interpretation of the emotional experience. I used to think fear was an intuitive omen prompting me to avoid what was ahead of me, but I learnt that it was a helpful reminder to tread cautiously. I don't let my fears hold me back from doing things that bring meaning and value to my life (and are safe) but I do let it guide me to be sensible and self-caring while I go about all these scary things.

Consider your values, intentions and priorities to bring perspective to emotion. If you can notice that the trigger for an emotion is in line with your internal compass, the experience is much more manageable. For example, learning a new skill like driving may be terrifying to some individuals. Say that friends and family are in line with a person's values and priorities, by reminding themselves that, once acquired, the skill will give the means and freedom to visit friends and family, then the fear will be worth it. I make it a general self-care rule to check in with my internal compass when I face unpleasant big feelings and ask myself, 'Is my emotion worth it for my values and priorities?' Using our values, by embodying them (acting in line with them) when emotional, helps us cope during times of unpleasant emotion and helps make meaning of the moment. It gives you a lifeline to live through that fleeting moment of challenge and makes it worth living.

If you find yourself overwhelmed by emotion, notice that, accept it, check in with its message and then turn your focus to embodying your values while you wait for it to pass. In the past when I have had social anxiety in a meeting or giving a talk, I choose to rest my attention on being warm, compassionate, fun and engaged with my audience. It is not that I am denying my anxiety, I am simply turning my focus on how I want to be and make others feel. In this instance, I know I am safe and recognise my emotion as unhelpful and that I need not act on it. I don't need to attempt to get rid of it, avoid or numb it, and I can choose how I will carry myself despite it. The moment may be unpleasant, but it has become meaningful and relevant if I am able to embody my values regardless. At night as I rest my head on my pillow, I may reflect on how the day felt hard and 'bad', but at least I am proud of my behaviour and conduct. I can sleep content, knowing it was a meaningful day and I lived my purpose.

Managing urges

Urges are inner-world experiences that motivate action and behaviour. They are the signals we pick up that tell us to do something. These may be things like shout, run, eat, sleep, pee or stretch our body. Whether or not we are conscious of it, all these actions are precipitated by an urge. Learning a little mastery over our urges is a key skill for **real wellness**. Being able to notice and then manage your urges is a priceless skill of human-mastery. (I'm sure we can all relate to inconvenient urges pulling us towards actions that may not be in our best interest.)

The first step to managing urges is to become aware of them and familiarise yourself with them. We have obvious urges, but also super subtle, almost undetectable urges that influence our choices. Urges exist because they are functional. Like emotions, they may be helpful messages to confront us with a need that requires attention and fulfilment. An urge may reflect a physiological or psychological need, like rest, food, or connection. It would be hard to remember to eat on super busy days if it weren't for our body's timely hunger cues and resultant urges to eat. Without useful urges, we may not know or remember how to look after ourselves and omit important self-care. So, we would not want to dismiss all our urges.

However, not all urges are useful or need to be acted upon, and some can be simply habitual or even manifestations of harmful conditioning or addiction. You can have urges to eat beyond satiety, drink beyond healthy limits, or pick up a cigarette to palliate boredom or anxiety. A vice is an unhealthy behaviour. Most people struggle at some point in their lives with a vice. These trip us up because of the urges we have for them and our difficulty in managing these urges. We would not engage in the vice if there was no urge, so learning to manage the urge is our opportunity for autonomy over the vice. Focusing on the vice will only get you so far.

Being attuned to your urges enables you to consider your impulses and make wise-minded decisions based on your long-term wellness needs and not just immediate gains.

Urges are tricky beasts! But as with thoughts and emotions, they can be manipulated to your advantage. Sometimes, you must act as your own parent and say no to things that you desire in the moment when they are not conducive to your best life. How do you stop yourself from indulgently feeding negative self-talk when it seems so loud within? How do you stop eating cake after multiple pieces when there's an urge for more? There may be a part of us that wants to do the 'fun thing'. But what is fun now may not be fun later. Delayed gratification is hard work but often what is called for.

If you have significant and disabling impulse-control issues, please see your doctor. There are medical conditions, like ADHD, associated with impulse-control struggles that can be treated.

If you're anything like me and love cake but can overdo it sometimes, building skills around managing urges to overindulge may help you enjoy cake in moderation. When indulging in sweets, use your attention to notice any urges for more. Noticing is always the first step, so use your mindfulness skills to check in without judgement what is going on for you. Notice any intrusive thoughts your mind pumps out around indulging the urge. Notice the associated physical sensations occurring during any urge. Then, rather than getting caught up in an internal argument around whether you want or don't want to act on the urge, forget the urge and its suggestion (i.e. eat more cake) and place your attention on the pursuit of caring for yourself. Consider what is going to set you up for a great day moving forward (i.e. drink some water, move your body and get on with your day knowing you can choose to eat more cake another time when it better works for you) and see if you can find any internal urges towards that.

Use the **Ideal You** skill if you're not sure what to do. Imagery is a brilliant tool when managing urges and determining a path of behaviour that will work for you. Bring to mind a vision of yourself healthy and content after only consuming one moderate portion of cake. Notice if this image feels good to you. Notice if you wish to embody (i.e. live out) this chosen image of yourself being masterful, autonomous and self-caring.

Bring your attention to this new urge – an urge to take control of your actions and do the thing that is caring towards yourself. Give the initial urge a name and tell it where to go ('No thanks, overeating cake urge, we are not doing that today!'). Without thinking too much, act in the direction of your useful vision towards self-care. Take the first step, then the next and keep your attention on each step, one at a time. If you get distracted by derailing urges, use your mindfulness to return your awareness to the image and task at hand. Place your attention on your legs as they walk away from the cake. Notice your excitement as you do this, relish it as much as possible. Cultivate a sense of pride. Then go reward yourself (just not with cake). If cake is not your bag, then switch this example for your vice (cigarettes, wine, online shopping, porn, yelling/projecting etc).

A key human-mastery hack to skill up on is the ability to sit with urges, to realise that we don't have to act or do anything at all following the experience of an urge, and to be able to continue on as we were prior to noticing the urge. This skill seems so easy and yet it can be one of the most difficult and seemingly impossible things to do. Urge-surfing, where you witness an urge arise and pass without acting on it, is a useful skill when overcoming unhelpful habits. The skill of urge-surfing describes an urge as a wave, with a peak and a trough. It describes the trick to overcoming unhelpful urges as to ride them out, like a surfer on a wave. You are not trying to stop the experience of an urge, its onset or duration. Rather, you are simply existing with them without acting on them. Urges can't last forever, so you can use your insight and awareness to remind yourself of their fleeting nature to help resist the temptation to act on them. The more you persist with riding out the urge waves, the more you realise how transient they are and that they have no control over you unless you allow them to by acting on them. Just like surfing actual waves, the more you practise surfing urges, the more experienced, resilient, and strong you become at doing so, and the more mastery you will feel you have over them.

Each time an urge is not acted on, it builds your neuronal ability to resist them. Your ability to sit with urges develops, and you can do so with less effort and more ease. So, as challenging, and even painful as urge-surfing may seem to you, take heart in knowing it gets better with repeated practice. When urge-surfing, you can stay engaged with your urges, noticing their manifestation in your body and their peak followed by their subsiding, or you can distract yourself from them while the wave runs its course.

There's a limitless number of ways to distract yourself as you urge-surf. Some ideas are cooking, walking, calling a friend, having a shower or swim, cleaning and going for a drive. If you want to curiously investigate the urge, you may like to creatively draw the energy of the urge as you sit with it; express the experience through art, journalling, or plotting it on a graph; or simply breathe into it as you notice it come and go.

Urges can cause suffering and struggle, especially if training yourself to abstain from a vice. Key to managing urges is the ability to manage your stress response to them. Stress is inevitably unpleasant, and we tend to want to avoid it. So, if we find experiencing urges stressful, we will find withstanding the urges unpleasant and may want to escape that unpleasantness by indulging in the urge just to get the stressful feelings over and done with. It is as if a part of us thinks the stress of the presence of the urge outweighs the consequences of indulging in the vice you're urged towards. I have noticed myself acting on an urge just so I don't have to deal with the stress of tolerating it. Furthermore, stress makes us more likely to choose from a place of heightened emotion and fear. So, we are more likely to act on an urge when stressed by it.

When you notice urges, if you can simply relax to combat the stress response, it allows you to calmly pause to consider your best move forward. If you accept and relax into the presence of the urge, you are most likely to utilise these wise-minded neural networks for considered choice. When relaxed, you can respond in a leisurely manner rather than frantically running from an urge. Instead of freaking out like a stressed-out mess at the experience of an urge, try to reassure yourself that an urge is just a fleeting inner-world experience, and that you are very safe in this moment even if you're also feeling an urge. As long as you don't allow your urges to determine your actions consistently, you are very safe. So, don't panic! Urges are harmless. They can't kill you. They have no power over you unless you choose to act on them. Be calm, breathe, and stay cool despite the sensations. Be curious about your response and tolerance around urges. Turn your attention away from the behaviour the urge is nudging you towards, and rather, notice how the experience of abstaining is for you. Are you scared of your urge? Get curious. Notice your response to your urges knowing you can look without fear of being unsafe.

I have bundled up all this advice into a hack. My recipe for urge management is to CRAP yourself:

INTERNAL-WORLD REGULATION

Call and name it ('I am experiencing an urge to …'). This is a diffusion strategy that helps you separate yourself from the experience and also prioritises it in your awareness so you can notice it fully.

RELAX. Limit your stress response in order to act wisely.

Accept the presence of the urge. Remember your humanness and that urges are a predictable part of life.

Problem-solve and plan (once cool, calm and collected):

a. Risk-mitigate by scanning for any potential problems you can solve — and thereby become less likely to act on the urge. An example is drinking water if thirsty instead of giving in to an urge to drink alcohol.
b. Plan how you can best cope throughout the experience — i.e. while the urge runs its course. You may need a hug, a shower, to go to bed …
c. Turn your attention off your impulse and notice all your options. Notice how you can move away and do many other things.
d. Worse case: if an unhelpful urge feels stronger than your ability to resist, you can remove yourself entirely from the situation to avoid acting on it. Or you may even like to ask someone to lie on top of you to physically hold you down and stop you from following an unwelcome urge.

While we have focused on unhelpful urges and how to prevent them from derailing us, remember that we can have super-helpful urges — ones that suggest action that will increase wellbeing, like an urge to hug, kiss, or thank a loved one. It's up to you to determine the nature of your urges — whether they are helpful or not, appropriate in the moment or not, conducive to wellbeing or not. Human-mastery and **real wellness** come from the attunement to urges – something you can develop – and flexibility in your response.

Don't be slave to your urges, be their master. Manage your urges by relaxing, making space for them, allowing them, and then turning your attention elsewhere. Use your wisdom to kindly remind yourself of your wellness needs and that whatever it is your unhealthy urge wants you to do, it is not necessary.

*

Once you have developed your inner-world noticing skills using mindfulness, if you can then learn to accept, listen, and care for your inner world, you have essentially mastered it. This outcome is the best you could ever hope for. With this mastery, you have created for yourself opportunity for optimal functioning and wellbeing. You can live peacefully, as an ally and colleague, with your inner world.

Case study

According to his medical history and previous clinic letters, the patient I was about to meet – Mr Arnold – had cirrhosis from decades of excess alcohol intake and was living with a traumatic brain injury sustained in a fall. To my surprise, when Mr Arnold walked through the clinic door he seemed groomed, content, sensible, sober, and relatively well. This wasn't what I had expected.

To my relief, Mr Arnold told me that a month earlier he had stopped drinking all alcohol. Already, he was eating and sleeping better, his thinking was clearer, and he wasn't having falls.

'How did you do it?' I asked.

'Well,' he said, 'I just stopped.'

It seemed too simple, so I probed a little more. Turns out his last intoxicated fall had frightened him. Suddenly, it was obvious to Mr Arnold that he had to stop or he'd soon be dead. At first, he found fighting the urge to drink hard, so he set about finding activities to replace his daily trip to the pub. Birds had always brought him joy, so he bought an old cage, cleaned it up then bought some budgerigars. Now Mr Arnold devotes his spare time to caring for them. His friends visit him at home to see the birds, and he has a scooter that he drives daily into town to get the newspaper, which he likes to read by the lake with a coffee.

Mr Arnold was incredibly masterful. He managed to acknowledge and accept his reality, using brutal self-honesty. He used his emotions to motivate helpful behaviour. He overcame his urges with activities and interests that were satisfying enough, and still social, to avoid needing the pub and a drink.

There's no doubt Mr Arnold will remain sober and will age a million times better as a consequence. But most importantly, I hope he lives out his days proud of his incredible lifestyle change and content within himself at having fostered healthier self-care and masterful self-management.

Take-home messages

- Internal regulation means noticing, accepting and caring for your human internal-world experiences (and even working them to your advantage) so you function optimally. So, these are the three steps: notice, accept, and care.
- Whether something you sense in your internal world bothers you or enlightens you depends on how you view it and relate to it. It is all about our relationship with what is happening inside us.
- Use your attention skills to focus internally where it suits. Sometimes, it's great to be lost in thoughts or feelings, and at other times, not at all. You can decide where you place your awareness and energy.

- As life flows on ceaselessly within and around you, with mindfulness you optimise your opportunity to notice things then use your values/priorities and self-care skills to make wise choices.
- Internal experiences are fleeting. They spark action only if you act on them! We are most likely to act on them thoughtlessly when we are unfamiliar with them or stressed by them. You have the power to decide how you behave.
- For thought management, try diffusion, challenge, reframing and radical acceptance.
- For feeling management, try reassurance, meeting any unmet needs, and stress management.
- For emotion regulation, learn to use these guys as messengers: read them, make space for them, process and learn to lovingly hold them.
- For urges, try surfing them or go CRAP yourself: Call and name it, RELAX, Accept the presence of the urge, Problem-solve and plan.
- For more hot tips, read about emotion regulation skills, Acceptance Commitment Therapy and Cognitive Behavioural Therapy.

Reflection

Next time you feel anger, try to confine it to your inner world: don't speak, don't move — simply wait until it runs its natural course. Notice any associated self-righteous thoughts and physical sensations in the body. Use your breath to breathe through the wave of emotion. Notice how it does pass. I apologise in advance for how hard this is. But you will experience for yourself how nothing may come of the anger other than improving your strength, emotional resilience, and distress tolerance (sages tend to say their trauma was their greatest teacher: irritating, but it can be true if you reflect and use what you learn wisely).

Conversely, if you manifest anger into speech, movement, and action, you have allowed it to project itself onto the world around you.

Now, don't get me wrong: expressions of anger are sometimes called for and may help cultivate self-worth and manifest a just external world outcome. Emotional expression, like all things, can be handled in a way that promotes wellness: you needn't suppress your feelings.

The instance of an emotion like anger is a useful message that you feel violated. When feeling angry, it may be that you need to express or protect yourself in some adaptive way. The self-mastery is the ability to notice the instance of an emotion and any associated urges, and the ability to enquire how you need to respond in order to remain safe but in line with the needs of your situation, your values, priorities, and intentions. With equanimity, you can then proceed in the way that will best work for you.

17

External-world Regulation

You are now familiar with a **Two Worlds** approach to living and human-mastery. So, just as it is masterful to acquire internal-world regulation skills, it is equally beneficial to learn to manipulate your external world to your advantage or, at least, understand how to manage your external world as best you can to make it work for you.

Our environment inevitably shapes us. The world around us determines our options, influences our values and beliefs, triggers our reactions, conditions us, and impacts our choices, habits, behaviour, health outcomes, and ultimately our quality of life.

Having some mastery of our external world makes a massive difference to our autonomy and wellbeing. The external world encompasses a multitude of factors that can impact our physical, emotional, and mental states.

- Social connections and relationships are crucial components: positive interactions with friends, family, and the community

contribute to a sense of belonging and emotional support, thereby enhancing wellbeing. We need others to co-regulate.
- Cultural and societal norms, as well as access to education and healthcare, also contribute to wellbeing. Inclusive and equitable societies that prioritise education and healthcare tend to foster healthier and happier populations.
- Workplace conditions and job satisfaction are additional external factors that can impact wellbeing. A supportive work culture and environment, fair treatment, and opportunities for personal and professional growth contribute positively to mental health. Conversely, high levels of stress, job insecurity, or an unsupportive workplace culture can have detrimental effects.
- Environmental factors, such as access to clean air, water, and green spaces, play a role in our sense of safety, influence our physical health, and contribute to a higher quality of life. Economic stability and access to resources play a crucial role as well.
- Financial security provides stability and the ability to meet basic needs, positively influencing mental wellbeing. On the other hand, economic hardships, poverty, and inequality can lead to stress, anxiety, and decreased overall life satisfaction.

The list goes on ...

*

Fundamental to wellbeing is living with a sense of environmental safety. If you are living in an unsafe environment, it is not possible to be optimally well, and your focus will be on survival. We need to feel safe to feel well. Clearly, the messages of this book are irrelevant to anyone living in a situation where there is threat to life, such as in a war zone, if living with severe and acute unstable illness, chronic exposure to violence, and other risk of serious harm. Tragically, many people do live like this, and if you don't, you're one of the privileged.

That said, stress is somewhat relative. What I perceive as stressful may not be seen the same way by someone else. I'll be the first to acknowledge that I'm a 'worried well' person. We all meet stress with different backgrounds, environments, conditioning, and sensitivity.

Regardless of your history and personal circumstances, the body's autonomic system will be dysregulated if you are living with trauma or in a chronically or extremely stressed state. When you live in an unsafe environment, inevitably you will perceive stress. Safety and living in a safe environment can mean varying things. There are many environmental stressors that may pose risks to your safety. These can be invisible and insidious, like some environmental pathogens, or, glaringly obvious and posing imminent threat, like physical violence and living with domestic abuse.

We need warm, dry, hygienic shelter with the means to meet our basic physical needs, such as nutrition, hydration, sleep, clean clothes and so on, and access to medical care to feel safe and secure, and to be well. We need to live free of bullying, harassment, violence and prejudice. We need to be loved and feel like we belong. We need to be seen, heard, and considered. We need a safe tribe, resources, and supports to turn to as required. We need to feel as though we are not alone and can ask for help when it is called for. These are our human basic needs, the things that cultivate environmental safety, and must be the priority for anyone pursuing **real wellness**. Once you have established a home base that is safe, you can begin to optimise your environment to thrive in your health and wellbeing.

*

Having a community and tribe that makes you feel loved, accepted, and gives you a sense of belonging is required for **real wellness**.

But these need not be a mass of friends or even involve people at all. Maybe your tribe is your home plants or pets? Or maybe your community is your immediate family circle of just one or two core people. Find your people, those beings who see you warts and all, and love you all the same. What I am speaking to here are the profound health and wellbeing benefits of connection. There is fascinating emerging neuroscience on the power interpersonal connections play on our brain chemistry, architecture and function. We need these connections to regulate and cope but also, with the emotional foundation of safety required they provide, we will thrive and be able to move mountains.

At home, having family you can lean on, share with, and listen to makes home feel secure and safe. It would be reasonable to argue that the life partner we pick largely determines our long-term health. I'm so blessed to live with someone who doesn't drink, smoke or eat poorly. Instead, my partner loves cooking, bike riding, reading and hugs. When I need a lifestyle change, if I explain why, he's supportive and often goes along with it. But it's our moments of connection, in between my busy days, that fill my cup, ground me, and keep me going. I need to return to that one safe person who chooses me, sees and hears me, and cares for me, and that is so very human and okay.

At work, having a mentor and colleagues you can run issues past for help makes work more fun and effective – and consequently more satisfying. The people you work with can make or break your career. I have worked very busy jobs with lovely colleagues and thrived. I have also had roles with cruisey terms but with unsupportive people and it has destroyed me. If you enjoy a workplace tribe of supportive colleagues, then you are blessed. Relish that support.

In your local community, having friends and neighbours you can help – and call on for help when you are in need – again creates an environmental foundation of support and safety. I'll never forget the support my local community bestowed on me when our son was a newborn. If something in the house broke down, there was always someone around who would come over and help fix it. Our supportive neighborhood was a reason to stay where we lived when thinking proactively about where we wanted to raise our child. If you can design a life with people who lift you up and make you feel good, then you'll be far more well than if you endure a life surrounded by miserable people.

My point is, yes: self-mastery is the path to **real wellness**, but part of this is seeking out connections and community. Self-mastery for **real wellness** is not all inwardly focused. As humans, we need each other to be well, and sometimes being of service is the medicine we need most.

*

The first step to external world regulation is to be aware of your environment and understand how it influences you and may work for you and/or against you. Social norms, culture, rules, regulations, and government policies collectively play a crucial role in shaping health, health behaviours, and overall wellbeing within a society. These factors contribute to the establishment of a framework that influences individual choices, access to resources, and the overall health environment. For example, cultural attitudes towards diet, exercise, and healthcare practices can shape an individual's approach to maintaining good health. In some cultures, certain health-related behaviours may be encouraged or discouraged based on traditional beliefs. The culture of our family impacts us. If your family culture values a strong work ethic and focus on achievement, then you may be vulnerable to conditioning around perfectionism and unrelenting standards. We tend to inherit the beliefs and tendencies of close and valued people in our lives, in part, due to people-pleasing and our deep need to fit in but also because we are biased towards what is familiar and what we know. What is your health culture?

Government-imposed rules and regulations, especially in areas such as public health, safety standards, and environmental protection, play a vital role in safeguarding the wellbeing of the population. Regulations on food safety, workplace conditions, and environmental pollution directly impact physical health and safety. Broader government policies related to healthcare access, education, and social welfare programs can significantly influence overall wellbeing. For example, policies that support affordable and accessible healthcare contribute to better health outcomes for the population. Governments often use public health campaigns to promote positive health behaviours. These campaigns can educate the public on topics such as vaccination, smoking cessation, healthy eating, and physical activity, influencing individual choices and behaviours. Social and economic factors, including income, education, and employment opportunities, are powerful determinants of health. Government policies addressing these factors can either mitigate or exacerbate health disparities within a society. Regulations governing the healthcare system, including insurance coverage, accessibility, and quality of care, significantly impact individuals' access to medical services and their overall health outcomes. Government-supported social programs, such as social security, unemployment benefits, and disability assistance, contribute to the overall wellbeing of citizens by providing a safety net during challenging times. How is your government influencing your wellbeing?

*

Wouldn't it be nice to have all the control in the world, including over our actions? Yet the reality is we, as humans, are profoundly influenced by what is available to us and surrounds us. Our behaviour is, in part, determined by our environment. This link between our external and internal worlds is one to get to know and understand for self-mastery. You can consider this more broadly on a social level or more intimately in terms of your most immediate environment. Get to know how your environment affects you. Become curious. Even the ideas and creations our brains come up with are limited by what we know and see around us. Random example, but have you ever considered how you could never have imagined Antarctica – the region of icy waters capped by an inland ice sheet containing roughly 90% of the world's total surface fresh water – had you not been told of it or shown pictures of it? Whether we like it or not, our environment is very much an intricately integrated part of who and why we are, how we will be, and what our minds come up with.

If you struggle to optimise your health choices, consider your environment. Have you ever noticed the development of an urge and craving triggered after seeing something? Like wanting chocolate after seeing an advert selling it. You might not have considered chocolate at all had it not been for this image influencing your brain's creation of an urge. When the weather is nice, do you find it easier to get outside and move your body? The weather can make outdoor movement appealing or unattractive. I know that when the seasons change and the months grow colder, I need to brainstorm creative ways to find warmth with movement. I tend to do more sauna stretch sessions and heated yoga in winter, otherwise I feel stuck and wretched. When the gear required for your hobbies is laid out and ready for use, do you think to use them more than when they are out of sight? If your exercise clothes are next to the bed as you wake in the morning, does it feel easier to put them on with less effort? I find it a lot easier to do some weights at home when they are left outside ready to be used.

If we surround ourselves with helpful supports and resources that we can easily see and access, we are far more likely to engage in healthy choices. Start by simply noticing how your environment is functioning, so you can plan ways to modify your environment to facilitate the healthy behaviours you wish for yourself. Surround yourself with the resources, supports and environmental structure needed to make these actions easy to do.

*

The last thing any of us would want is to live a life engulfed by barriers and obstacles that hold us back from meeting our needs, but if barriers are part of 'business as usual', then it may be that we don't recognise them as such. If you do an audit, you may realise that your environment is working against you – that you may have been taking the path of most resistance and struggling unnecessarily. Have you ever tried to work and concentrate in a loud café with teenagers gossiping, letting out inevitably disruptive and irritating high-pitched giggles? Well, if you have, you will know the situation is futile and you might as well give up or move your place of work.

Obviously, moving and adjusting is preferable to giving up! Discard and remove as best you can anything that is holding you back from reaching your self-mastery goals. Remove any booze or crap food from your workplace and home if this is something you are trying to limit in your life. A highly effective way I limit evening chocolate snacking is to not have it in my house (or I store it so inconveniently that when I'm tired, I can't be bothered to get it and instead go for a grapefruit).

Removing negative influences from your environment may mean changing your social circle or the way you engage with each other. Swap an afternoon tea and cake catch-up for a walk and talk. If you need to cut out the booze and your friends are big drinkers, take a rain check on social meet-ups until you know you are safe to abstain in the face of their drinking. If your mates care for you, they will understand any suggested tweaks to your interactions – especially if you are vulnerable and explain where you are at. If they don't, then it says a lot about the role of your relationship to them. Sometimes, as friends, we can enable each other's unhelpful habits.

Take an inventory of the environments in which you live, such as your home, work, and local community. Consider the healthy resources and supports you have in each of these domains, along with the obstacles and challenges. Can you build on the enablers and minimise the barriers? Consider your access to unhelpful and helpful things that influence your wellbeing. At home, you may have a pantry of crap food, making poor eating choices more likely than if this food was not available and instead you kept a large fruit bowl centre-stage on the kitchen bench. Reflect on any environmental microstressors, such as poor lighting, clutter, and noise that may contribute to sensory overwhelm, cognitive load and stress. Notice whether elements of your environment, such as interior design or access to windows and fresh air, are conducive to your peace and health or are barriers to it. The orientation of your environment matters. Is your house lay-out concentrated on a couch and TV, making sedentary living and screen-time the family focus. Or do you have an open-plan home with easy access to the outdoors, making exercise and being in nature more likely?

Set up your environment with stuff that helps you be well and make healthy choices. Brainstorm strategies to strengthen your resources and prioritise healthy behaviours that are conducive to your sense of **real wellness**. If you want to start writing that book, make sure you always have the writing materials/resources on you in case you can get cracking during unexpected pockets of spare time. Develop strategies to make your environment work for you, even if you live on the move.

I travel a lot for work, and among the techniques I implement for my wellbeing is booking accommodation with a pool or gym or that is close to running tracks. As well, I keep spare walking shoes and yoga clothes in my car so if I fancy a spontaneous run or yoga class, I can do it straightaway. I hunt down the local yoga studios and other after-hours activities to keep me busy and entertained. To avoid eating out all the time, I pack a few kitchen supplies and shop for fresh foods and veggies.

*

I wish I could say that we have the power to determine our health and wellbeing, regardless of our external world and environment. But that is not possible, given our vulnerable human nature: it's simply not true. Our reality is that we are significantly shaped and influenced by our environment, and that is the way it is. We need to understand that, accept it with self-compassion, and then work with this truth. The power we do have is the ability to learn and develop insight into how our environment is impacting our choices, habits and wellbeing. Then, we can start to manipulate our surroundings to our advantage by building on our resources and supports, and modifying the barriers and obstacles as best we can, thus optimising our environment so we may function at our peak.

To achieve five-star self-mastery standards, you may also consider how your environment is impacting others in your community so you can support the wellbeing of the collective. We are all in this together and absolutely need each other's care and support.

Case study

About five years after graduating, Yanni started a new role. He shared an office with an older colleague who had been with the company for years and worked part-time. Yanni was a busy but organised guy who was performing well at his job. He was proud of his achievements and excited for his career ahead. Why was it, Yanni wondered, that every Sunday afternoon he would feel intense dread about going to his workplace the next morning?

Yanni lived a structured life that gave him the sense of control he needed. At home, his space was minimalist and decluttered. His spare time was carefully divided up into down time, exercise, chores and family time. At work, Yanni took the same meticulous approach to scheduling: he had to hit the ground running each day as his job had lots of demands and he managed a team that was equally as busy. The work and pay were okay, so it confused him that his outlook at the start of the week was so negative.

One day, on a morning run before work, Yanni listened to a podcast on environmental microstressors – small irritations, hassles and frustrating demands – and how they may add up until they have a negative effect on our mental health and cognition. It was a lightbulb moment: when he compared his home and work environments, he realised one was cluttered and unpleasant while the other had order, design and an aesthetic that was soothing to him.

At home, he had large windows he would open during the day to keep air coming through; he had indoor plants that made the room feel fresh; the walls were white, the living spaces uncluttered; in the evenings he often lit a scented candle or played chill music to help unwind. Everything at home had its function and its place; there were only a few spaces allocated to clutter – like the laundry cupboards and his bookshelf, which worked as a bit of a short-term dumping zone for stuff to be sorted as time permitted.

What a contrast with his work environment: the walls were a nausea-inducing yellow, the windows were big but permanently shut, there was a stale smell and no music. But what most irritated Yanni was that his shared workspace was filled with papers, never-consulted books, and redundant IT equipment – all of which had been there since he'd first moved in. With this insight, he approached the colleague he shared the space with and suggested they do a clean-out and redesign. He was apprehensive about the idea, given his colleague had worked there so long with the room as it was. But to Yanni's surprise, his colleague said, 'Go for it! Do whatever you like' but added that he was too time-poor to assist.

Yanni started staying back on Monday evenings, after he'd completed his tasks. He would put on some music and get to work on improving the office. Nothing was wasted: he collected all the equipment, papers, and other miscellaneous objects, placed them in an appropriate area and invited his colleagues to go through and take what they could use. Soon the space felt lighter, neater, fresher and more pleasant to spend time in. Impressed by how much it lifted his mood, Yanni emailed his manager asking her permission to paint the walls and requesting that maintenance investigate whether the windows could be made to open. He let her know that he planned to bring in some plants, air fresheners, a chair from home for visitors to sit in, and a Bluetooth speaker for music.

By the end of the month, Yanni had painted the walls white, could open his office windows, had sorted the perfect work playlist and enjoyed watering a few pot plants each week. From then on, the end-of-weekend dread was far less heavy, and being at work more pleasant. His preoccupied colleague scarcely seemed to notice, but Yanni's secretary certainly did. Routinely, when people dropped in for meetings, they would comment on how nice his office was and seemed to relax and brighten when sitting in his visitor's chair.

Yani felt as though he could work there with a new sense of lightness – and that the lift in his spirits was sustainable. It was an enormous relief for him that his Sunday afternoons felt happier.

Take-home messages

- The external world significantly shapes our overall wellbeing through its impact on social connections, physical environments, work conditions, economic stability, cultural influences, and access to essential resources and services.
- Awareness of these external factors and efforts to create positive changes in them can enhance individual and collective wellbeing.
- The interplay of social norms, culture, rules, regulations, and government policies creates a comprehensive societal context that shapes health behaviours and overall wellbeing. By understanding and addressing these factors, governments and communities can work towards creating environments that promote positive health outcomes and contribute to the overall welfare of their populations.
- Identify the enablers and supports around you as well as barriers and obstacles. Leverage your resources.
- Brainstorm to implement ways of manipulating your environment to optimise your sense of safety, autonomy and peace.

Reflection

Consider whether there are environmental spaces in your life that cause stress? Identify the factors that stress you (e.g. lighting, noise, clutter, aesthetic).

Are there any factors you have the capacity to modify? If so, make a plan to do so and notice the effect it has on your peace of mind.

18

Compassionate Self-discipline

Sometimes, you simply have to make yourself do (or not do) something. Sometimes, what we need to be well is not what we have any urge or desire to do: we may not feel like doing that thing. Sometimes, we need to do the hard thing to care for ourselves. This is the skill of compassionate self-discipline – more accurately, it is self-compassionate discipline. Executing this is not self-punishment or restriction. It might feel like that initially but, in the end, the long-term benefits of exerting some self-compassionate discipline when it is truly called for are evident and worthwhile. Having this skill is fundamental to self-management and living a life of **real wellness**.

Some of our needs don't align with our desires or impulses, which makes them feel hard to meet. You may really want something, like a new pair of shoes, but it may not be at all what you need. We all have work to complete, and at times it may build up and become overwhelming. In these instances, it is common to avoid the work as it seems so large and difficult. Many people procrastinate in this situation, which only makes matters worse. When you're in a place of paralysis from having a lot of tasks, try applying a little self-compassionate discipline to start achieving some of your goals one tiny step at a time. Motivation won't always be high, but with self-compassionate discipline, you do it anyway.

Motivation waxes and wanes, so do not fall into the trap of cueing your behaviour based on whether you 'feel like' doing it. Things that take effort and a little hard work are usually good for you (as long as they are safe), so although these things may feel hard, they may be the compassionate plan of action. The best things in my life have been a shit ton of work. I am grateful for my skill of self-compassionate discipline as it allows me to work on the things I value and prioritise with an intention of loving kindness, no matter how 'hard' it may feel. I'm also grateful for my morning coffee and the boost it gives to my focus and determination: I thrive on it. But, once that caffeine buzz and drive wears off and the wear of the day starts to take its toll, I am able to tap into mindful self-kindness to gently guide the course of my afternoon and evening. Using this more loving and caring approach, I can do what I need without harshly forcing myself or cultivating a sense of restriction and lack. I have the intention of self-care and the motivation to give myself what I need in order to be well – even if it is not the fun option.

This skill breeds self-trust and leads you in a direction that will work for you. When you learn you can meet your needs, even when it's tough, you create an internal sense of security and safety. When we are young, if we have good parents, they do this for us. Once older, it is up to us to meet our needs and protect ourselves from harm. In my opinion, we need to have this sense of self-trust to thrive. When I know I can do hard things, I know I can be very honest. I know I am determined, that I never give up. I also know I am very human, and my ego may not always want what the rest of me needs. I feel safe in myself and my skills to know I can survive big challenges and permit myself the time and space for restoration and recovery so I can return to baseline.

*

I find it useful to break the skill of self-management into five steps. Understanding the role each one plays is paramount to being able to remember and apply it. Developing your ability for each of these five skills and following this step-by-step 'recipe' will strengthen your capacity for self-compassionate discipline:

Step 1 = Self-honesty
Step 2 = Wise mind
Step 3 = Committed action
Step 4 = Mindfulness
Step 5 = Self-kindness

Step 1: Self-honesty

Self-compassionate discipline requires self-honesty. It's all too easy to deny your needs – especially when they're not appealing or part of your agenda. Say your day is packed full of jobs you want to get through, but you notice that despite all the tasks ahead of you, you're quite fatigued and your body is calling for a rest. Take the rest! Trust and honour your body. Taking rest in this moment may feel inconvenient or impossible, as you may want to smash out the jobs you've set yourself – especially if you're a doer like me. In this instance, it's common to kid yourself that rest is unnecessary and that instead you need to kick on and punch out your to-do list. But with a little break or quick lie-down, your productivity for the rest of the day will be higher and you're likely to get the work done without becoming exhausted.

If you are especially tired or sick, and simply not in the state to push yourself, then radically accept your predicament and park the work for another time (or delegate it). In this instance, proceeding would not be self-compassionate and may even be harmful.

Without self-honesty, we can fall prey to our egos and ideas while missing out on our reality, our intuition and the needs of our whole self – body and soul included. There's a tendency to feel we must do a lot more each day than is really the case. Usually, taking needed rest amounts to improved quality and quantity of work anyway. But you have to be honest with yourself!

On the flip side, if you are less of a doer and more avoidant in behaviour, don't fib to yourself that you need rest simply to avoid doing hard things. Your skill in self-honesty is important and one to take seriously with integrity. For one person, going to the gym for a movement session may be exactly what their whole self needs while, for another, rest may be called for. Only you know this wisdom. You know when you are being avoidant or not. Just be honest with yourself. More often than not, I may feel a little tired and avoidant, but I know that this feeling is not a reason to avoid self-compassionate discipline for action. In this instance, I would suck it up and get onto Step 2.

The ability to be honest with yourself is so liberating and conducive to sustainable **real wellness**. Watch your BS and use your self-honesty skills to adequately appraise the situation and identify the things you need to do for you to be well. Cut out the crap and be straight with yourself.

Step 2: Wise mind

There is wisdom in knowing effort for long-term gain is worth it. A wise mind is aware of and acknowledges the body's emotional state, along with the facts of your situation, and comes to a balanced appraisal of reality to aid your decision-making and motivation.

You may feel a little tired and avoidant but recognise that you'll be better for it if whatever it is you need to do gets done.

The gratification – warm fuzzy feelings – we get from meeting our needs may be delayed, making it less appealing to do what is required immediately. But if we use our wise adult thinking to see that meeting the need has value in the longer term that makes it worth the strain in the present, we can commit and apply ourselves to achieving it with less struggle. Saying no to that last alcoholic drink before bed may be less immediately rewarding, but it will probably feel good the next day!

Getting to a yoga class may feel hard sometimes, but a wise yogi knows that the class amounts to so much good that questioning whether to attend is not required. When feeling a little resistant to a class, I gently remind myself that I can always skilfully rest in Child's Pose and simply attend to my breath if needed. I have a motto: 'When in doubt, go to yoga.' If I were into making T-shirts with slogans, that would be one of them!

Step 3: Committed action

Now that you have honestly identified and wisely appraised your path toward the needed action, completely commit to it. Commit without waiver. Commit 110%. Plan the process, write it out, tick off the steps, visualise your efforts and achievements, and cheer yourself throughout the action until it is complete. In other words, just get on with it.

With this step, the trick is to not overthink it. Once you've done the work to identify the action required that aligns with your values and priorities, and you've used your integrity and skill for self-honesty and wise-minded decision-making, you need to stop the internal deliberation and get the action happening! Don't get stuck in internal deliberation, don't waste energy delaying things, just commit and do the thing. You have done the thinking already –

so, don't let your monkey mind hijack your efforts with further deliberation and rumination on the matter. Instead focus on action.

Avoid the trap of allowing waxing and waning motivation to determine whether you pursue your needs and goals. That stuff is a fleeting internal sensation that need not define you. Turn away from low drive and limiting thoughts and use your values and priorities as your internal compass to remind yourself of why, how and who you wish to be. Your values and priorities serve as a powerful reminder to choose the behaviour that will ultimately work. Remember your focus in Step 3 is on action.

Step 4: Mindfulness

Mindfulness allows a state of internal awareness and equanimity. Without mindfulness, it is hard to overcome urges, thoughts, feelings and emotions that may derail your efforts for discipline. As you commence your task, you need to notice any distractions and turn your mind back to your commitment. Our minds are expert in creating stories and sentences for us to take as gold to justify our impulses and, especially when it assumes and predicts that a planned course of action is going to be taxing or difficult in some way. Can you recall a time when you avoided something good for you and noticed a limiting thought like, 'I can't be bothered' (you can), or my usual thought line, 'There's nothing I can do' (actually, there is a lot I can do, and my actions moving forward are pivotal to my outcome)?

It's surprisingly easy to create a delusional story to justify a lack of nurturing willpower. But that is okay and pretty much to be expected. You may notice a tempting but counterproductive thought like, 'It will be all right' (but there's no denying that if you give in to the temptation, it may well have negative consequences) or 'It's only a little bit of …' (it all adds up, and a little bit may still amount to a lot of trouble).

Being able to mindfully notice your thoughts, diffuse them and thereby resist any potential derailments – in other words, stick with discipline – is tough mindfulness but entirely doable and oh so worth it. Can you see how this is masterful, regulating and conducive to wellbeing?

Step 5: Self-kindness

The difference between simply forcing yourself to do something and using this wellness-focused approach to overcome inner resistance and live your full potential is the integration of self-compassion. You are not being cruel or harsh. You are not judging yourself or enforcing unrealistic expectations or standards. Rather, you are gently reminding yourself of your humanness, that resistance is something everyone experiences and nudging yourself towards your holistic health needs as best you can. Lovingly bring to mind your wellness needs and consider how overcoming your inner resistance will allow you to better meet those needs.

Think of yourself as your own parent, soothing yourself through the pain of meeting and moving through the resistance. Although I may look like an adult from external appearances, deep down, I still have an inner child to manage. This is the part of me that wants the immediately gratifying thing – the fun and easy thing. It's also the frightened and worried part of me that doubts my abilities. I may whine, whinge and complain (adults have tantrums all the time). But I can care for her and discipline her when needed and in a kind way – just as I lovingly police my son's desire for TV!

*

The best things in life may be free and/or simple – like taking a daily walk, eating healthy foods, getting eight hours sleep, and relaxing – yet accessing them may feel really difficult. Why is this? Well, it's because we get in our own way. We experience tremendous feelings of resistance that seem elusive, but if you use your mindfulness skills to look within, you might identify some off-putting thoughts and unpleasant physical sensations. As you now know, that stuff is fleeting and not necessarily truthful or helpful, so simply allow it all and make the move towards your goal anyway. You're likely to discover that the resistance is all about starting.

Get to know this predictable resistance so you can confidently and efficiently dismiss it when needed. I know that before I enter the ocean for a surf, I will feel extreme resistance (to be honest, I feel it before I've even put the wetsuit on, which is no fun whatsoever). In this instance, I consider myself as having two basic options. Choice 1: I allow this internal sensation to prevent me surfing or Choice 2: I simply disregard the resistance as predictable and fleeting cerebral junk so I can go enjoy a surf. Want to start exercising? Put on your walking shoes and get out the door. You don't need to feel excited or happy to do it. The resistance to doing it isn't an omen or sign not to do it. Use your mindfulness skills to notice it, let it be, and turn your attention to the task at hand. Besides, action builds momentum. Once I'm in the water, it's easier to stay in the water and start surfing.

Take heart that once you have applied some self-compassionate discipline and begun whatever it is you choose to do, then it gets easier, and less discipline is required each time you initiate the action. This is the beginning of forming a habit (see Chapter 21). At the end of a surf retreat, after days of consistent practice, I'm pretty good at jumping into the water. The resistance is still there, but I get better at dismissing it and getting on with the surfing.

Case study

Claudia lives with depression, which she manages with medication and therapy. She wanted to increase her wellness levels and hoped that one day she could come off the meds. While she knew the benefits of exercise for managing mood, she had always found it a struggle. Jumping out of bed to go for a jog before school was not her thing. However, she fantasised about becoming one of these active types. She idealised fit people and wished she could enjoy the benefits of exercise.

A big fan of self-help books, when Claudia read one about how to coach yourself, she learnt about committed action and how you can't rely on motivation to get things done. This was a revelation. Like so many people, Claudia had been inclined to listen to her motivation and had exercised only when she felt like it. Problem was, she almost never felt like exercising.

She made a commitment to try the program set out in the book, which showed her how to overcome her internal resistance and start exercising, even when she did not feel motivated. Before going to bed, Claudia would put out all her exercise gear so she wouldn't have to think about it in the morning. Also she set a loud alarm and made sure she could be out of the house for 20 minutes and still have time to get ready for school. She made a fun playlist to listen to while being active and, last but not least, she took her dog Buster with her. For years, her mum had been walking Buster each evening, so at first he didn't know what was going on when she woke him early and then slipped his lead on him. Buster thought it was Christmas and absolutely loved getting out in the morning, which in turn made Claudia feel good and encouraged her to keep the habit up. The first week, she managed to do three 10-minute walks; the next week she did a little more. Slowly and steadily, she was able to increase her frequency and duration, and then she started jogging. She noticed better sleep and appetite.

She noticed how proud she felt. She enjoyed that she had become one of those people she had previously fantasised about.

Eventually, Claudia was running most mornings. One day, she tried a local Zumba class, and when she found it hilarious, she started attending it regularly – wearing an '80s leotard, just for laughs. The momentum kept building and she found she could set SMART goals and meet them: she was mastering the ability to live beyond her comfort zone and enjoy embodying her fantasy self. Two years after she began starting her day with a 10-minute walk, Claudia had weaned herself off her meds under the supervision of her GP and parents.

Exercise remains a core coping mechanism for her mental health and wellbeing. Nowadays, she loves it and will always be grateful for the self-mastery it has gifted her. Her movement therapy helps release the stress of university. When her mates go to the pub after class, she goes to the pool for some laps. But her favourite form of exercise is the No Lights No Lycra dance class, held in the community hall on Wednesdays, which she discovered one evening on a run.

Take-home messages

- What we need is not always what we want – cue self-compassionate discipline.
- Self-compassionate discipline requires self-honesty, wise-minded consideration, mindfulness, committed action, and self-compassion.
- Don't brutally force yourself to be disciplined; rather, be non-judgemental and loving about it. Remember your humanness and remind yourself that we all struggle to do the right thing by ourselves sometimes.
- You don't need to feel good or motivated to be self-compassionately disciplined. But you do need to accept, allow,

and move through your inner resistance to be disciplined, and you do this with loving kindness, keeping your values and priorities top of mind.
- Connect your needs to your values and priorities.
- Once you have identified your need and the connection to yourself, don't overthink or overfeel things. Focus on action and the tiny little steps required to gently nudge yourself to meet the need.
- Use the 5 steps to work through this skill to use in your self-management tool kit for **real wellness**.

Reflection

What is something you want to do but have been putting off because it feels especially challenging? Write it down and consider why it might feel so challenging. What are the thoughts and feelings you notice creating this sense of difficulty? Can you allow them, but make plans to start your desired activity in spite of them?

What's one thing you can do now to initiate this thing you want, even though the resistance may still be there? Be kind to yourself when you begin. Remember, this is hard for all people, and it's a human thing to experience inner resistance to new things. It's okay and it's not a reason not to start. Be your own parent – kind, loving, ensuring safety but also getting the job done!

Hot tip: figure out when you work most efficiently. For me, self-compassionate discipline is most effective first thing in the morning (and after coffee), when my motivation and energy is highest. Later in the day, I tend to be more fatigued, and willpower wanes. So, I have learnt to schedule hard things for the morning, when I have optimal determination and focus.

19

Self-care

Simply put, self-care means meeting your needs. Every person requires a certain amount of daily self-care. It's easy to see this in relation to kids. They need to be fed a balanced diet, kept hydrated and warm, bathed daily, changed regularly, occupied with a mix of creative and physical pursuits, and finally, they need emotional attunement and connection: to be seen, heard, and their feelings validated. Most need regular cuddles or some sort of human affection many times throughout the day. Adults need all these things too – not to mention other adult-conditioned, acquired, and nuanced needs, like a particular brand of coffee or skin-care ritual. If we neglect meeting our individual holistic needs for long enough, we are vulnerable to feeling and becoming unwell.

To an extent, and most of the time, we must all meet our basic physical needs. When meeting your physical needs, ideally you feel safe and secure in your environment, eat a healthy diet – and not too much – get sufficient quality sleep, treat any acute illness, stay hydrated, and keep warm and clean. When you are meeting these needs, you can physically function without being unduly vulnerable to illness and communicable diseases.

But over and above your basic physiological needs there are less obvious self-care needs, and we refer to these as holistic needs. In rehabilitation medicine, we take a biopsychosocial-spiritual approach to considering a patient's health needs and prescribing their care. This helps to holistically appraise their whole self rather than focus on only body systems and medical issues. I like to use this approach when I think of self-care. When our more holistic needs are met, we are likely to feel balanced, most well, restored, and grounded. This is when you have fostered a healthy relationship with yourself and life and may feel the sense of **real wellness**.

*

In my opinion, human holistic health and self-care needs include:

1. Biological (basic, physical and physiological): healthy food; fresh and clean water; sufficient sleep, downtime and rest; safe shelter and physical safety; warmth; clean air; sanitation; personal space; sexual expression; movement and exercise; and medical care.
2. Psychological (behavioural, mental and emotional): to be seen, heard and accepted; self-trust and healthy self-perception; internal- and external-world awareness and regulation skills; coping skills and adaptive behavioural management; boundary-setting with yourself and the world around you; interpersonal skills; sense of belonging; psychological safety; and problem-solving.
3. Social (environmental): friendships, mentors and supports; home and community life, including roles, responsibilities and demands; awareness and management of societal and cultural norms, pressures, values, expectations, environmental microstressors and income.

4. Spiritual (soulful): opportunities to express your values and engage in your priorities; playtime, fun and pleasurable activities, creativity; intellectual stimulation; sense of connection to the world around you and beyond you; alignment with your true essence or higher self.

While it's universal to all humans to have self-care needs, exactly what these are and how we effectively meet them is up to us as individuals. What you come up with has to be unique to you for it to work. It's your recipe tailored specifically to you. We may share some needs but ultimately, just as your recipe for **real wellness** is personal and yours to create, your holistic health needs are also unique to you and yours to decipher. Noticing and being willing to experiment with new things is helpful when creating your recipe. For some of us, we meet our needs to belong and feel connected to others at a church or in a walking group or simply within the pages of a good book to characters grown close to you.

When it comes to implementing your self-care, note that *what* you do is less important than *why* you do it. To me, self-care means a little downtime to practise loving kindness, compassion, and relaxation – there are many ways to meet this need and, in my opinion, some of the best ways are free of charge. I could achieve the same positive outcome by permitting myself some time chilling in a park – out in the sunshine, without my usual distractions, and away from the pull of the business of life. I do not need to spend $50 on a pedicure, but that is also a perfectly valid option if that fits with my values. Please be mindful that the wellness industry feeds off the culture of 'self-care'. You could spend all day indulging in saunas, spas, facials, and eating overpriced 'clean' meals. But if you undertake these activities without the intention of self-care, you may end up more depleted than before. For some, getting all their daily 'self-care' rituals in can be stressful, time-consuming, and costly. Marketing pulls us towards the *what* to sell us the *why*. But with mastery, you will know that the *what* is flexible if you consciously know your *why*. In order to feel liberated, fit and empowered, I can go for a run at no cost. I could also spend a lot of money on the latest wellness exercise equipment and not necessarily achieve the same outcome for my wellbeing, depending on my intentions. Maybe I accidentally lose myself to an unhelpful intention to fit in with the fashion.

Taking time to identify your needs and the ways you can meet them in your everyday life or regular schedule is an insightful process that builds self-awareness, self-acceptance and facilitates self-care. I teach self-care audits at wellness retreats and promote these personal inventories to be self-directed whenever you feel unwell. If you take time to enquire within, you may notice gaps in your self-care or moments of fulfilment from activities that bring you joy, so you can highlight these in your awareness and do them more. Noticing and consciously taking time to consider your holistic needs is the first step to optimising your capacity for self-care and will reveal clues that help pave your way towards adequately meeting them for **real wellness**.

*

Self-care can get a bad rap. Some people view it as selfish or a waste of time that could otherwise be spent achieving and 'doing' things. But without reserving time to meet your needs and restock your resources, you can burn out, become resentful and lose your capacity to rise to occasions and be there for others. Sure, self-care may entail taking time out for yourself and all the jobs of the external world to focus on your own care needs. But it results in a more resilient self, one that is most able and likely to optimally manage themselves in challenging life situations and when acting in service to others.

Self-care is in and of itself a need. If we don't care for ourselves, who will? As adults, we need to take ownership of this responsibility. We aren't kids anymore. It's up to us to check in with ourselves and figure out what we need.

An easy way to determine what self-care you need at any moment is to simply ask yourself the question, 'What do I need right now?' The answer will come from an inner wisdom. With practice, you will hear it as what you would tell a friend in your circumstance, or your child.

All living things need rest and recovery – including you. Muscles fatigue with prolonged use, even when we ingest an abundance of calories from good nutrition. Happily, all our human systems have an inbuilt repair mechanism. We are constantly changing, stressing our body, which keeps flipping back into repair. This is called allostasis (stress flexibility and adaption) for homeostasis (our body's natural drive to keep all the systems balanced to maintain function). Without this life-sustaining balance, things don't work long-term – we burn out or break. View your self-care as a life-sustaining activity – required to not only thrive, but also survive. I use the visual of pulling a rubber band. When I take the self-care I need, I see it like the pulling back of the elastic before a launch forward: in other words, as preparation. Before I know it, I'm being of service and achieving jobs.

The overused oxygen mask analogy is apt: in the event of a flight emergency, to help others, you need to put your own mask on first. Here's a personal example as well. In my 20s, as a young doctor-in-training I was struggling with myself. After pretty much two decades of life focused on school and then medical studies, while my capacity to study was highly developed, I lacked skills to cope with stress and to wind down. I had difficulty switching off after work, and was plagued by imposter syndrome, perfectionism and people pleasing when at work. I felt I didn't have time to relax and be social. After becoming burnt-out, I learnt the hard way to live with more work/life balance and to prioritise my holistic health needs. I needed to work out who I was, what I stood for, what my boundaries were, and what I needed to do in my life day-to-day to stay and feel optimally well despite all the stress of working in medicine. This journey of self-awareness and self-acceptance took some time, and I needed professional guidance, which was amazing. My beautiful dad, who holds himself to high standards of integrity and public service, used to say I'd do better if I focused more on others and society's issues and less on myself. But what he didn't understand was that, for many years, I needed – and had little choice but – to focus on my relationship with myself to function optimally. Only then could I look outwards and be altruistic in my profession.

It may seem somewhat narcissistic to prioritise your relationship with yourself and your self-care, seemingly at the expense of your work or other commitments, responsibilities, and roles. In my case, I felt I couldn't 'do it all', and chose to take some time off medicine to work on myself. We all need a stable foundation of self-awareness and self-acceptance in order to self-care, so we have the bandwidth and reserve to care for others. Including that brief time-out, it took me a decade to figure out how to achieve that, and that is okay. It is what it is. Our personal journey to **real wellness** cannot be rushed and will take as long as it needs.

Something that took both Dad and me by surprise was that during my seemingly narcissistic 20s, some of my fellow health professionals were watching with interest! It turns out I wasn't the only one who'd struggled with their relationship with themself. A number of individuals told me privately that I inspired them with my commitment to packing a healthy lunch and doing my daily exercise, and that my honesty around my challenges was validating for them. By focusing on and building my capacity for adaptive self-care, not only was I setting myself up to be able to sustainably and durably be of service to others, but I was also inadvertently acting as a role model. The word 'doctor' is Latin for 'teacher', so I like to tell myself that I've been a great doctor from way back.

It's worth bearing in mind that while you're putting in the work to master a state of **real wellness** – developing your self-awareness, self-acceptance, and self-management – you're showing others that positive change is possible, thereby bringing hope to those who need it. So, don't worry if it feels a little indulgent. Your self-care is an investment in society as well as in yourself. We never really know how we influence others, but being the change you wish to see in the world is generally a great way to live life and is conducive to **real wellness**.

- If, on an individual level, we invest in ourselves, we create optimal conditions to invest in each other and participate fully in life. Forgive yourself for seeming self-absorbed.
- Living with self-care means you're better placed to be of service and serve as an inspiring role model to those watching who may be struggling with their own wellness.

Quite frankly, people who stigmatise self-care as selfish or as a sort of unnecessary luxury are being judgemental. If they impose this judgement on themselves, they may be prone to unhealthy living – at the mercy of this unhelpful belief.

Being of service and looking after others is, for many, a lifeline. But if you are a giver but can take on the perspective that a bit of self-care serves you, so that you can serve others, then you'll be more likely to overcome any false guilt when acting in care of yourself. Furthermore, you will be more resilient and well to care for others. Is going for a massage or a girls' trip once a month selfish? Or will it help you be a better partner or parent once you're home again and feeling good? Does it make you 'bad' to miss a family evening meal to get to a yoga class or will it help you be more present once you are home with your family? Is making time for movement during a busy workday wasted work time, or is it one of the best things you can do for your job productivity?

*

We have discussed how **real wellness** is spiritual – when we can live fully and freely aligned with our values and purpose. Remember that while self-care is a requirement for survival, it is also the path to living to your full potential. This stuff takes lots of work. It ain't easy. It may entail asserting challenging boundaries, speaking up, moving beyond your comfort zone and through moments of fear and self-doubt. These things may be initially stressful and draining – remember to facilitate recovery with good food and rest. We need to take time to develop self-mastery in order to actualise our best life. Without solid self-care, it is hard to live your best life. Without good self-care, over time you inevitably become burnt out. It isn't sustainable. So, if you want to live optimally and make the most of what you have, you need to fuel yourself with all you need. Think of yourself as an athlete of life. As an athlete, you will need premium care to function at a high level. That's not to say you need to be training all day and eating nothing but chicken breasts and protein pancakes. But it does mean knuckling down on your self-care.

Working full-time has always been a struggle for me: it simply doesn't suit me. I thrive working part-time, whereby I can do other things on the side for my holistic self-care, like creative pursuits, with time to chill, relax and hang with my loved ones. I learnt the hard way that this kind of work–life balance is actually a need for me. At one point I was working full-time, intending to get through my training and maximise my earnings. The trouble was that I ended up unwell, so it was plain that my intentions were off: working towards them was coming at the expense of my wellness and happiness. Over time, I came to some realisations about my needs. Firstly, I didn't need to smash out my training so fast, and secondly, I didn't need to earn the maximum amount possible. I could get by with less income – provided I shopped more carefully and cut back on the non-essentials. It wasn't worth the toll it was taking on my wellness.

Poor self-care is not a character flaw but will eventually affect your physiology and human form. To be able to seize your life and spiritually be your best version, you need premium self-care to fuel your body, mind and soul. We need to be able to manage ourselves optimally to thrive. So, cultivating skills in self-management is pivotal to our pursuit of **real wellness**.

*

Self-care is not always me-time, massages and moreish meals. Sometimes self-care may take the form of a loving restriction. It might look like avoiding sugar, completing a task before its deadline rather than resting on the couch, getting up a bit earlier to exercise instead of sleeping in, or ending the day early – without squandering precious rest time scrolling on your phone – to optimise quality sleep. As already mentioned, sometimes doing the thing you need to do to care for yourself is not always the fun option or the thing you want to do. Often, self-care is mundane, feels hard, and requires discipline. Just as parents may impose boring routines on their kid to ensure their care, we need to be our own parents and enforce regular self-care. Self-care may create a sense of FOMO (fear of missing out). But that is okay. Once this skill is developed, you will grow to relish JOMO (the joy of missing out).

Use your self-honesty skills to identify your self-care needs and any unhelpful judgements around meeting them that are holding you back. It may be time to lovingly challenge some of your beliefs around self-care. Are you fibbing to yourself and making excuses to avoid meeting your needs due to internal resistance? I have witnessed friends who say they don't have time to exercise because of various responsibilities (parenting, work, [insert excuse], bla, bla, bla, bla, bla). But really, I suspect they are lazy and not wanting to get out of their comfort zone. Use self-compassion to honestly appraise your relationship to self-care, challenge limiting beliefs and harness your power to thrive and live fully.

*

Lastly, creating a ritual of daily exercise for your self-care may well be one of the most useful habits you could choose for yourself and your life, both immediately and in the long run. In my opinion, exercise is the best medicine. End of the story. I believe there is not a single holistic health need or health condition that does not benefit from some form of movement. I feel obliged to have this paragraph somewhere in the book – I'm a Specialist Physician of Rehabilitation Medicine who routinely prescribes exercise as medicine to her patients (way more than any pharmacological medications). But also, I am a vulnerable human who knows the benefits of daily movement on a personal and holistic level. It saves me every day. We were born to move. Having daily exercise as a staple in my holistic health diet helps my longevity and resilience.

If I could offer one piece of health advice to my patients, it would be to self-care through movement. But exercise must be your own thing that works for you and your body. If you are paralysed by spinal cord injury, then you may need to use mental imagery to move breath and energy through your body.

Not everyone gravitates to the same movement. A lot of people benefit from dance lessons. I'm not much into those but I love my daily vinyasa yoga. Maybe chair yoga is perfect for your holistic health needs. Create your own morning stretch routine, do what works for you. You need not go to the gym or do what your friends are doing. Find what forms of movement light you up and keep you coming back for more. Exercise is allowed to be nurturing, enjoyable and even relaxing! But for gosh sakes, if you're over the age of 40, get into those weights. Resistance training is a must to age well.

Real wellness is all about experimenting with ideas aligned with your internal compass so you can find the things you need to keep you well. Keep open to new ways of exercise as you may find that what works one year doesn't the next. The more flexibility and adaptability you have with the abilities of your physical self, the easier it will be to always find some way of moving your body in the pursuit of self-care. You may not be able to do CrossFit or run marathons forever, but there is always some way to move. If you need help, please see a health professional. Change things up, mix up your repertoire but always keep it right for you.

Case study

Bill was a hard worker. He was a labourer and breadwinner for his young family. His self-care looked like beers and take-out in front of the TV each Friday night after work. When he entered his 30s, Bill's weight slowly increased. His blood pressure became elevated, and his blood analysis showed some negative effects of poor diet and high blood sugar levels.

When Bill and I met, we discussed the risks to his health and function if things weren't managed appropriately. We discussed what healthy living would look like for him, and he admitted his current lifestyle bore little resemblance to it. Then we identified and challenged Bill's unhelpful beliefs around planning healthy meals and making time for exercise. To Bill, these behaviours were a waste of time when he could be working. There was little indication that he was ready to make changes.

Despite medication, Bill's health continued to decline, so he eventually agreed it was his lifestyle that needed to be first-line therapy. By then, it was in need of urgent rehabilitation.

With his wife on board, Bill was able to implement some changes to his diet and weekly schedule. On workdays, he swapped the tradie diet of bought, mostly processed food for a packed healthy lunch. For dinners, the family started using delivered balanced meals, and most evenings, Bill and his wife would go for a walk together. He still enjoyed winding down on a Friday, but he reduced his beer intake. Not only did Bill's relationship with his wife improve, but he quickly lost weight, lowered his blood pressure, and weaned himself off some of his medications. Bill learnt that self-care was something he needed to attend to in order to be well.

Take-home messages

- Self-care is meeting your holistic health needs. In other words, physical/basic, spiritual/soulful and emotional/psychological, and environmental/social needs.
- The way we may meet these needs is unique to the individual. Sometimes the best self-care is simple and free.
- Be honest with yourself in order to realise your needs.
- Acts of self-care may feel like a treat, but they're essential health behaviours that keep you well and functioning. Sometimes they may be hard work.
- Self-care is not selfish but is necessary to health and wellbeing – remember the oxygen mask analogy (make sure you are breathing before helping others) and the natural mechanics of the human body (day to day, we need rest and recovery).
- Role-model self-care for others.
- Try to incorporate movement into your everyday life. Do what you can and that which works for you.

Reflection

Write down all the activities and moments this last week that made you feel good, strong, empowered, rested and restored. Start to notice when you do something (or don't do something) that makes you feel well and add this to your list of self-care tools. Start to schedule these needs into your everyday lifestyle.

20

Self-soothing

A key skill for self-management is an ability to self-soothe: it is fundamental for human-mastery. Self-soothing skills enable us to cope during times of increased stress, maintain positions of high challenge that push you out of your comfort zone, and achieve big life goals without burnout. Without self-soothing skills, you may rely on others or external means to cope and are vulnerable to developing a chronically dysregulated nervous system that can lead to health issues.

For whatever reason, many of us lack the ability to self-soothe. Some people may be unaware of the relevance and utility of this skill. Others may simply forget its importance and lack time to apply it while living a busy adult life. We can learn and relearn this skill. In my opinion, self-soothing is a responsibility to be prioritised. If you need help, there are entire books on this skill, and you can seek professional help. In fact, maybe my next book will cover this topic in hectic detail.

Ideally, we can lovingly comfort ourselves like a responsible and present parent would to their children. Imagine a young kid sick with a fever. As a carer, you can't go through their illness on their behalf or wave a magic wand and take it away from them, so instead you comfort them as their illness runs its course. You make sure they feel safe and loved, and that their needs are met as best you can to avoid matters getting worse and to optimise their recovery. This may look like providing cuddles on your chest; keeping the child warm, hydrated and comfortable; resting them; being there for them when they flit in and out of a fever; and providing nutritious fuel. As adults, we need to be able to do this kind of thing for ourselves. Self-soothing is comforting and regulating yourself when needed.

Essential to falling asleep is the ability to self-soothe. We must have a sense of safety and peace to let go of thinking and tension to drift off to sleep. We must be able to let go of the day and our conscious life and slip our awareness into a place of comfort and ease. Just as babies need soothing to sleep at night, we do too. As parents we rock them, sing lullabies, and stay present while they learn to fall asleep with us. As adults we must put ourselves to sleep, and this can be tricky for many people (I still struggle with this). Sleep hygiene is an art form. Helpful behaviours for sleep are taking baths, ceasing screen time and caffeine intake early, avoiding stimulating activities before bed, journalling, essential oils, hypnosis, relaxation techniques, mindfulness, and stretching. Keep your room cool, uncluttered, safe feeling, and dark. There's an array of techniques out there to assist insomniacs. I use journalling, making a tomorrow to-do list, reading, practising relaxation or self-hypnosis, and having a big warm and cosy cuddle as my usual bedtime routine. For me, sleep is my number one wellness resource, and my routine starts when I wake. I aim to wake and sleep at the same times daily, I get sunlight and exercise every morning, ensure sufficient hydration and nutrition through the day, take no caffeine after 2pm, read before bed, and avoid using screens in the hour or so before I want to close my eyes. When I've been slack and given in to that particular vice, I curtail my scrolling addiction by charging my phone outside of my bedroom. Find what works for you.

*

But self-soothing is not only about getting to sleep. Some of our awake moments are our most stressful. You may notice stress building at work or when out and about driving. It may be helpful throughout the day to check in on your inner state. Ask yourself how you are feeling. Acknowledge any stress accumulating. Practise rating your stress using a Likert scale of 0 (cool calm and collected) to 10 (nutbag territory). If you're more than 4 or 5, it means things within are about to tip into more stress than not. It would be wise in this moment to practise some self-soothing to better balance your nervous system and prevent a build-up of tension and stress that may be even harder to manage and regulate by the evening. This may look like making a herbal tea or taking a brief walk outside and connecting to nature.

Inherent to the skill of self-soothing is the requirement for mindfulness. Mindfulness allows you to tune in to yourself to notice the state of your body, mind and soul. With mindful attention we can pick up stress cues then institute some internal regulation and self-soothing. Without it, we can run around busily from dawn to dusk only to arrive home in a state of amplified physical tension accumulated throughout the course of the day that we failed to notice. We also lacked the awareness to consciously take a minute to relax our body and rest briefly. Being able to notice your stress levels rise throughout your day and exerting a little self-soothing to counterbalance and avoid development of distress may simply mean pausing to gaze at the clouds in the sky.

A simple technique that you can use while seated at a desk is what I call the 'sipping breath', where you use your breath to activate the parasympathetic (rest and digest) nervous system. Take a huge inhale and just when you can't fit any more breath in your body, take another little sip. Then, exhale fully through the mouth. Do this four times or until you feel your score (that is your self-assessed stress level, on a scale of 1 to 5) shifting downwards.

I find the hours after work and before dinner my most important when it comes to self-soothing as, despite my best efforts, the day's stress has usually piled up within me and I tend to have 12 hours' worth of interactions to process and inner critic thoughts to dismiss. I'm generally pretty spent after a day working at the hospital. I've learnt it's helpful to end my workdays with some purposeful action to shake off any excess stress. I may walk my dog on the beach, take my son to the oval to play soccer or, if I'm super lucky, head to a hot power vinyasa yoga class. Find what it is that grounds and settles you.

There are all kinds of ways to soothe the mind, body, and soul. Basically, soothing yourself requires making space to check in with your needs, then choosing a way to allow the body and nervous system to settle and the influence of the mind to soften. Self-soothing results in a settled and grounded state called ataraxia. This is my favourite word. Ataraxia describes that state of internal bliss we can experience when we feel at ease, peace and safe. Emotionally, cognitively, and physically we are at ease. To embody ataraxia, you may use rituals and behaviours, vagal toning exercises, pranayama and breath work, time in nature or with loved ones, certain drinks and foods that nourish you, activities of self-expression or other body work.

There are internal and external means of self-soothing, and finding adaptive tools that work for you is key. Use the external senses (sight, touch, taste, sound, smell) and your internal skills to regulate yourself. Think nice smells, sights, sounds, and textures. Think comfort and safety. When I self-soothe at home, I get into comfy and cosy clothes, light some incense, turn on some chill music, get warm, and sip a hot drink. Learn some somatic (body) techniques like bilateral tapping, heel drops and eye scanning.

SELF-SOOTHING

Google nervous system regulation strategies for a world of tips to try.

Many people respond to day-to-day stress by potentially harmful external means. They may reach for drugs, food, cigarettes, gambling, sex, shopping, and other things in order to cope. But it is important to your health to limit addictive external mechanisms of coping and to build your capacity to engage in adaptive self-soothing activities. It's very common to use alcohol to wind down. While this may not be harmful if done in moderation and with loving intention, having an ability to soothe in other ways prevents reliance and promotes self-mastery. We can become heavily reliant on all sorts of things to cope, and not necessarily drugs of addiction. I used to be addicted to yoga classes. I would show up to classes daily and sometimes even twice daily. I felt I needed the yoga. This was not an issue as a trainee doctor; in fact, my yoga addiction worked well to get me through all the drama of that period of my life. Back then, that studio yoga was an adaptive lifeline. In those days, religiously attending a class had few repercussions: I had no kids, my husband wasn't home as he was training too, and the studio was down the road from the hospital. But over time, as I had more responsibilities at home, the travel time made in-studio practice difficult. My reliance on studio practice was no longer working for me. I saw how I'd been relying on this one coping skill and needed a broader repertoire of ways to regulate my nervous system and self-soothe. So, I investigated other ways of coping, and I soon realised I did not need to attend the yoga class each day after all. In fact, I was more than capable of doing my own yoga at home when it better suited my lifestyle – or other things that worked equally well to self-soothe and regulate. It was great to feel independent in this way. Having said that, I am still a massive fan of the studio practice! However, it is empowering and freeing to be able to cope just fine without it.

In the same way that we may rely on external substances to cope, we can become reliant on other people. It is super helpful to acquire the skill of independently self-soothing to ensure this is a choice rather than a need. Of course, humans are social animals and we absolutely do need each other to cope. Co-regulation is a powerful healing tool, and sometimes being in the arms of your loved one is the single most efficient and effective way to self-soothe. Some evenings I simply need a hug. Returning to the subject of my yoga studio addiction, there are numerous health benefits to practising in a group. It provides us with a sense of community, belonging and connection. The co-regulation from being and breathing with your yogi peers feeds the soul. But sometimes we are alone or not in a position to connect with another or our tribe. We may not always have direct access to the comfort of our loved ones, so having some skill to soothe ourselves when alone is important for **real wellness.**

Being able to nurse yourself through difficult times is empowering, masterful and an effective skill that can lessen the impact any challenging experience may have on you. If you can rely on yourself when needed, you free yourself to cope anywhere, anytime. You become a free-range human. A simple technique that I find helpful is to find a comfortable position in which to rest peacefully, mindfully, and safely and then place your hand on your heart space. Simply feel your chest. Connect to the rhythm and beat of your heart. Just feel yourself in this place of rest. Enjoy the heaviness of your hand resting over your heart. If you like, you can place your other hand over your belly, close your eyes, and breathe deeply and slowly into your chest. Feel the rise and fall of the abdomen as your body breathes you. If you feel freaked out and flighty, for whatever reason, try repeating within, 'I am safe' on the inhale and 'I am here' on the exhale.

*

Just a little self-soothing may be enough for your day-to-day self-care regime. But sometimes, when life is particularly challenging, such as when starting a new career, you may need to up your self-soothing game to manage the increase in stress. It is helpful to predict this when big a change is in the pipeline. When in crisis or overwhelm, self-soothing becomes paramount.

In this instance, it involves radical acceptance of your situation and your pain. You need to surrender to your circumstance. During an instance of emotional overwhelm, you need to park problem-solving until you have regulated your inner world, and your mind is more focused and balanced in thinking. Choosing to stay present with pain and challenge it without avoiding it, numbing out to it, or problem-solving, is a tough ride. It helps to have faith that the moment of overwhelm and dysregulation will pass. If in a safe environment and you can, it may help to lie down, get cosy and comfy, and give yourself a big cuddle till it does. Don't make matters worse – and, yes, things can get worse sometimes, but usually because we are not being skilful. Self-soothing actions cultivate resilience and help to avoid making matters worse. It means choosing nurturing, mindful and loving strategies over escapist behaviour, numbing out and acting impulsively.

When in crisis or protracted overwhelm, be sure to talk with your supports and check in with your doctor for help. You may think you need to cope alone but you don't. You may think there is nothing others can do to help but you are wrong. Together, any problem is solvable, and there is always something that can be done to improve things. Sometimes, booking in to see your GP is the self-soothing act you need.

To recap, have a mix of internal and external tools that work for you and supports you can call on when needed. With self-soothing skills, you are unstoppable. An ability to self-soothe allows autonomy over your physical self and behaviours, it develops your self-mastery for self-management, it cultivates a healthy relationship with self, and it can prevent stress, distress, and even some illness. Put simply, self-soothing is showing up for yourself in the present moment with loving kindness and a commitment to hold yourself safe, to settle and reset.

Case study

Karen had endured some traumatising incidents and used smoking as a way to manage the anxiety she lived with. Smoking was her self-soothing crutch. But Karen also suffered from asthma: she had to stop smoking.

To keep her hands busy and prevent herself from picking up a cigarette, Karen started doing crochet and sewing. When she became rattled, she learnt to take comfort in prayer. Interestingly, Karen wasn't religious, but she found praying to a higher power useful. She was aware of how contradictory it seemed for someone who didn't believe in God to utilise prayer as a self-soothing technique, but it worked so well she didn't care. Asking for support, protection, and guidance somehow enabled her to settle a little and carve out some calm for herself. Prayer created a sense of connection, safety and peace within. She couldn't explain it but it helped. The way she looked at it, her idiosyncratic praying seemed far more sensible than smoking and choosing a life of airways disease.

Take-home messages

- Self-soothing is a skill of self-management for **real wellness**.
- Self-soothing is regulating your mind, body and soul.
- Self-soothing may utilise internal and external tools and strategies.
- Use your mindfulness skills to check in on yourself throughout the day to see if you need some self-soothing.

- Having a healthy balance of tools reduces the risk of addictions and dependence and promotes self-mastery.
- An ability for self-soothing allows you to combat stress and care for yourself in loving ways.

Reflection

Take time to reflect on the ways in which you cope to regulate and unwind.

Are you leaning on external means too much? Are the ways you cope with stress working for you?

21
Habit Autonomy

Habits are a natural product of the human body and mind. They enable behaviour to be efficient and effective. For instance, as adults, our skill for walking is so automated we don't think of it at all. If we did have to consciously think about each movement, walking would occupy an immense amount of our time and headspace. Our habits can work for us, but some may contribute to poor health. Many illnesses and disabilities are caused by unhelpful habitual lifestyle choices, and all are affected by our self-management. Our habits form our lifestyle, affect our identity and self-esteem, and they significantly impact our future. To manage ourselves optimally for **real wellness** we need to have some skill in managing our behaviour and everyday choices.

Habit autonomy means being able to choose wisely how you live your life and care for yourself. When you have this autonomy over your actions and responses, you feel safe, free, and proud. It is a calming and happy way to be.

Changing habits can be a source of struggle and distress. Whether you look towards doing more of something healthy, or less of something unhelpful, changing habits and behaviours is not always easy. You would not be alone if you struggled with certain vices and behaviours despite knowing they do not help you to live optimally or feel well. This is a very human thing!

Having some knowledge around what helps form and break habits is useful when embarking on a journey of living with **real wellness**. Once you know a little about how and why your habits exist, you can start to modify them and choose ones that work for you. Having autonomy over your behaviour will allow you to make choices that work for you and keep you well.

Forming habits

When it comes to starting new habits, there will often be internal resistance preventing the desired change. Simply understanding, accepting, and expecting this resistance is helpful when forming helpful habits. The resistance itself may be obvious, but its origins may be less clear or possibly subconscious. A sense of resistance results from negative thoughts and assumptions (like 'I can't do that'), distracting and avoidant urges (like an impulse to snack or run for the hills), emotions (like a feeling of impending doom), and sensations (like a clenching nausea in the tummy). If you relate to this, it probably has something to do with your humanness, or upbringing, and what you learnt from the world around you. If you had role models who displayed ability and ease in being proactive and problem-solving, then your level of internal resistance to putting in place new behaviours is likely going to be lower than that of a person who was raised in less functional environments and consequently lacks confidence. Be kind to yourself, wherever you land on the spectrum of resistance to new things and change.

*

Can you recall a time when you considered starting something new and unfamiliar? Did it feel hard? If you suffer from self-limiting beliefs – as do 99.9% of us – then internal resistance is likely to arise when new activities are introduced. Resistance may be subtle, vague, and therefore tricky to notice. It can negatively affect your initiative without you even realising and make just the prospect and idea of engaging in a new behaviour feel 'hard' before you have even tried. That invisible effort and cognitive load is real and exhausting. That is the resistance I am talking about! It may be the hardest part of starting something new and harder than the physical action of doing it. With change, newness, and uncertainty comes effort. It is inevitable that these growth experiences take a toll on our energy levels and mood. So, when jumping out of your comfort zone and modifying habits, you often need to up your self-care and rest to optimise your resources and strength. Double down on your healthy habits: meet your basic needs with good sleep and nutrition (and don't forget that coffee).

It's easy to misread our internal cues. If you misinterpret fear as an intuitive warning not to proceed, you will miss out on a growth opportunity. As long as you are safe, then proceed with your goal cautiously. The fear is not some wise intuition guiding you to stop new action; rather, it is a helpful reminder to take care because it is something you have not done before. Fear is a predictable by-product of new action. Safely and compassionately progressing, despite the fear, is the medicine you need to reach your aspirations, grow and empower yourself. It can be as slow and cautious a journey as you like. Slow and steady may not win the race but it will get you there eventually!

To help proceed with action in the face of fear, reflect on your values and priorities and link them to your goal. For example, I have often taken on professional roles outside of my comfort zone to maximise the time I spend at home with my family. Experience has taught me that the fear and resistance that inevitably arises with any new job I start is easily overcome – and I consider the discomfort as worth enduring – when it means I get to live being a present and engaged mum (my value) and enjoying time with people who mean the most to me (my priority). Being tuned in to this drives my capacity for self-compassionate discipline and committed action.

Use your mindfulness skills to notice when internal resistance arises so you can choose whether you allow it to halt action and affect your choices. If your new habit aligns with your values, priorities and goals, expect the resistance, make space for it, relax, and don't be scared of it. Use your internal regulation skills to minimise the impact of it by challenging the resistance, or simply dismiss it entirely and turn your attention elsewhere. You can label any internal resistance as neurological junk, disregard it and just punch on, because you know it is safe to do so, the feeling is normal, predictable, human, and you choose to grow through it. Call it and name it (there goes that resistance again). Using language that resonates for you, label the internal-world feelings – maybe to you they're junk, crap, nonsense, unhelpful. By overriding them, you lessen their grip on you. Use mindfulness to notice the junk arise, let it flow, and turn your attention back to your pursuit.

To overcome resistance, you must relax to accept the resistance and then flow ahead with it. Physically relax. Slow your breathing and extend the exhale. Be chill. Whatever you're feeling and sensing, it's cool. Remind yourself the resistance cannot hurt you. It has no power over you unless you allow it to change your actions. Remind yourself that you are safe. By relaxing in this way, you prevent secondary stress and reduce the internal physiological response to fear. It means your body is better primed for calm action, and your brain primed for wise-minded reasoning. Consider it appropriate to experience a few internal alarm bells so we remember to move forwards with caution and care. See them as a helpful reminder, but not a reason to stop your progress. Thank the resistance and tread carefully forward all the same: 'Oh hello there, predictable resistance, thanks for being here. Please excuse me while I get on with what I need to do. Make yourself comfortable.'

Recall other times you overcame a similar amount or type of resistance when trying a new thing and survived. You'll be able to draw on a multitude of past experiences as evidence of your ability to thrive during new challenges. Change is an inevitable part of living. No doubt when you were a kid, learning to do new things felt hard and you were wary at times. Just because you're an adult now doesn't mean you shouldn't continue to grow and develop in that same way; nor does it mean new things won't feel hard and you won't feel wary.

Doing the thing you hope to become a habit – despite your resistance, motivation, energy, thoughts, and feelings – is how you start to automate a habit. Repetition is the path. The path has resistance, and the resistance progressively lessens the further down the path you travel. Doing the thing regardless is the work that needs to be done to form behaviours into habit.

An automatic habit feels easy and the experience flows. This is the goal. Automatic behaviour is like being on autopilot. Driving to work each day may be something you do without much thought: because it is automatic, we don't think about it so much. This is great because thinking and feeling and pausing before action is where all the effort lives. So, being able to action things that you choose without internal deliberation feels easy, thus we do it more, and it becomes a part of our lifestyle. Automating a habit doesn't necessarily mean you've eradicated all internal resistance; it simply means you engage less with the resistance and consequently there is less struggle and hesitation over initiating it. It's done without much conscious consideration and deliberation, so less energy and time is expended.

To automate a habit, you need to use your skills in committed action, no matter what your feelings and energy levels are. Habit formation requires repetition and consistency. It is only human to wax and wane in motivation (I have said this several times now, but it cannot be said enough). Regardless of what your internal world may be bringing up for you, without unwavering committed action, you may not consistently repeat the desired habit enough for it to become automatic. For committed action you need commitment to your values and priorities. Be aware of *why* your habit is meaningful and important to you and how it links with your values and priorities. Resistance is hard to move through, so your *why* needs to be crystal clear. Turn to this *why* when motivation and energy are low. It can override any fleeting thought, feeling, or urge getting in the way of the consistency and repetition required to form your desired new habit (as long as your self-care is on point, otherwise you may not have the cognitive resources and actually just need some self-compassionate rest and to go meet your needs).

The good news is that once you begin your new behaviour, it gets easier with repeated practice. Neuronal plasticity means that the more you do something, the more your brain is wired for it. Neurons that fire together wire together. The nature of the brain and our nervous system means that we do things more easily the more they are done. This is a fact. You can reassure yourself of this. It is the reward for all your hard work. I can confirm that you have a brain that is plastic (malleable). So, despite what your monkey mind may tell you, if you do the work repeatedly, you will achieve automation due to the neuroplastic reality of your nervous system.

Allow yourself to be fascinated with the process of change. Notice how stuff is easier over time. Notice with curiosity the level of resistance to things and how your habit may become easier to complete. With repeated exposure, any internal resistance may even become replaced by an urge to do it!

Habit hacks

I have many clients who say they want to do something for themselves but struggle to start. Why is it that some habits are easier to form than others and some people are more successful in starting new habits than others? Are there tricks to habit formation? Yes. Yes, there are. Here are some ideas:

- When you do something pleasant, it feels good, and you want more of it. So, if you start a habit that feels good, you'll be more likely to repeat it.
  - Reward yourself following completion of a new behaviour, like buying yourself a gift.
  - Pair the habit with another activity that makes you feel good. For example, if you like having coffee at a cafe and want to start writing, then schedule some time to write at a cafe while enjoying a coffee. (As I write, I'm editing this book for the millionth time in my favourite place, Byron Shire, New South Wales.) Knowing that each time you do something you get a treat makes doing it more appealing. That is right: just like dogs and kids, we respond well to treats too.
  - Maximise and amplify any good feels during or after achieving the task to enhance the rewarding properties and the effect it has on the process of habit automation. Acutely notice the full breadth of any good feelings brought on by the behaviour. Mindfully relish them and magnify them in your awareness by focusing fully on them.
  - Write down how good it felt, why, where you were, and how you did it, to consciously reinforce any benefit.
  - Sometimes doing new things is more enjoyable and easier with a friend and some support. Seek out a habit buddy or

even consider group practice or lessons to make your new habit more social and fun so it is easier to form.
- A habit needs to be obvious, so you are reminded to do it. If it's not obvious, you may be distracted by an alternative that is more accessible, familiar, and tempting. Consider your environment and modify it to make any desired new habit more visible, accessible and easier to do.
  - If everything you need to do the habit is laid out in front of you, it's a lot easier to do. An example of this would be filling your kitchen with healthy foods if you are aiming to upgrade your nutrition.
  - Set up your environment in a way that facilitates your chosen habits. I always keep a spare set of yoga clothes and sneakers in my car so I am always able to pop into a class or go for a random jog if the opportunity arises when out and about.
  - You can use environmental cues to trigger habits, like leaving a candle by your bedside as reminder to do some meditation before sleep.
  - You can use post-it notes on the fridge for prompts to add veggies to your dinner.
- Keep focused and clear on your new helpful habit goal so you remember to do it. Do things that reinforce your goal in your conscious mind.
  - Meditate on it, use a mantra, journal, use post-it notes on your mirror or fridge, try a goal tracker app on your phone, and get an accountability mate – someone you can chat to regularly about your progression, to keep the goal alive and stay on track. These things keep your habit top of mind.
- Turn your habit into a routine or incorporate it into an already existing routine. Using daily structure and routine takes away the thinking and is a useful way of making habits stick.

- For example, I like doing my exercise in the morning. It is how I love to start my day. So, when I wanted to build more strength, I added some weight training to my morning exercise routine.
- When you boil the kettle, do some mindful breathing.
• Schedule time for your new habit. Make protected, conscious and sufficient time to do the reps. Feeling time poor and a sense of time pressure makes doing difficult things all the more difficult. Not having enough time can easily turn into an excuse not to progress with your goals.
  - Write down the habit into your daily task list or calendar. Quarantine time for it by rescheduling anything that might interfere with it (maybe use a slow cooker so dinner is being cooked while you are drafting that novel).
  - Be clever about when you schedule your habit. I always schedule into my day the hardest, scariest, newest and most challenging thing first for when I'm fresh and have the morning vitality and time to get cracking (not to mention caffeine on board, which is probably my biggest habit hack).

Breaking unhelpful habits

Over the years, simply because you are human, you may have developed unhelpful habits you now wish to limit or cease.

There may be some habits you need to drop or limit to help you feel well. For example, alcohol disrupts quality sleep, destroys your microbiome, causes anxiety and weight gain, and, when used to cope with stress, robs you of experiencing your sober ability to independently manage yourself (this is just to name a few unwanted side-effects of this socially accepted poison). Don't get me wrong: I drink sometimes and enjoy it (hello, French champagne). But using alcohol to cope in life can become an unhelpful habit that makes matters worse and may lead to dependence. When I'm going through an unwell patch or growth period with lots on my plate, cutting out the booze is top of my list to re-set, restore, and optimise my function, but most importantly to empower myself.

Just as forming new habits can be hard, breaking old ones is difficult, if not more so. It is a wise move to make sure that behaviours you adopt and carry out repeatedly work for you and are sustainable before they automate! Once automated, you need to undo all that neuronal plasticity and neural change that mounted up from the years of repeated practice. When breaking unhelpful habits, expect the journey to be equally as hard and long as the one you took to get to where you are. But there are skills and hacks you can master to make unforming habits and rewiring your brain easier.

In the same way that internal resistance may arise to put you off starting a new habit, there will be internal resistance when attempting to break an unhelpful one. Again, we need to understand, accept, and expect internal resistance. Apply the relevant habit formation skills, such as mindfulness, calling to mind values and priorities, and self-compassionate discipline. Make the habit you wish to break difficult to do, unattractive, less obvious, and limit any spare time you would use to do it: in other words, fill it with other activities.

Manipulate your environment. For example, if you are trying to reduce your chocolate intake, put your stash up high and out of sight so it takes effort to reach for it, and you don't see it to think of it – better yet remove it from your house completely while you get some distance from the habit. Get accountable with a friend or group, track your habits, and use mindfulness as well as tools like journalling, SMART goal setting, visualisation, and mantras to keep on track.

To overcome a habit urge, we need to be mindful. If automation (zooming through action with little awareness, consideration, or deliberation) makes a behaviour into a habit, then it makes perfect sense that, to break a habit, we need to slow things right down and be super mindful of ourselves. Decelerate the whole process to purposely notice all the little steps and cues to combat. We need to be able to pause before the action. We need to be mindful to notice when we are triggered and notice the urges that precipitate our action. With this mindful awareness we carve out some space and time between impulse and action to masterfully consider the potential consequences of acting on this habit, return to our why, values and goals, and consider alternative responses. An application of mindfulness is necessary and inherent to this process of dealing with impulsive thoughts, urges, and emotions. You need to be able to notice them, understand them, familiarise yourself with them in order to manage and overcome their hold on you. It is these fleeting internal thoughts, feelings and sensations that drive the vice. Mindfulness decreases your impulsivity and increases your chances of picking up on a habit urge and noticing alternatives.

*

Habits have a cue, routine and reward. To understand your unhelpful habit and why it's so sticky, identify its triggers (cue), the context of it (routine) and the benefit (reward). Then, systematically address and replace these with alternatives to break a habit cycle. Sit with yourself and enquire into the habit triggers. What are they? Identify their purpose. Why do you think you do it? What does it give you? Work out any routines to it. Where do you normally do it and in what context? The more you understand the habit, the more opportunity you have to act effectively in an alternative way. Let's say, for example, that you want to stop smoking (habit), which is your way to unwind (purpose and reward) after dinner, and a habit you normally indulge in three times as much at the pub (trigger and cue) on a Friday after work (routine). You could instead schedule a tennis lesson or social walk on a Friday (new routine) after work, go for dinner at a non-smoking restaurant (reduced cue and trigger) afterwards and use a relaxation technique or book a massage after dinner to unwind (different reward that meets the same need). This work is fiddly and confusing so, if like me, you struggle to do it alone, then use a workbook or get a coach to help identify in detail your blind spots.

It's not sustainable to omit a habit without replacing it. The existing habit is serving a need. You cannot omit a need. For as long as it's there, it's there. It is a real need. Identify the need it is meeting and think of alternative ways to meet it. Remember, you can't deny your needs long-term as you will become unwell. So, you have to find new and healthier ways to meet the need to stop needing the unwanted habit. (Writing this, I feel like Dr Seuss!)

Experiment with new and healthier ways to serve your needs. Get busy with new skills. Being busy also means you have little time for your unhelpful habit. So, don't go cold turkey. I don't think that works (certainly, it has never worked for me). Have a replacement habit ready to swap in. For example, if you want to stop smoking, then learn a new skill that occupies your hands, like drawing, journalling, or knitting. You need something else to do. Without an effective and useful swap, you will be left dealing with cravings without any alternative distraction or reward. While I hate to say it, typically, a substitute habit is not as effective in reward initially. That's why 'bad' habits can be so strong and addictive. Think about replacing scrolling Instagram with reading a book. In this instance, there's probably less dopamine firing through your brain's reward pathways reading than when engaging in apps designed by the smartest people in the world to be as addictive as a pokie machine. But for most people, some relief is better than none, and it's more helpful to read than simply lie in bed doing nothing but abstaining from scrolling. With time and abstinence from your vice, any high you felt from it becomes less familiar and, as your brain rewires, your expectations around pleasure and reward adjust, making less rewarding alternatives more fulfilling. Recovered addicts discuss how gratitude and enjoyment of simple things, like the beauty of nature, return after abstinence from substances that provide extreme unnatural highs, such as heroin. Have a repertoire of replacement behaviours so you can try numerous alternatives without going cold turkey. Create a whole toolkit of coping mechanisms and distractions. Use them all at once if you have to.

Consider the benefits of your unhelpful habit so you can try to meet this need with a replacement. For example, going for after-work drinks is common, and people may think the reward from this ritual is the drink. But for a lot of us, it may also be the opportunity for social interaction, a laugh, some playtime away from responsibilities, and last and almost incidentally enjoying a delicious drink. So, if you are trying to reduce alcohol and want to break the habit of after-work drinking, be sure to replace it with something social, fun and not too serious – like going to a comedy show with friends. You can still have your delicious drink, just make it alcohol free!

Educate yourself on the real negative consequences of the habit you wish to omit. Earlier, I listed a few about alcohol. Find the facts. Debunk any BS your mind tells you. Challenge any unhelpful thoughts and beliefs around the habit. If trying to reduce your use of alcohol, consider whether alcohol is doing the things you use it for and how it is affecting your life and body. Some people believe alcohol alleviates anxiety, but in fact it causes it. Others think it helps them sleep but it destroys sleep architecture and also robs sleep of its restorative quality. Talk to experts and your doctors. Read quit literature about your unwanted habit and learn from others. Empower yourself with the facts to ensure your actions are well informed.

Once you have completed your research, try not to focus on the habit you wish to break. If you tell yourself the story you are not allowed something, then you set yourself up for a deprivation mindset and may inadvertently crave it more. Humans tend to want what they believe they are not allowed. So, instead focus on what you do want, what you do want to be doing and put your energy into developing a clear understanding and vision of that. Imagine an alternative version of you living free of the habit you wish to break. Use the Ideal You skill. What are the things you do with your time? How do you look? What are you wearing, eating, saying? How are you feeling and acting? Ask yourself, 'How do you wish to be?', 'What would you like to be doing?' Focus on that. Journal, use visualisation and mantras to solidify into your awareness a new reality for yourself. The more you do this, the more your subconscious mind with be able to get on with all it does to manifest it for you. Let go of any unhelpful deprivation mindset and stay acutely aware of the benefits you are choosing for yourself with your lifestyle change. You deserve **real wellness**.

Up your resources and support when breaking an unhelpful habit. There is no reason to do all this alone. In fact, isolation breeds shame. Shame extinguishes motivation. It is so draining and demoralising. Join a group. Get a coach. Access the vast amount of knowledge and resources that exist about whatever it is you're working towards. Find help: you deserve the support. If you have the means, then why is it that you should go without expert guidance and help? Be kind to yourself. Draw on family, friends, health professionals, hobbies, support groups, podcasts, quit lit, recovery sites, nature, pets, community, and volunteer work. We may have a world of resources at our fingertips without realising it.

In this scenario, the most influential and powerful support person, the one integral to any change process, is yourself. You are the one with the power to apply your skills. You are the one who can do the mindfulness, values awareness, visualisation, mantra, journalling, and distracting activities. You are ultimately the one who drives this. You are the one who does the work. Only you can do this. Only you can change yourself. So, invest in yourself and take care of yourself as a priority. Make sure you meet your holistic needs as best you can. Increase sleep and optimise your nutrition and relaxation. Reflect on all the activities, places, people, and things that give you strength, peace, calm, and contentment. Work out what it is that you can do to keep yourself feeling grounded and well, then factor this stuff into your week. Simple things like doing some morning movement, enjoying a loved hobby, and cooking a healthy meal at home may help. How can you regularly schedule these things into your day?

Be self-compassionate as you change. Accommodate and forgive yourself for your struggle and humanness. Recommit to your path daily and work towards your goals in a loving and kind way. Beating yourself up and punishing yourself depletes your resources. Instead, be encouraging, warm and forgiving. Learn to use yourself for optimal support. Replace unhelpful thinking with supportive thoughts, cheerlead and applaud yourself along this journey of change. You've got this, you can do this and maybe you already are doing this! Make sure you have fun things to look forward to, to avoid a sense of lack. It is easy for the mind to make us feel as though we are missing out. FOMO is real. So, keep the rewards and treats coming to reduce any false sense of deprivation, and keep busy so when FOMO arises you have something to do. Shower yourself with lovely self-care when undertaking this hard work. You deserve it, and it will make the process easier.

HABIT AUTONOMY

*

Finally, please remember, if you're struggling to break a habit or start a new one, it isn't because you're weak, or whatever story your mind may be creating around your experience. Rather, it's because you're human, and you have neuronal and physiological limits. Neuronal plasticity is a rate-limiting factor that cannot be avoided: that is to say, the process cannot be rushed. Expect breaking and forming habits to feel difficult as your brain and body adapt, and you slowly rewire your system. However, with time and repetition, change requires less effort and feels easier.

Expect the process to take time. The time it takes depends on the time it takes to rewire the brain. All you can do is repeat the reps as much as you can, eat well, sleep sufficiently, and have faith. There are slow and tiny changes to dendrites, neurotransmitter levels, receptors, cell types, and the structure, clustering, and connection of neurons. Neuronal plasticity has a fixed rate–limiting factor that needs to be understood, expected, and accepted. Be kind and patient with yourself. Accept and expect the process of behavioural change to require consistency. Without consistency in your behaviour, the neuronal changes are shortlived. So, be as consistent as you can with your choices.

Lapses in our desired behaviour are the norm, unfortunately, but don't give up. Just reset and recommit as quickly as you can. Take any judgement out of the situation and try to see things objectively. You are not a failure: you are a human doing something hard that requires time, effort and practice. There is no wasted time along this journey of behaviour change. There are only lessons galore and skills to build.

Because some unhelpful habits are a great deal more harmful than others, they may require a different approach. Addictions and behaviours that contribute to poor health need to be taken extremely seriously. In this circumstance, you must seek evidence-based specialist care and qualified health professional support. Be sure to see your GP. Seek support from experts and allow yourself to be supervised. The brutal reality is that some habits can be lethal without you even knowing.

Case study

Sharon and her husband were in the habit of enjoying a glass of wine with dinner every night. They had an overseas holiday coming up. In the lead-up, Sharon wanted to shift some weight and get fit, so she decided to cut out alcohol but then enjoy some wines on her trip. When Sharon explained her goal to her husband, he was keen to follow her lead and support her.

They discovered the world of non-alcoholic beverages at the liquor shop. But the drink Sharon grew to love was a home-made soda water with fresh lemon and a dash of apple cider vinegar. She found this a perfect substitute: refreshing and satisfying enough to sip. It even had no calories! Sharon lost a little weight and felt great for her trip. Having experienced the benefits of non-alcoholic alternatives, she didn't return to drinking wine every night with dinner.

Take-home messages

- Internal resistance arises when changing habits. Expect it.
- Use your mindfulness to limit engagement with the resistance and delay tactics.
- Be committed by drawing on your values and priorities.
- Be consistent despite resistance.
- To develop a habit, make it obvious, attractive, easy, and make time for it. To break one, make it hidden, unattractive, difficult, and unsatisfying.

- Expect the process to feel hard, take time, and require consistency. Remember that neuronal plasticity is a rate-limiting factor: in other words, there is no shortcut when it comes to rewiring the brain.
- Be kind to yourself when embarking on behavioural change. Invest in yourself as your greatest resource. You are the one who needs to do the draining work.
- Increase your supports and resources, and seriously consider obtaining professional help and supervision.

Reflection

Be mindful of the next time an opportunity arises to start a new desirable habit and of the resistance you experience that holds you back.

- Notice if this resistance is a certain thought or feeling. What are your assumptions, beliefs, and the reasons you resist it?
- Brainstorm solutions to these barriers and challenge their reality.
- Come up with creative ways to maximise the appeal and satisfaction of your desired new habit.
- Make doing the habit obvious and easy by modifying your environment.

22

Holistic Skills for Self-mastery

Think of this book as a kind of starter pack. My aim is to give you some concepts, some stories, and some techniques and strategies to try on for size, and for you then to take charge of your learning. **Real wellness** is all about what is right for you. Create your own repertoire of holistic tools to manage yourself. Keep open to learning new aproaches to wellbeing. Read widely. Try new things. Never stop your education and development of self-mastery. Avoid being put off by ideas that may initially seem silly, juvenile or to 'woo woo'. If you come across an ancient skill, something tested over the ages and still in use, there is likely some knowledge there and you would be a fool to dismiss it. Give things like that a go. Conduct your own experiments and create your own evidence based on your personal experience.

In this chapter, for quick reference, I bring together my favourite holistic techniques. They are each techniques that I use extensively and believe that they may be of benefit to you too.

- *Visualisation*: In Chapter 14, I explained how to use your mind's brilliant ability to imagine in order to cognitively prepare yourself to do things. In a nutshell, you bring to mind whatever it is you wish to do and use visualisation to practise it. Athletes are taught to visualise in preparation for competitions. In the same way that they train their muscles and cardiorespiratory systems with exercise, they can also train their minds with visualisation. This technique helps to improve your willingness and confidence to change your behaviour. The visualisation provides you with imagined practice. It helps you to feel more familiar and comfortable with whatever scene you imagine. If you have an intimidating event or task coming up, try using visualisation to improve your courage and motivation and to practise how you wish it to unfold. This tool is also useful when brainstorming ideas and your dreams for manifesting. In my experience, if I can picture it, it is more likely to happen.
- *Mantra:* Thousands of years ago in ancient India, sages started teaching the practice of repeating – either silently or out loud – sacred words, phrases, sounds or syllables, which we call mantras. With contemporary understanding, we can view mantra as a mind skill. Reciting a mantra helps tame the mind and cultivate focus. Repeating self-affirming phrases can empower the growth you want for yourself: you can use a mantra to speak of your goal as if it has already been achieved. For example, if you want to quit smoking, repeat morning and night: 'I no longer smoke. I don't need cigarettes. I am whole and complete and calm without these toxins.' Reciting a mantra is another way of cementing your intentions into your consciousness. It promotes personal responsibility and self-agency – kind of like cheerleading self-talk but in commanding phrases. It is a motivating act that helps prepare you for change. It can be helpful to use a mantra when meditating or calming yourself. As you breathe in, you can repeat to yourself 'let'

and as you exhale you say 'go'. This simple mantra, when continually recited rhythmically with the breath, is effective in calming yourself, focusing on the present, and soothing the nervous system. Yoga uses mantra as one of many holistic tools for human-mastery.

- *Prayer:* Like mantra, prayer uses language, and the words of a prayer may be said aloud or repeated in your mind, The use of prayer is an act of conscious intention setting. It brings to your awareness what concerns you and what you hope for. It consolidates your dreams and desires and reinforces your priorities. Prayer need not be religious, and you can direct your prayer to a higher power, to the natural world, or even to yourself. Prayer can be an act of radical acceptance and surrender to something more than yourself, cultivating a sense of spirituality and wonder, and expressing awe about the unknowable aspects of existence. It can be soothing and settling to acknowledge the great mystery of life, release some of life's responsibility and turn to a source beyond yourself to cope.
- *Journalling:* This is freely expressing yourself in written form – to offload your worries and pressures in a stream-of-consciousness way, with no constraints on what you write about or how you go about it. By putting your feelings and thoughts and inner experiences into words, you are able to process them more effectively, with more conscious awareness and insight. You need not be a literary superstar. I journal in dot point! I find that my mind goes too fast for my writing, so I scribble illegibly, doing my best to capture the thoughts that flow during the process. While you can't really read my words, this method of journalling is proving to be cathartic and effective at purging my inner talk and releasing what's within onto a page. Do what works for you and don't have a fixed impression of how journalling needs to be. Journalling helps you process and express your inner world and puts confusing internal influences

onto paper, making them clearer and more tangible. Journalling can be used to imagine overcoming hurdles and brainstorming changes you wish for yourself. When creating change, write out your desires, how your days would go, how you would feel, what you would wear and look like, and what you would do if you were living your best life and overcoming any obstacles to achieving the changes you aspire to. This future-oriented journalling helps to shift your identity from the person you are now to the version of yourself you wish to become. It helps to overcome resistance and troubleshoot obstacles to change, as you may find yourself discovering solutions as you write through them. Like visualisation, journalling can be a motivating act that helps build confidence for change simply by imagining it.

- *Cultivate a sense of faith:* Having faith means you face every day in the knowledge that life is impermanent, things are forever changing, *and* that this means there is always potential for new developments and growth. There is beauty in this. Faith is leaning into the natural flows of life. The faith mindset is that things will be as they are and that is okay. With faith, you learn to reassure yourself that you will get through even if your efforts or plans do not work out. Faith does not require positive thinking but does require confidence in the face of adversity. Even if your worst-case fears present, you will still be okay, and life will go on. Having faith provides the fuel you need to stay in the game of life, resilient and courageous every day.
- *Build your self-worth*: Your own estimation of your merit as a human can stem from internal sources, like your self-assessment of your character, but also external ones, like achievements and aesthetic. If you give a lot of weight to external indicators of your value, you will be prone to negative mental states. This is because positive messages from the external world may not be sustainable, and even if they are, may not fully satisfy your intrinsic need for personal validation, which must come from

within. An intrinsic sense of self-worth is developed by: living a life aligned with your values, priorities and intentions; fostering a healthy relationship with yourself through self-care (including showing up for yourself with self-compassionate discipline, even when it feels hard or not fun); and by expressing yourself to those you love, sharing aspects of your inner world to see you are accepted and loved for your whole self – ugly truths, worries and all. If you treat yourself with loving kindness and care, you grow to trust yourself. With self-trust, self-compassion and self-care, your sense of self-worth will grow.

- *Spend time in nature*: Whether it's spending time in your garden, gazing up at the night sky, watching a coastline or forest bathing, being in nature is grounding, soothing and settling. Has being immersed in nature ever facilitated a complete shift in your perspective? Contemplating nature has a special knack for getting us humans to see the bigger picture. It helps us accept and surrender to difficult things. It grounds, comforts and soothes us. There seems to be some sort of special coregulation that occurs between a person and a natural landscape. I experience this every time I set foot on my beach. Being in nature is humbling and healing. It may facilitate inner peace. There is a sense of serenity and peace when you accept what is natural. What is natural is impermanence, connection, empathy, and recycling. What is natural is for life to come and go and flow. Nature helps us relinquish the need for control and instead accept what is so we can flow into it and along with it, with more ease and less struggle.
- *Maintain a balanced, healthy lifestyle:* A balanced lifestyle that meets your needs is conducive to synaptogenesis and neurogenesis (change and neural growth, respectively). Some lifestyle suggestions for optimal physical health and function are:
  - Eat a balanced diet full of fresh fruits, vegetables, and whole grains (there is good evidence for a Mediterranean diet).

- Daily exercise and movement (in my opinion exercise is the best medicine).
- Get sufficient quality sleep: 7–9 hours every night.
- Manage stress.
- Decrease or eliminate smoking, alcohol and illicit drug use.
- Spend quality time with loved ones, getting sufficient hugs and intimacy.
- Enjoy creative pursuits, learning, getting out of your comfort zone and trying new things.
- Foster ways for connection with nature, animals, and your sense of spirituality.
- Cultivate meaningful relationships with others and your community so you have the support you need and enjoy a sense of belonging.

- *Gratitude practices:* These are intentional and reflective activities that involve acknowledging and appreciating the positive aspects of your life, fostering a sense of thankfulness and contentment. These practices have been increasingly recognised for their profound impact on overall wellbeing, both mental and physical. One common gratitude practice involves keeping a gratitude journal: regularly writing down things you're thankful for, whether big or small. This process encourages a focus on the positive aspects of life, promoting a more optimistic outlook. Expressing gratitude towards others, either through verbal appreciation or handwritten notes, is another powerful practice. Acts of kindness and generosity can also be incorporated into gratitude rituals, creating a feedback loop of positive emotions. Research indicates that engaging in gratitude practices is associated with reduced stress, improved mood, enhanced sleep quality, and increased overall life satisfaction. For instance, taking a moment each day to reflect with gratitude on specific moments, such as the support of friends during challenging

times or the beauty of nature, can contribute significantly to an individual's wellbeing.
- *Somatic therapy:* The Greek word sōmatikos means 'of the body'. Somatic therapy recognises the significance of bodily experiences in psychological health and emphasises the mind–body connection. It involves exploring and addressing the impact of physical sensations, movements, and posture on emotional and mental states. This therapeutic modality operates on the premise that unresolved emotional issues may manifest as physical symptoms or tension in the body. By fostering awareness of bodily sensations and encouraging mindful attention to them, somatic therapy aims to release stored emotions and promote healing. Techniques commonly employed in somatic therapy include breathwork, movement exercises, and body-focused mindfulness practices. For example, a somatic therapy session might involve guided movements or gentle touch to help an individual reconnect with their body and release tension held in certain areas. This approach has proven effective in treating conditions such as trauma, anxiety, and chronic stress, as it seeks to integrate the physiological and psychological aspects of wellbeing, ultimately fostering a more balanced and harmonious relationship between the body and mind.
- *Energy work:* This refers to a range of holistic practices that focus on the manipulation, balancing, or channeling of the body's energy to enhance overall wellbeing. Rooted in various cultural and spiritual traditions, energy work operates on the principle that disruptions or imbalances in the flow of energy within the body can contribute to physical, emotional, or mental ailments. Practitioners of energy work, such as Reiki, Qi Gong, or Healing Touch, aim to influence the body's subtle energy fields to promote healing and relaxation. For instance, in the Japanese technique of Reiki, practitioners use their hands to transfer healing energy to the recipient, facilitating a sense

of harmony and balance. Many energy work practices focus on the chakras, which are believed to be energy centres within the body. By clearing blockages or replenishing depleted energy, these practices aim to alleviate stress, reduce pain, and enhance the overall vitality of an individual. While the mechanisms underlying energy work may vary, its goal is to optimise the body's energetic flow, fostering a sense of holistic wellbeing.

- *Self-hypnosis:* By bringing your mind and body into deep relation, hypnotists theorise they can access brain states conducive to reprograming our subconscious thinking to positively impact our filtering and behaviours. Self-hypnosis can be taught and practised to overcome habits, unhelpful thinking, and to create meaningful change.

Case study

Caleb felt dissatisfied with his life but was unsure what to change. He wasn't in a position to employ a life coach and wasn't keen on therapy.

His girlfriend made it her practice to journal each night in bed. Caleb dismissed it as a waste of time and would read while she wrote about the events of the day. One night, he decided to try writing out how he felt to see what it was like. Words started pouring out of him: Caleb found himself expressing his dislike of work, his jealousy of other people's ability to work flexibly, and his dreams of travelling. The next night, he repeated the exercise, and the night after that as well. Soon Caleb found himself craving the journalling, as it helped him feel lighter and sleep better. He could see that it was helpful. It revealed to him his own innermost thoughts and feelings, which was something he previously avoided as it felt overwhelming and hard. But journalling wasn't overwhelming or hard, and the benefits were worth the initial effort of starting.

A year on, Caleb had clarified his goals – to work part-time from home and be able to travel as he did so – and was committed to achieving them. The journalling had brought into his awareness some useful guideposts and clues towards the changes he needed to make in order to feel well and content.

Take-home messages

- There are numerous holistic ways to improve your self-mastery. Be willing to experiment with new ways of coping to find what works for you.
- Maintaining a healthy, balanced lifestyle that meets your holistic needs is key to **real wellness**.

Reflection

Start your morning by visualising the day ahead and how you'll carry yourself.

What do you look like? How do you act and carry yourself? What are the things you will do?

Final Words

Okay, so here we are – the end! Well done. Bravo. Incredible work. You have just read my **real wellness** manifesto! Huge congratulations to you for reading all this juicy content and getting this far in your own journey to embracing and enjoying optimal you. Simply letting these words enter your awareness and allowing the content to soak into your soul is a great start to living your best life.

You are now aware of all the tips, tricks, and truths that support my clinical practice and my own wellbeing. I turn to this stuff day in and day out. It is the real deal. It is my path of practice and I hope you incorporate a little of it – maybe even a lot of it – into yours. You now know my self-mastery framework for managing your humanness. I truly hope the contents of this book give you some useful ideas to write your personal prescription for self-mastery and **real wellness**. I want you to move forward in your precious life accepting of your humanness, validated, included, worthy *and* masterful in the way you live as you. Make the most of unique you in a loving way.

I hope you have let go of the media-fuelled BS image of wellness and instead replaced it with a more attainable and compassionate view. I'm not promising everlasting happiness, a perfect path, pristine health or living free of challenges. These falsehoods are unfair, so unhelpful, and can derail us from enjoying the beauty of what is. I am not promoting or selling you an aesthetic or specific practice – this truly is not that approach to wellbeing. Rather, contentment and mastery come from embracing the real you. Give yourself the caring permission to be flawed and immortal *and* show up more fully in life. Giving these skills and concepts a go should cost you pretty much nothing and it might save you $$$$, not to mention a life lost in unrealistic comparisons and self-shame.

The best you'll ever feel is when you foster an adaptive, insightful, accepting, and self-compassionate relationship with yourself. It doesn't come from a pill, surgery, or quick fix.

You don't need to do tantra, meditation, or saunas; there's no need to lose weight, dye your hair, dress in designer leisurewear, track your macros and sleep, or take a bunch of supplements. You do need to foster community, social connectivity and supportive relationships; to exercise, eat a balanced diet with plenty of plants, get adequate sleep; avoid misusing alcohol, smoking, and other substances of addiction; invest time and effort into learning and understanding yourself; forever work on self-acceptance; and develop some skill in self-care and mastery over your actions. To achieve **real wellness** requires mindful awareness; the commitment to live a life aligned with your priorities and values; capacity for self-honesty; and autonomy over the habits that are the building blocks of your lifestyle and ultimately shape your health and wellbeing. Invest in these things. Give it a shot!

To sum up the message, being well does not mean living free of disease or disability or inhabiting a world free of stress and pain. That would not be human. That would be the most unhelpful health message any health professional could impart. That would not be compatible with human life. **Real wellness** is achieved when you adaptively manage yourself, meet your holistic needs and function as boldly in life as you can. I passionately believe that **real wellness** is possible for anyone, no matter their circumstances. The three pillars of **real wellness** can be learnt and practised.

My dream is that, in the future, these human-mastery skills will be incorporated into our public education system. You're never too young to learn these essential skills. And it's never too late to start either.

Once you understand and accept yourself, you can then experiment with ways to manage your humanness. The choice of habits you adopt and the practices you incorporate into your life to develop and maintain these pillars is really up to you, and they need to be tailored to suit your unique needs. Rather than being sucked in to all the marketing messages of what stereotypical wellness looks like and asks of you, tune in to yourself to experiment with ways of being to develop your self-mastery. Experiment with anything and everything that aligns with your values, priorities and intentions. Optimise your environment to work for you. Be sure to continue your practice of self-awareness and self-acceptance for your entire life, and never stop trying new ways of self-management aligned with your soul.

There's no such thing as a perfect life. There will always be tough times and hard days. The pursuit of wellness is dynamic and fluctuating. Our struggles and imperfections don't mean we're broken and need fixing or healing. Accepting this and being able to manage this reality adaptively is a part of the quest. Don't expect robotic or godlike abilities from yourself. Stay humble and real. It's okay – and expected – to have slips, slumps and far from ideal moments. Just reset and keep trying. Just do your best – that's all any of us can ever do. Never give up on yourself and never lose sight of the beauty inherent to experiencing this incredible life. Come back to these skills time and time again to save yourself and get back on track. To me, pursuing **real wellness** is a lifestyle and spiritual commitment. It is your life's purpose. It is so much more than defending my ego and fiercely avoiding failings.

If you're embarking on a journey to **real wellness** and feel that you're not making progress with building the self-understanding, self-acceptance, and self-management skills you need to make effective changes in your life, then please do consider seeking professional support. If this option is available to you, it might fast-forward your progress. There is no shame in leaning on experts trained in matters of human function. There are many wonderful people out there with the credentials to support you, so don't hold back from benefiting from such privileged resources. Assert your power and access the support. Your local family doctor might be able to suggest some good people. With help, I wholeheartedly believe that, if you develop your skills in self-awareness, self-acceptance, and self-management you will cultivate your own sense of **real wellness**. All you need is skills practice, and to cultivate supportive connections (with yourself and others) while holding a loving commitment to each day and gratitude for all that you are now.

*

The coverage of this material has been exhaustive and in depth, yes; yet there is always more to learn and share. Please join our tribe – Ataraxia Collective – where skills and ideas for **real wellness** are shared. There are such rich rewards to being connected to community and cultivating a sense of belonging. We welcome you! www.ataraxiacollective.com.au @axcollective on Instagram.

Please sign up for future books – there will be more! This journey of self-mastery and optimal health is ongoing for us all. We are all learning and growing. Let's rally around each other: do it together and thrive in numbers as we move closer towards our most optimal selves.

Final take-home messages

- **Real wellness** is attained through a life of self-mastery.
- Self-mastery requires self-awareness, self-acceptance, and self-management.
- These core self-mastery skills can be learnt and practised.
- There is a lifetime's worth of knowledge, concepts and tools for you to acquire along your journey towards self-mastery.
- **Real wellness** is a lifestyle – a lifelong commitment to living your best life and making the most of all that you are.
- All humans are imperfect: we make mistakes and slips in our behaviour; we struggle; we experience pain and loss; and are vulnerable to ageing, disease and disability. And we can *all* be well.

Acknowledgments

Writing *Mastering Real Wellness* has been a deeply rewarding journey, and it would not have been possible without the support, guidance, and encouragement of many remarkable people.

First and foremost, I want to express my deepest gratitude to my beautiful husband, whose unwavering support and love have been my anchor throughout this process. Your belief in me and this project has been most appreciated. To my family and friends, thank you for your encouragement, insightful edits, and for being my biggest cheerleaders. Your faith in my vision has been invaluable.

A heartfelt thank you to my editor, Anne Reilly who truly gave her heart and soul to this book. Your dedication, meticulous attention to detail, and unwavering commitment to excellence have elevated this work in ways I could never have imagined. I am profoundly grateful for your hard work and passion.

To my dear friend's dad Graeme Jones of Kirby Jones Typesetting, your patient guidance, valuable contacts, and the incredible work you did typesetting the manuscript have been instrumental. Your generosity and expertise have made this journey smoother and more enjoyable, and for that, I am sincerely thankful.

Thank you to my cover designer Christa Moffitt of Christabella Designs who provided prompt and gorgeous concepts, so many that it felt impossible to choose a final design. Thank you for the extra information and support you gifted me with tolerance and kindness.

I extend my appreciation to all the experts from whom I have learned the skills and knowledge that form the foundation of this book. Your insights and teachings have profoundly shaped my understanding of wellness, and I am honoured to share this wisdom with others.

My practice of yoga and the local teachers who support this lifestyle have been a cornerstone of my personal journey to wellness. Your teachings, encouragement, and the sense of community you foster have been a constant source of strength and inspiration.

Finally, to my health practitioners who have supported my journey to real wellness, thank you for your care, expertise, and dedication. Your support has been crucial in my personal transformation and has enriched my life in countless ways.

This book is a testament to the power of community, support, and the shared journey towards wellness. I am deeply grateful to each and every one of you for being part of this journey.

With heartfelt gratitude,
Dr. Susannah Ward

Dr. Susannah Ward is a specialist physician in rehabilitation medicine based in Newcastle, New South Wales, Australia. She holds degrees in Medical Science and Medicine with honours from The University of Sydney. In 2018, she was awarded the prestigious Fellowship prize from The Royal Australasian College of Physicians. Dr. Ward's professional life spans clinical practice, research, and governance, with numerous publications to her name.

With a keen interest in wellness and holistic health, Dr. Ward has been a dedicated advocate for the wellbeing of health professionals, passionately promoting a nurturing and supportive medical culture.

Dr. Ward resides by the beach with her husband, son, and dog. In her leisure time, she enjoys studying self-mastery, writing, yoga, gentle jogs, and connecting with nature. A certified mindfulness meditation and yoga teacher, she also runs retreats and events as the founder of Ataraxia Collective (@axcollective; www.ataraxiacollective.com.au).

Mastering Real Wellness is her debut book, with plans for many more to follow.

www.ingramcontent.com/pod-product-compliance
Lightning Source LLC
Chambersburg PA
CBHW072148070526
44585CB00015B/1048